# "A BETTER COUNTRY"

**Recent Titles in**
**Contributions to the Study of Science Fiction and Fantasy**
*Series Editor: Marshall Tymn*

MARTHA C. SAMMONS

# "A BETTER COUNTRY"

## The Worlds of Religious Fantasy and Science Fiction

CONTRIBUTIONS TO THE STUDY OF
SCIENCE FICTION AND FANTASY, NUMBER 32

Greenwood Press
*New York • Westport, Connecticut • London*

**Library of Congress Cataloging-in-Publication Data**

Sammons, Martha C., 1949–
  "A better country".

  (Contributions to the study of science fiction and
fantasy, ISSN 0193–6875 ; no. 32)
  Bibliography: p.
  Includes index.
  1. Fantastic fiction, English—History and criticism.
2. Christianity in literature.  3. Theology in
literature.  4. Myth in literature.  5. Science fiction,
English—History and criticism.  6. Lewis, C. S. (Clive
Staples), 1898–1963—Influence.  7. Tolkien,
J. R. R. (John Ronald Reuel), 1892–1973—Influence.
I. Title.  II. Series.
PR830.F3S35    1988      823'.0876'09382      87–23639
ISBN 0–313–25746–9 (lib. bdg. : alk. paper)

British Library Cataloguing in Publication Data is available.

Library of Congress Catalog Card Number: 87–23639
ISBN: 0–313–25746–9
ISSN: 0193–6875

First published in 1988

Greenwood Press, Inc.
88 Post Road West, Westport, Connecticut 06881

Printed in the United States of America

The paper used in this book complies with the
Permanent Paper Standard issued by the National
Information Standards Organization (Z39.48–1984).

10  9  8  7  6  5  4  3  2  1

This book is dedicated in memory of Clyde S. Kilby

# Contents

" . . . they were longing for a better country—a heavenly one."

—Heb. 11:16

# "A BETTER COUNTRY"

# Introduction

C. S. Lewis once remarked to J. R. R. Tolkien, "There is too little of what we really like in stories. I am afraid we shall have to write some ourselves." Humphrey Carpenter explains that what "they had in mind [were] stories that were 'mythopoeic' but were thinly disguised as popular thriller" (*The Inklings*, 65–66). Lewis saw the need for a mixture of the kinds of writing done by Novalis, George MacDonald, James Stephens, H. G. Wells, and Jules Verne. He also wanted a form that would "give the Christian story a fresh excitement by retelling it as if it were a new myth" (*Inklings*, 66). W. H. Lewis admitted that "any amount of theology can now be smuggled into people's minds under cover of romance without their knowing it" (*Letters of C. S. Lewis*, 167). Thus was born a new type of novel that presents the spiritual and mythopoeic under the guise of a popular format. Tolkien called this genre "romance" or "theologized science fiction"; G. K. Chesterton called it "alternative theology."

Because critics disagree about the definition of fantasy literature in general, a definition of *religious* fantasy is even more difficult. Manlove defines fantasy as "a fiction evoking wonder and containing a substantial and irreducible element of the supernatural with which the mortal characters in the story or the readers become on at least partly familiar terms" (*Modern Fantasy: Five Studies*, 1). Another important characteristic is the creation of another world or presence of things not found in ordinary reality. In *An Experiment in Criticism*, for example, C. S. Lewis defines fantasy as "any narrative that deals with impossibles and preternaturals."

Although a wide spectrum of books may fall into a definition, religious fantasy as it will be discussed in the following pages is a work that integrates aspects of Christianity with elements of fantasy, including science fiction. Not only does the "religious" element vary, however, but authors use a variety of forms. Even Lewis and Tolkien disagreed about the role and nature of the writer and the degree to which religious elements should appear in a story.

Fantasy, chosen as the "fictive analogue" for the writer's Christian world view, presents as real and credible the supernatural world outside our perception. In addition, it does not deal with things as they are now but what they ought to or will be. A major element is thus the real but unseen spiritual world, particularly supernatural beings, because the main purpose is to show the reality of this world and humans coming to terms with it. Another key element is magic. Lin Carter defines fantasy as a story in which magic really works (*Imaginary Worlds*, 6). But in religious fantasy, the magic comes from God, and a central theme of the book is usually the characters' relationship to Him. However, books differ in how explicit the references to God are.

Religious fantasy also presents theological concepts, issues, or moral values. Leland Ryken defines Christian literature in general as presenting or alluding to some aspect of Biblical doctrine, values, or symbolism, or touching on concepts such as God, providence, forgiveness, salvation, eternal life, sin, fallen creatures, and the creator (*Triumphs of the Imagination*, 124, 156–157, 170). These themes are also found in Christian fantasy, including others such as the creation, the reality of the supernatural, the end times, the importance of the individual, obedience, the inner quest, and the afterlife.

While good versus evil is the plot of most fantasy, in religious fantasy, good wins because God is considered the sovereign and absolute power. In addition, the hero chooses the side of good, often after a long inner battle. Because this moral struggle is the primary focus of the story, the character's journey is often symbolic of an inner spiritual quest. Reader identification with this character is thus an effective technique for encouraging changes in the reader's own attitudes and values. For this reason, characters are often converted or morally changed.

Christian Research Institute's *Forward Magazine*, says that behind the fantasy world "there must still be a supreme being who provides a basis for authentic morality. Absolute morality can only be sustained in . . . a universe sustained by a transcendent, holy God" (Scheer, 32). This call for "authentic morality" in Christian fantasy illustrates that the most important aspect of a work is the ideas that apply to our "real" world. Even though the work may contain an imaginary world, the meaning is considered true. This genre is therefore more contemplative than other types of fiction; some might call its intent didactic. Motivated by Christian concerns, it exists not just for the sake of entertaining but rather deals with "eternals."

However, the "message" is ideally conveyed through fantasy and

Biblical images, symbols, characters, and events. Since the imagination is considered a better source of images than the natural world, many writers have transferred or transposed spiritual truths and religious beliefs into the objective devices of fantasy literature such as secondary worlds, talking animals, magic, and so on. Religious fantasy "tries to catch . . . a clear vision of the truth and it offers it in the only language in which truth can be clothed—the language of symbol and archetype" (Melrose, *Nine Visions: A Book of Fantasies*, 4). Other common techniques involve supposition (asking "what if . . . ?") and re-mythologizing (converting Biblical names and events into a different language and mythology). Each technique affects the reader and conveys Biblical principles differently.

By taking the "religion" out of the normal world and translating it into a fairy-tale world, Christian fantasy is able to present Christianity in a different "language" for certain audiences who are otherwise repelled by or cannot understand traditional terminology. One writer describes a Christian fantasy writer as "a person who knows God intimately enough to take everlasting truths, clothe them in completely new symbols and events, and proclaim them with heart-stirring originality" (Pinzon, "Drunk on the Wild Sweetness," 7). In "The Fantastic Imagination" (in *The Gifts of the Child Christ*), George MacDonald writes that this type of writing gives new embodiment to old truths, thereby transfiguring Christianity into a wholly new form.

A number of books have recently been published that follow in the tradition of Lewis and Tolkien. Yet few use the same forms, exploring instead other types of fantasy. The intended audiences range from children to adults, and the forms include secondary world fantasy, fairy tale, animal stories, dream voyage, historical fantasy, science fiction, and myth. Each form has certain advantages, depending on the author's purpose, themes, and audience. But it is difficult to achieve believability and effectively integrate the message with the story, thus avoiding the extremes of either blatant allegory and didacticism or obscurity. As a type of literature that has the ability to actually change the reader, however, it is unique. Effects include not only changed moral values but also recovery, restoration of the Medieval metaphors, satisfaction of desires, and consolation.

Religious fantasy is becoming a distinctive class of science fiction and fantasy. The sub-genre seems to be growing, paralleling and perhaps tapping into the popularity of secular fantasy. Gary Wolfe believes that

writers who seek new mythic patterns for Christian experience rather than merely replacing it with a scientific myth, or who like [David] Lindsay attempted to create wholly new myths on intellectual rather than doctrinaire bases, have been far fewer in number in fantastic literature, but have begun to emerge as the most profoundly influential figures in all of modern myth-literature ("Symbolic Fantasy," 206).

For this reason, he believes "symbolic fantasy," as he calls it, has become increasingly important. Thomas Howard encourages writers to

keep on telling tales of realms in which . . . things make sense. . . . And so with the other things that you find in myth but that you can't find in our imaginative landscape. Any Christian suspects that those things are there forever. One way or another, we have to tell the story about them ("The Uses of Myth," 21).

While other studies have examined individual Christian fantasy writers such as MacDonald or Lewis, few are available on religious fantasy as a whole. And because this genre powerfully affects many readers at the spiritual level, the techniques used should be identified. In addition, because religious fantasy is controversial, its aims and benefits ought to be understood. Those who attack fantasy, for example, argue that the word "fantasy" suggests something made up and therefore a lie or simply entertainment. Others object that if Christianity has to be romanticized in fiction, it implies the Bible is inadequate, or that fantasy attempts to be an avenue or companion to theology. Fantasy has also been viewed as overvalued, escapist, useless, false, even a tool of Satan ("Satan's Fantasy"; Basney, "What about Fantasy?", 18). Some may even argue that to avoid alienating secular audiences, the message has to be watered down. Ironically, however, the most successful contemporary religious fantasy novels have been published by secular publishers.

The aim of this book is therefore to explore why fantasy is used to convey theological principles, and the forms and methods used to achieve various effects. While it will examine the theory and general techniques used by the "founders" of the genre—Lewis, Tolkien, and MacDonald—it will focus on many newer writers who continue their tradition yet explore new techniques and forms for conveying theology through fantasy.

# Chapter 1

# "The Perilous Realm": Elements and Themes of Secondary World Fantasy

Most good fairy stories are about the *adventures* of men in the Perilous Realm or upon its shadowy marches (J. R. R. Tolkien, "On Fairy Stories").

## THE CREATION OF OTHER WORLDS

The most important characteristic of secondary world fantasy is, of course, the creation of another, secondary world, an invented milieu. Lewis and Tolkien agree that the work must have "at least the hint of another world" (Lewis, *They Asked for a Paper*, 452), and this world is often more real than our own. Manlove observes that in religious fantasy "the 'real' world is often not our universe, which to the writers is no less fantastic than those they have created, but is equated with the final Reality from which all worlds stem" (*Modern Fantasy: Five Studies*, 2). In addition, John Timmerman observes that another world makes "it possible to confront more openly and daringly a spiritual reality too often ignored in our world of system and fact" ("Fantasy Literature's Evocative Power," 535). Because fantasy deals with the truth and reality of the human heart, which is "devalued in daily life, one must look to another world where such realities can be restructured and given credence and value" (535).

Secondary world fantasy, says Tolkien in his essay "On Fairy Stories," is about "*Faerie*, the realm or state in which fairies have their being." Most fairy stories are about "the adventures of men in the Perilous Realm or upon its shadowy marches." Faerie contains

many things besides elves and fays, and besides dwarfs, witches, trolls, giants or dragons: it holds the seas, the sun, the moon, the sky; and the earth, and all things that are in it: tree and bird, water and stone, wine and bread, and ourselves, mortal men, when we are enchanted (9).

One also finds "beauty that is an enchantment, and an ever-present peril; both joy and sorrow as sharp as swords." He distinguishes fairy story from traveller's tales, dreams used to explain marvels, and beast fables. The works of George MacDonald or *Alice in Wonderland*, for example, may not be considered invented milieu fantasy because these works are dreams, and the details used present a strange rather than realistic other world.

According to Lewis, David Lindsay was

the first writer to discover what "other planets" are really good for in fiction. No merely physical strangeness or merely spatial distance will realise that idea of otherness which is what we are always trying to grasp in a story about voyaging through space: you must go into another dimension. To construct plausible and moving "other worlds" you must draw on the only real other world" we know, that of the spirit (*On Stories and Other Essays in Literature*, 12).

Thus other planets in fiction are "good for" spiritual adventures, says Lewis, because they satisfy the craving of our imaginations, suggest "otherness," and convey "wonder, beauty, and suggestiveness" (*On*, 64).

Because it is difficult to describe "marvels" when our world is already known, you must go to faerie for something other than what we have on earth: "It is not difficult to see why those who wish to visit strange regions in search of such beauty, awe, or terror as the actual world does not supply have increasingly been driven to other planets or other stars. It is the result of increasing geographical knowledge" (*On*, 63). This other world can be earth in the distant past or future, another planet, or a parallel universe.

Because a reader may be more willing to enter a secondary world and accept what happens there, he may be more open to any ideas in the story. Recognizing that the work is fantasy, he willingly suspends his disbelief and accepts another world with its own laws. For example, when a character is taken to another world, he can experience anything without straining credibility, and when he returns to earth he can apply the things he learned. Moreover, since the secondary world serves as a mirror or metaphor for ours, things that happen in that world, including ideas the reader and characters learn, can be applied to our world.

Finally, the other world, by showing us things in a different way, can shed light on our world and help us return to it with a renewed vision. Ursula Le Guin writes, "Scientist and science-fictioneer invent worlds in order to reflect and so to clarify, perhaps to glorify, the 'real world,' the objective Creation" (*The Language of the Night: Essays on Fantasy and Science Fiction*, 113). While "the science-fictioneer imitates the Creation," the "fantasist imitates the Creator." However, writers have disagreed about whether art is an imitation or copy of what God has already created or whether creation is on-going and can be a newly created imaginary world.

### Historical Views of Artist as Creator

How and why a Christian fantasy writer achieves his expression of faith begins first with his concept of the relation of his art to God's Truth, as M. H. Abrams traces in *The Mirror and the Lamp*. While the idea that poetry is inspired by the gods is ancient, Plato began the controversy by condemning art as an imitation that leads us away from reality. Explicit reference to the poet's invention being similar to God's creation of the universe is found in late fifteenth century Florentine writers. For example, in *Commentary on Dante* (1481), Cristofor Landino writes,

The Greeks say "poet" from the very "piin" [sic] which is half-way between "creating" which is peculiar to God when out of nothing he brings forth anything into being, and "making," which applies to men when they compose with matter and form in any art. It is for this reason that, although the feigning of the poet is not entirely out of nothing, it nevertheless departs from making and comes very near to creating. And God is the supreme poet, and the world is His poem (Abrams, *The Mirror and the Lamp*, 273).

In 1561 Scaliger made the influential statement that while other arts "represent things themselves just as they are, in some sort like a speaking picture, the poet represents another nature and varied fortunes, and in so doing makes himself, as it were, another God" (Abrams, 273). But, more important, the concept of poet as creator in God's image began in English criticism by Sir Philip Sidney, who believed the poet is a second creator of a second Nature. He used the Roman definition of poet as "vates" or diviner, foreseer, or prophet, and the Greek word "poiein" or maker. Sidney wrote that the poet is not tied to Nature but "lifted up with the vigor of his own invention, doth grow in effect into another nature in making things either better than Nature bringeth forth, or, quite anew, forms such as never were in Nature, as the Heroes, Demigods, Cyclops, Chimeras, Furies, and such like" ("The Defense of Poesy," 607).

Since God made man in his own likeness, he "set him beyond and over all the works of that second nature: which in nothing he sheweth so much as in poetry, when with the force of a divine breath he bringeth things forth surpassing her doings" ("Defense," 607). However, because of the Fall, our "erected wit" makes us know what perfection is, but our "infected will" keeps us from reaching it. Still, art does not become didactic. Lewis comments, "The 'Golden World' which it presents must be set forth 'in so rich Tapistry' as Nature never knew, must lure us into itself. The images of virtue are not mere *moralitas*, no powder hidden under jam" (*English Literature in the Sixteenth Century*, 346).

In 1589, George Puttenham, in "The Art of English Poesy," wrote, "It is therefore of poets thus to be conceived that, if they be able to devise and make all these things of themselves without any subject of verity, that they be—by manner of speech—as creating gods" (640). Abrams notes that this idea that the artist is a God-like creator of a second nature was kept alive by Italian and English neoplatonists who applied the word "creation," though casually, to poets such as Dennis, Donne, and Pope. They used the terms to explain and justify supernatural elements in a poem copied from life. These elements, they said, belong to a second "supernature" created by the poet.

Lewis explains that neoplatonists such as Scaliger, Sidney, Bacon, and others presented a Christianized Platonic dualism, in which the material world is inferior to that of the soul: "The man who, in his 'feigned history,' improved on Nature and painted what might or ought to be, did not feel that he was retreating from reality into a merely subjective refuge; he was reascending from a world which he had a right to call 'foolish' and asserting his divine origin" (*English Literature in the Sixteenth Century Excluding Drama*, 321).

In the eighteenth century, Addison added to these ideas:

There is a kind of Writing, wherein the Poet quite loses sight of Nature, and entertains his Reader's Imagination with the Characters and Actions of such persons as have many of them no Existence, but what he bestows on them. Such are Fairies, Witches, Magicians, Demons, and departed Spirits. This Mr. Dryden calls the Fairy way of Writing, which is, indeed, more difficult than any other that depends on the Poet's Fancy, because he has no Pattern to follow in it, and must work altogether out of his own Invention ("The Spectator," 406).

By 1740 the idea existed that the poem can be a second creation that is not a replica of this world but creates its own world subject to its own laws, thus giving it an inner coherence. There were seen to be two kinds of truth: rational and poetic. By the nineteenth century "create" was routinely used to describe what the poet does. For example, in "A Defence of Poetry, " Shelley writes, "Poetry lifts the veil from the hidden beauty of the world, and makes familiar objects be as if they were not familiar" (487). In addition, it "makes us the inhabitants of a world to which the familiar world is a chaos. . . . It creates anew the universe after it has been annihilated in our minds by the recurrence of impressions blunted by reiteration" (505–506). Similarly, for Coleridge, Imagination was the gift of the artist and reflection in man of God as Creator, "a repetition in the finite mind of the eternal act of creation in the infinite I AM" (*Biographia Literaria*, 167).

## Other Writers on Creation

One of the chief influences on religious fantasy, George MacDonald is more conservative in his views of the artist, claiming it is better to use the word "creation" for "that calling out of nothing which is the imagination of God." "Everything of man must have been of God first" (*A Dish of Orts*, 3). Man simply rearranges and recombines elements God has made. But by using materials from our world and drawing on reality, the author can express truths that cannot be expressed or explained in any other way.

MacDonald believes the main function of imagination is "to inquire into what God has made," apprehend spiritual truth, and give form to thought. The word "imagination" means "an imaging or a making of likenesses" (*Dish*, 2). He was influenced by the German Romantics, who said imagination and intuition receive truth, then reason apprehends it. Thus imagination and intellect must work together. But imagination is the faculty most like God's and man's highest mental faculty, existing in the subconscious. Imagination gives form to thought; form comes from nature, and nature comes from God. Therefore, God inhabits this area of the mind, controls what it does, and is the source of thoughts. The artist, then, has no control over the products of his imagination.

MacDonald's prescription for constructing a fairy tale came from Novalis. It should have "a narrative surface bustling and incoherent, supported by an underlying musical harmony" deriving from "an orchestration of themes" (Hein, *The Harmony Within*, 55). Because they are formed by principles above our apprehension, even though works of the creative imagination may seem chaotic, incoherent, and dreamlike, they are about God, in God's language, and expressions of spiritual truth. Since God invests nature with meaning but truth is hidden, man, through imagination, can come to know truth if he is in harmony with God: "The 'harmony within,' the hidden unity and coherence of all things is with God, whose meanings and purposes infuse the entirety of this apparent chaos with a higher order. The spiritually mature artist is able to catch glimpses of the true import of things" (Hein, 154).

It is the artist's job to create anew hidden patterns in his own work. A "man may, if he pleases, invent a little world of his own, with its own laws; for there is that in him which delights in calling up new forms—which is the nearest, perhaps he can come to tradition" ("The Fantastic Imagination," 23–24). If they are new embodiments of old truths, he calls them products of the imagination. If they are mere inventions, they are Fancy. Thus MacDonald holds to the value of presenting truth in a new way: "Law is the soil in which alone beauty will grow; beauty is the only stuff in which Truth can be clothed; and you may, if you will, call Imagination the tailor that cuts her garments to fit her" (Hein, 148).

Other theoreticians about religious fantasy have expressed their own views about the nature of creation. In "The Mirror," G. K. Chesterton contends that it is the business of the artist to make the world over again like a God. Even if he tries to paint things as they are, he will inevitably and unconsciously paint them as they ought to be. In *The Mind of the Maker*, Dorothy Sayers draws an extended comparison between God as creator and writing a book. Sayers argues that instead of the words "copy" and "imitation" we should substitute the words "image" or "image forth" because an image expresses something unimaginable. She quotes Paul's words: "God . . . hath spoken to us by his Son, the brightness of his glory and express image of his person." Christ is the express image of God, "not the copy, or imitation, or representation of the Father, nor yet inferior or subsequent to the Father in any way" (*The Whimsical Christian*, 84). God is known to us only by this image.

She believes that while God created out of nothing, we build and rearrange in new forms. Yet the artist is not limited by matter:

The components of the material world are fixed; those of the world of imagination increase by a continuous and irreversible process, without any destruction or rearrangement of what went before. This represents the nearest approach we experience to "creation out of nothing," and we conceive of the act of absolute creation as being an act analogous to that of the creative artist (*Mind*, 29).

Francis A. Schaeffer agrees that we create from what has already been created. But the word "create" is appropriate because man takes what is already there and makes something new; an unmannish part of reality is transformed into a mannish one:

God, because he is infinite, can create out of nothing by his spoken word. We, because we are finite, must create from something else that has already been created. Yet the word "create" is appropriate, for it suggests that what man does with what is already there is to make something new. Something that was not there before. Something that began as an unmannish part of reality, is transformed by the mannishness of man and now reflects that mannishness (*Art and the Bible*, 35).

Schaeffer concludes that fantasy and imagination should not be a threat to Christians:

Christians . . . ought not to be threatened by fantasy and imagination. . . . The Old Testament art commanded by God was not always "photographic." There were blue pomegranates on the robes of the priest who went into the Holy of Holies. In nature there are no blue pomegranates. Christian artists . . . have a basis for knowing the difference between them and the real world "out there." The Christian is the really free person—he is free to have imagination. This too is our heritage. The Christian is the one whose imagination should fly beyond the stars (61).

Finally, Harold Myra, in his fantasy novel *Escape From the Twisted Planet*, suggests that the reason God did not create this world complete was because he allows us to share his creativity:

He lets us share in his making of worlds. He could have created our planet ready-made. . . . But we are "made in his image" as you say, and we become a part of his creativity, joining with one another to make beautiful civilized worlds out of the rough material he gives us. He could as easily have kept all the joy of making to himself (130).

## Lewis on Creation as Reflection

Lewis and Tolkien disagreed about the relation of art to God's Truth, as Randall Helms discusses in his essay, "All Tales Need Not Come True." Lewis' view of reality, involving man's separation from his heavenly potential, can be described as Platonic. Briefly, Plato believed that the real, stable, permanent part of the universe exists in a supernatural, super-sensible "heaven" as Ideas or Forms. The physical world is only the realm of appearances rather than solid reality—illusory, transitory. In this way, it is only a shadow or copy of the "real" world. Thus the artist is three-times removed from reality. Lewis similarly considered reality static, God absolute. Because there is an objective, eternal Truth, God's "story" is already complete. However, "Lewis apparently entertains contradictory notions on the question of whether the romantic experience really *mediates* revelatory reality or merely *reflects* and points to a truth which has never been revealed in another form" (Urang, *Shadows of Heaven*, 39).

Lewis uses this concept of art in his fiction. Aslan's followers, for example, go to His country, only to find the real Narnia and the real England, the imitations of which they had known all their lives. As they go "further up and further in," they find a garden containing an even better Narnia than the one Aslan destroys. From the mountains they see a Narnia that is "as different as a real thing is from a shadow or as waking life is from a dream. . . . It's all in Plato." Aslan's country is like the old Narnia but "more like the real thing." Lewis describes the difference as like a reflection of a landscape in a mirror, where the reflection is real but "somehow different—deeper, more wonderful, more like places in a story."

In *The Last Battle*, Lewis' Platonic ideal is a solid, concrete reality where "every rock and flower and blade of grass" seems to "mean more." Similarly, in *The Great Divorce*, Lewis finds that things in heaven are much more solid than the ghostly earthlings who travel there and that you could cut your finger on the grass. Life is weak and flimsy compared with the solid reality it reflects. That is why, in *Perelandra*, Ransom is told, "You see only an appearance, small one. You have never seen more than an appearance of anything." "I have lived all my life among shadows and broken images," he sadly concludes.

Dennis Quinn attacks Lewis on the grounds that such Platonism "denies or diminishes the reality of the sensible world and substitutes for it a world that exists only in the mind" ("The Narnia Books of C. S. Lewis: Fantastic or Wonderful," 109). In discussing *The Faerie Queen*, for example, Lewis points out that neo-Platonism allowed the artist to imitate the reality in his own mind rather than external Nature, thus scorning faithfulness to fact, and glamorize the spiritual world at the expense of the real. The Narnia tales, Quinn argues, deny the reality of the created universe. "Fantasy is harmful to the imagination . . . because it encourages the reader to turn inward and to distrust if not despise reality" (119). It implies there are no wonders or marvels in our world.

Since Lewis believed everything originates with God, imaginative inventions must reflect God's Truth. There can therefore be no genuine creativeness because one can only reflect the universe's order and beauty: "I think that all things in their way, reflect heavenly truth, the imagination not least. 'Reflect' is the important word. This lower life of the imagination is not a beginning of nor a step towards, the higher life of the spirit, merely an image" (*Surprised by Joy*, 167). The New Testament clearly uses the word "originality" as the "prerogative of God alone," so our duty and joy should be found as simply "reflecting like a mirror." It "leaves no room for 'creativeness.' " Thus the author should not bring "into existence beauty or wisdom which did not exist before" but rather try to embody in art "some reflection of eternal Beauty and Wisdom" (*Christian Reflections*, 6–7). Because the New Testament uses words like "mirror" and "imitation" to describe life itself, literature certainly should not aim at being creative, original, or spontaneous.

As a reflection of ultimate reality, art is also only a rearrangement of what is there. In *Letters to Malcolm: Chiefly on Prayer*, Lewis, for example, says poets, musicians, and inventors never "*make*. We only build. We always have materials to build from. All that we can know about the act of creation must be derived from what we can gather about the relation of the creatures to their Creator" (73). He thus feels the word "creation" cannot really be applied to human writing:

We re-arrange elements He has provided. There is not a vestige of real creativity de novo in us. Try to imagine a new primary colour, a third sex, a fourth dimension, or even a monster which does not consist of bits of existing animals stuck together. Nothing happens. . . . We recombine elements made by Him and already containing *His* meanings (*Letters*, 203).

Art and imagination are, however, a path to understanding God. In *The Great Divorce* the Ghost tells the artist that his paintings were successful because they allowed others to "see the glimpses too. But here you are having the thing itself. It is from here that the messages came. . . . Light itself was your first love: you loved paint only as a means of telling about the light" (80–81). Lewis also felt it was the artist's duty to worship God by inventing.

### Tolkien on "Sub-creation"

According to Lewis, then, while man can create, he cannot do so *ex nihilo* as God can. Stories can only rearrange or retell what already exists; thus many of Lewis' works are attempts to re-tell or "explain" the Bible. J. R. R. Tolkien, however, took a more liberal view of the idea of man being made in God's image, calling the artist a sub-creator, i.e., a creator of images not found in our world. He not only expands on, rewrites, and changes the Genesis story but considers his myth a supplement to the Bible.

To Tolkien, on the other hand, fantasy is "a human right: we make in our measure and in our derivative mode, because we are made: and not only made, but made in the image and likeness of a Maker" ("On Fairy Stories," 55). In response to C. S. Lewis, who once described myth and fairy stories as lies, Tolkien wrote: "Man, Sub-creator, the refracted Light / through whom is splintered from a single White / to many hues. . . . Though all the crannies of the world we filled / with Elves and Goblins . . . 'twas our right . . . we make still by the law in which we're made" ("On Fairy," 54).

Tolkien disagreed with the distinction Coleridge made between imagination and fancy because he thought it inappropriate and inaccurate. Tolkien defines fancy as "a mode of memory emancipated from the order of time and space" and analogous to understanding. Imagination is "the power of giving to ideal creations the inner consistency of reality and analogous to reason," the power of image-making. Art is the link between imagination and its final result, sub-creation, which gives the "inner consistency of reality" ("On Fairy," 46–47). "Fantasy" is his word for that "which combines with its older and higher use as an equivalent of Imagination the derived notions of 'unreality' (that is, of unlikeness to the Primary World), of freedom from the domination of observed 'fact,' in short of the fantastic" (47). Since it can create images not found in our primary world, it is thus the most nearly pure form of art and difficult to achieve. Lewis says the best example of sub-creation is *Lord of the Rings* because the "direct debt . . . which every author must owe to the actual universe is here deliberately reduced to the minimum" (*On*, 84). He considers Tom Bombadil and the ents the "utmost reach of invention, when an author produces what seems to be not even his own, much less anyone else's" (86).

In discussing the Truth that art should reveal, then, Lewis looks back to the One Story God has already created; Tolkien looks forward because he sees Truth as a story still in the making. In "Leaf By Niggle" he uses the analogy of a Tree of tales to which all can contribute. Artist Niggle, who has always painted trees, ultimately sees his Tree complete in heaven: "All the leaves he had ever laboured at were there, as he had imagined them rather than as he had made them; there were others that had only budded in his mind, and many that might have budded, if he only had had time." In "On Fairy Stories" Tolkien suggests that in fantasy the artist "may actually assist in the effoliation and multiple enrichment of creation," thus implying that one day the artist's creations may be given real life in heaven.

In his letters, Tolkien explains that *Lord of the Rings* itself is essentially about the relation of Creation to Sub-creation. Sub-creation is freed from the channels the Creator has already used. Thus certain things not theologically sound are acceptable within an imaginary world and, in fact, can elucidate truth (*The Letters of J. R. R. Tolkien*, 189). Fantasy is made out of the primary world of simple, fundamental things but rearranges primary matter in secondary patterns (*Letters*, 298). While he felt that all art must reflect and contain elements of moral and religious truth, it must not be explicit as in the real world (*Letters*, 144).

Tolkien nevertheless maintains that the sub-creator "hopes that he is drawing on reality: hopes that the peculiar quality of this secondary world (if not all the details) are derived from Reality, or are flowing into it" ("On Fairy," 70). Traditionally, fantasy was associated with the unreal and imaginary. But by defining it as sub-creation with an inner consistency of reality, Tolkien makes it a reality apart from ours:

Fantasy is a natural human activity. It certainly does not destroy or even insult Reason; and it does not either blunt the appetite for, nor obscure the perception of scientific verity. On the contrary. The keener and the clearer is the reason, the better fantasy will it make. . . . For creative Fantasy is founded upon the hard recognition that things are so in the world as it appears under the sun; on a recognition of fact, but not a slavery to it ("On Fairy," 54–55).

Tolkien considers his myth a supplement to the Bible because writers of the Bible and of fairy stories, "both works of fantasy, become coworkers with the Great Author, sub-creators working but in accord with the Creator" (Helms, *Tolkien and the Silmarils*, 26). He insists that his stories arose in his mind as "given" things; he did not invent them but rather he had the sense that they were revealed to him or that he was simply recording what was already there" (*Letters*, 145). But he expands on and changes the Genesis account. *The Silmarillion*, for example, tells the story of the creation, fall, redemption, and apocalypse but with changes. He thus describes it as a "monotheistic but sub-creational mythology" (*Letters*, 235). God is "not embodied and is remote." Although there is a fall of angels in his cosmogony, he says it is different from the Bible in form (*Letters*, 147).

One variation on the Bible is that the Ainur were allowed to create some elements of the universe and take material form on earth as Valar. Another difference he cites is that in the Bible the Fall of man is a consequence of the fall of the angels and evil brought into the world by Satan: "The rebellion of created free-will precedes the creation of the World (Ea); and Ea has in it, subcreatively introduced, evil, rebellions, discordant elements of its own nature already when the *Let it Be* was spoken" (*Letters*, 286). So the original design of the universe was spoiled even before man's fall because of Melkor's conflict with the Valar. Another example is Gandalf's "incarnation" after his death. Tolkien says that while one might be reminded of the Gospels, "it is not really the same thing at all. The Incarnation of God is an *infinitely* greater thing than anything I would dare to write" (*Letters*, 237).

In describing the fantasy writer, contemporary fantasy writer Robert Siegel seems to agree with Tolkien:

God has honored not only our physical being but our desire to be subcreators; that is, to help him in the matter of creation. . . . He has graciously allowed us to extend and efoliate—I love that word of Coleridge's—*efoliate* the creation. I mean, he may have created the tree, but we're branches of that tree; we are there extending some of the leaves of it. . . . Man really has been given license in his art to take the humble materials of creation and to help extend it (Fickett, "A Conversation with Poet/Novelist Robert Siegel," 36–37).

He believes our ability to create makes us most like God:

We are subcreators, participating with God in creating the world. It's as if God made the trunk, branches and bird of the Great World Tree and allows us to participate in bringing out the foliage, in the finishing of each leaf. It's important to take seriously our talent to create—to extend the creation (Miller and Miller, "Exploring Myth," 2).

In "On Fairy Stories," Tolkien distinguishes between the creation of a secondary world and Magic, which produces "an alteration in the primary world" and seeks power. He prefers the term "Enchantment," the creation of a secondary world into which both designer and spectator can enter. Yet magic is a key element within the Perilous Realm itself.

## MAGIC

The Creator whom the fantasist imitates is often likened to a Magician. In "The Ethics of Elfland," for example, Chesterton says, "I had always believed that the world involved magic: now I thought that perhaps it involved a magician." The essential nature of fairy story is magic, and in the case of religious fantasy the source of magic is usually the supernatural. John Timmerman believes the association of God with magic shows his miraculous and incomprehensible power (536). In "On Fairy Stories," Tolkien adds that, depending on the author, the work may also have the element of the mystical and supernatural or be a mirror for man. He distinguishes between two kinds of magic in *Lord of the Rings*, "magia" (good) and "goeteia" (bad), although either can become good or bad depending on the "motive or purpose or use." For example, a bad motive is to dominate the free wills of others or deceive, whereas magia is used for "specific beneficent purposes." Magic is an inherent power that men cannot possess or obtain and is not achieved by spells (*Letters*, 200). In most contemporary works, the Supreme Being, the source of good magic, gives his followers power that they often evoke through the magic aid of prayer. But evil creatures selfishly misuse magic by seeking to control others.

In his trilogy, which he admits intentionally imitates Lewis' Narnia chronicles, John White contrasts these two types of power ("Fantasy: A Habit of Mind," 8). In *The Tower of Geburah*, the Christ-like Gaal tells Kurt that power is not evil, only dangerous, yet is needed to do good. In *The Sword Bearer* magic is "the mystical power of the Changer" (God) which is greater than all other powers. The guide Mab calls himself a prophet or seer, as opposed to a magician or wizard, and he performs miracles by using the Changer's power in the Changer's service. Whenever Mab has used his power when Changer has not told him to, it did not have any lasting good.

In contrast, Qhahdrun, the chief sorcerer, is lord of the evil Qadar and uses power for himself alone. Magicians like him were brought from other worlds by Changer when Anthropos began. But they chose to serve themselves, and their magic is stolen power. In the end, however, "all power will go back to the Changer from which it came." Similarly, in *The Iron Sceptre*, the witch twists Gaal's laws and uses his laws against him through sorcery.

A magic aid is Gaal's name, prayer, or Gaal's words. For example, in *The Tower of Geburah*, Lisa commands a wall of fire to go away and opens a tunnel in Gaal's name. When she is placed on the stone altar, all she can think of is the name Gaal, even though she does not know who he is: "Gaal, give me something real," she says. Then there is a change. "The feeling inside her, the very faint feeling that something *did* matter grew slightly stronger. . . . 'Gaal, Gaal' she said again. 'I don't know you. Can you help me? Will you?' " (164). Then she is sent a blue light and a pigeon to lead her. This same pigeon helps the children at the Tower of Geburah when they pray to Gaal after making "a mess of things." Kardia suggests that Wesley pray to Gaal even though he, too, does not even know who Gaal is: "Pray to Gaal? Wesley had never been taught to pray to anyone." Nevertheless, he prays that the door of Lisa's dungeon be broken down, "not knowing to whom he said it," and the door shatters.

The four lines Gaal teaches the children in *The Iron Sceptre* are called "deep words" that will make the three circles of enchantment powerless:

Gaal is the Lord of far and near.
Gaal is the Lord of light.
Gaal is the Lord of sea and fire.
And Gaal is the Lord of Ice (229).


In *The Sword Bearer*, the Changer's name has power. But one cannot just say "in Changer's name" to have something happen, but rather, "in the name of *my* Changer."

Evil magic usually seeks to possess and reduce one's being by subduing the will. In Stephen Lawhead's *In the Hall of the Dragon King*, the power of the sorcerers is said to be the way of death. Durwin gave it up so it could not be misused and because one cannot serve two masters. "Who is the other master?" he is asked. The Most High God, the One, "demands your life as well. But in him there *is* life, rather than death—which is where Power always leads in the end." One may be tempted to use more and more power until it becomes your Master, ending in slavery and death.

Throughout Lawhead's books, prayer is used whenever the characters are in trouble. It is always answered and is more personal than the kind Quentin is used to, that of praying to the old gods. For instance, when Quentin first hears the prayer of the god at Dekra, he is surprised to hear that the elder can pray without fear, self-consciousness, and lack of assurance. He actually feels the god's presence. Quentin prays whenever he is in a fix on his quest; he needs a means of escape from wolves or a waterspout, or simply needs hope. For example, when the group is about to be attacked by Nimrood and Jaspin's army, their only recourse is to pray to "the Most High. He is the only one who can save us now."

In *The Warlords of Nin*, Alinea similarly realizes that prayers can do for Eskevar what magic potions cannot.

In Paul Gallico's *The Man Who Was Magic: A Fable of Innocence*, a Christ figure is associated with Magic. A strange thin traveler named Adam comes from Glimour, behind the Mountains of Straen, to Mageia, the city of the world Magicians, to learn from the Guild of Master Magicians. However, his Magic is True, whereas the Magicians use trickery and deceit. Adam teaches the child Jane that the world contains magic such as a tree growing from an acorn or a cow producing milk. But most important, her head is like a magic "box with many compartments. Each one you can call upon for anything you want or desire. It contains the greatest magic of all." Adam then points out to her the wonderful things inside her own mind.

Afraid that Adam will put them out of business, the Magicians rise in anger to kill him. But when he produces gold for them, he escapes as they greedily gather it:

Through their own human weaknesses they had failed to recognize one whose innocence of heart had endowed him with powers that transcended theirs and who meant them no harm. The long-feared magician who might some day appear to show all of them up as tricksters and against whom they had barricaded themselves behind high walls had proven to be no more than a simple, friendly young man who had come modestly to sit at their feet and learn from them. They had stoned him from their midst and he had repaid them with gold (191).

In the classic *The Secret Garden* by Frances Hodgson Burnett, magic is also associated with the supernatural, although it is not overtly mentioned. Contemporary fantasy writer Madeleine L'Engle calls this a Christian book even though it never mentions Jesus, and it is because the message "doesn't show" that it succeeds. L'Engle comments, "Mary's journey into love is, in fact, her journey into Christ, though this is never said, and does not need to be said" (*Walking on Water: Reflections on Faith and Art*, 123).

Two sickly and bad-tempered children, Mary and Dickon, become healthy and emotionally transformed because of the magic of a secret garden with Edenic parallels. Because Dickon's mother died by falling off a branch of a tree in the garden, the garden has been locked and allowed to grow wild. Although the tree is now dead, roses grow over it, symbolizing the growing of good from evil. But the garden also represents the children's souls: "Nobody has any right to take it from me when I care about it and they don't. They're letting it die, all shut in by itself," cries Mary. When Colin, the children's friend, sees the garden he feels he shall "live forever and ever." This feeling of immortality, says Burnett, similarly can come briefly when one sees a sunrise, sunset, stars, the sound of far-off music, or just a look in someone's eyes.

Mary and Colin attribute good things to good Magic and evil to wrong Magic. There is a lot of Magic in the world, but "people don't know what it is like or how to make it." Colin observes, "Magic is always pushing and drawing and making things out of nothing. Everything is made out of Magic," including people. To show their thanks to the Magic, they sing the Doxology. As a result, the gardener realizes, "Perhaps it means just what I mean when I want to shout out that I am thankful to the Magic. . . . Perhaps they are both the same thing. How can we know the exact names of everything?" (239).

Robert Don Hughes' trilogy (*The Prophet of Lameth*, *The Wizard in Waiting*, and *The Power and the Prophet*) is the best example of a developed religious secondary world fantasy in which a supernatural "Power" is the source of magic. God is described as the Power, the source of all powers. This Power works "on men as a magician works on the wind and fire," but the magic is "painless—and cleansing." The Power, who lives on a Mountain in the North Fir forest, finds Pelmen there and changes him:

He was no longer his own. The Power had placed a stamp upon him, and part of that mark was a humility born of uncertainty. He could never be sure, now, when he might be summoned. Often, in responding to that call, he'd witnessed his own careful plans evaporate in the shift of circumstance. Yet he wasn't unhappy in this. There burned within him a sense of personal purpose that had always been lacking when he'd called himself his own (*Power*, 66–67).

The Power meets Pelmen wherever he is, gives him a sense of peace, and preserves him from danger. He also "leads you to do what you should—and furnishes the energy with which to do it." Most important, the Power gives Pelmen the ability to be a Powershaper, one who shapes powers as though they are extensions of his mind. If he focuses his thoughts, the powers do as he asks. Pelmen says when he shapes he first feels terror. Then "I sense a power, I begin to shape, then somehow, inexplicably, it begins shaping me." He feels an "enormous warmth engulf him," a "rushing presense," "elation born far beyond human experience," and "abundant joy." A Powershaper also can become an alter-shape when the need for a new identity arises, and this shape reflects his personality. Some of the Power's followers, however, do not discover this "gift" of shaping because they "grab at the trappings of faith without experiencing faith itself." Each person must take his own approach to the Power.

Pelmen often invokes the Power for help. Usually kneeling, he talks to the Power with a hint of "simple, genuine warmth . . . he spoke to One he knew as a friend." For example, he asks for a "wall of invisibility" and a "cloak of protection" around himself. The Power also sends a wind to help him find his way out of a castle. But the "Power did not jump when he called. He had no assurance that his every request would immediately be met." Usually, he had to exhaust his own resources, seek new ones, or else the Power would come unbidden. In contrast, his friend Rosha believes the Power is like a safety net whom he calls on only if he gets in trouble.

Hughes shows the conflict between followers of the Power and those of a false faith. The people of Lamath once disagreed about whether the "powers of the air" could be controlled by powershaping, magic, or by physical means. Thus they created a two-headed dragon, Vicia-Heinox, who lives in the center of the world, so that they would cooperate to kill him. But because they needed something to believe in, some became Dragonfaithers who believe in the dragon's lordship. Skyfaithers, on the other hand, believe in the Power and are called such because their blue robes are the color of the sky. They destroy the dragon statues and scatter throughout the countryside "spreading the precepts of the book and explaining the Power." Various factions emerge such as Divisionists, who believe the dragon is both good and bad, thus explaining evil in the world. In contrast, the orthodox Coalescence Mainstream believe he is both one and two persons, thus creating a tension.

An ancient, Bible-like book of strange runes is about "recognizable events" and people just like Pelmen. The ideas and symbols threaten him because "each passage only deepened his conviction that the words spoke of him." The book places "an enormous burden on someone's shoulders," and he resists being the one to bear it. Rosha, a Skyfaither, is to keep reading this book to the people of Lamath to tell them the "truth."

Although the Power helps Pelmen kill the dragon, Flayh, an evil and powerful shaper, impersonates the dead dragon and renews the Dragonfaith. To kill Flayh, an ancient crystal weapon designed to kill the dragon must be used to absorb Flayh's power. Pelmen is to be sacrificed by building an altar and placing the crystal over his heart. But Flayh is stabbed first, and in a great explosion, all powers return to the Power. The Power saves Pelmen, however, and allows some power to remain with him as a shaper.

Hughes states that the purpose of The Prophet of Lamath was entertainment rather than apologetics, especially because he submitted it to a secular publisher, Lester del Rey. The second novel, The Wizard in Waiting, was written as he prepared to go to Nigeria as a media missionary: "More of my faith wanted to come out in that rewrite, so I let it. I began to be consciously apologetic" ("Crossing Over: A Tale of Two Markets," 18). Since the characters already existed, he said he was not tempted to make them allegorical and still tried to make the book "light." The third book of the Pelmen trilogy, The Power and the Prophet, was written when he was a missionary in Africa: "It became more than just a book, for it dramatized the things I was experiencing: Spiritual failure in the midst of 'professional success,' the carnality of my own 'baptized ambition,' and the high cost of romanticizing the call of God." But he was bothered by the fact that the trilogy did not "seem to take evil as seriously as I do, and while it was obviously theistic, it wasn't Christological" ("Crossing," 18).

Hughes believes there is a problem in determining the purpose of Christian science fiction and fantasy: is it to evangelize and focus on non-Christians to "give an explanation of the hope within us?" Or should it focus on Christians and nurture their faith through a religious publisher? He leans toward the secular publishers: "'Mainline' SF & F remains a viable playground where we can still enjoy the company of non-Christians—and they can enjoy us. And perhaps be influenced *by* us? . . . Good Christian writers can have a real impact on the SF & F world at large" ("Crossing," 20).

Because of the length of the Pelmen trilogy, Hughes is able to develop the theme of Pelmen's relationship to the Power. This is a central theme in religious fantasy because it shows the reality of the supernatural and its interaction with individuals.

## REALITY OF THE SPIRITUAL WORLD

The magical element in Christianity, Lewis points out, is that heaven is the realm of objective facts: "One cannot conceive . . . a more 'magical,' fact than the existence of God as *causa sui* (*Malcolm*, 104). Another purpose of creating other worlds is thus to show the reality of the spiritual world and characters attempting to come to terms with it. As J. R. R. Tolkien explains in "On Fairy Stories," the secondary world created by the imagination presents the world that lies behind appearances. Since this world is even more real than the world of "fact" seen in space and time, we need both worlds to see the whole picture. According to Madeleine L'Engle, a great fantasist teaches about life in eternity, "life in that time in which we are real." A common theme in religious fantasy is therefore showing that there is more to reality than what we see.

The Bible itself presents the theme of two worlds or two levels of reality, the physical and spiritual, and the presence of spiritual reality in the physical world. According to I Corinthians 2:14, spiritual truths are not discerned intellectually but spiritually. Such things cannot be explained in natural terms: "By refusing to allow reality to be conceived solely in terms of known, observable experience, biblical literature transforms the mundane into something with sacred significance and evokes a sense of mystery of the divine" (Ryken, *The Literature of the Bible*, 17–18).

Just as the Bible shows that it is this spiritual world that gives meaning to life, so too the focus of contemporary religious fantasy is on the unseen, transcendental world. Fantasy reveals that there is a supernatural world within or beyond the natural and presents a vision of it. This ability is especially important as our perception of the spiritual world has dimmed. Lewis observes that "giants, dragon, paradises, gods, and the like are themselves the expression of certain basic elements in man's spiritual experience. In that sense they are more like words—the words of a language which speaks the else unspeakable" (*A Preface to Paradise Lost*, 57). George MacDonald was attracted to fantasy "because he saw the potential it had to assert the presence of . . . transcendent yet immanent reality and to explore the moral imperatives it places upon men's lives" (Hein, 114).

Nancy Willard's *Things Invisible to See* takes place in the "real" world but shows how the supernatural pervades and influences it. Throughout the book, God is shown to control events:

In Paradise, on the banks of the River of Time, the Lord of the Universe is playing ball with His archangels. Hundreds of spheres rest like white stones on the bottom of the river, and hundreds rise like bubbles from the water and fly to His hand that alone brings things to pass and gives them their true colors (1).

He often responds in heaven to character's comments on earth. For example, when Ben Harkissian believes "it hardly seemed worth God's time to make an island that had so little on it," God replies, *"Where were you when I broke the sea for its decreed place and said, 'Hitherto shalt thou come but no farther, and here shall thy proud waves be stayed'?"*

Ben accidently hits Clare Bishop in the head with a baseball. Both Clare's mother and Ben pray for her healing: " 'But will God know we're talking about a baseball?' persisted Ben. 'Couldn't He—I know this sounds funny, but there are so many big problems' . . . 'He looks into our hearts,' " his brother Willie replies. Mr. Knocken, Death dressed in a black suit, is a spiritualist summoned to help Clare. The spirits claim that a woman called Cold Friday is the one who can heal her.

Clare has a guardian spirit, the Ancestress, who teaches Clare to let her spirit leave her body: "Weightless and fleshless, Clare hung in the air beside the old woman and stared down at the slender body that had housed her so faithfully for seventeen years." When Ben is starving during the war, the ancestress sends him food and helps Clare appear to him as an albatross. During the time Ben is gone, a friend Sol Lieberman (soul lover?) teaches Clare to throw a baseball.

Willard compares life to a baseball game. Father Legg, the coach of the men's softball team, "was fond of using baseball analogies in his sermons. Wouldn't you like to pitch for God's team? Don't let temptation get you out!" While marooned on an island, Ben is visited by Death, who makes an agreement to play a baseball game: "If the Dead Knights win, Death shall take the South Avenue Rovers. If the South Avenue Rovers win, Death shall give the members of this team a new lease on life." Proceeds are "to be given to the Red Cross."

Father Legg observes that the odds against them are tremendous. "But we have in our midst a power that no other team can boast. We have a power that never fails. We have love. . . . A miracle would be nice." He becomes hesitant to ask "of God a thing that could not happen according to natural law." Before, he had always said, "Thy will be done. He was afraid to say it now."

Meanwhile, Cold Friday cures Clare and explains,

You is conjured with one of the old spells the devil sent out when he took his third of the earth. . . . They come from the darkness that moved on the face of the waters 'fore the earth *was* . . . that spell got itself handed down, hand over hand, 'cause that spell is so evil (245).

She takes the spell off by sending three doves and two other birds out the window, then calling, "Lord . . . come on down and heal her Yourself."

As Clare, now able to run, prepares for the game, she is not nervous because "there was only the game and the no-game, the players and the watchers, the inside and the outside. Right now only the inside mattered . . . . *The very hairs of your head are numbered*, said God." She glances over the bleachers and sees

a vast, silent throng that receded as if on invisible waves, the women in white, the men in black, the lovely fabric of their presence growing faint among the far-off dead, turning in those farthest from her to feathers, wings, the faces of birds (259).

This same group keeps the plane of Clare's father, Hal, from crashing as he returns home. While the pilot believes the clouds played tricks on them, only "Hal believed his eyes. The engines were silent. But under the wing he saw the ghostly shapes of children, animals, birds, bearing them up."

As the pitcher throws a ball,

In Paradise, the Lord of the Universe tosses a green ball which breaks into a silver ball which breaks into a gold ball, and a small plane lands safely at Willow Run and Hal Bishop climbs out, singing for joy . . . . Clare starts running and Ben runs after her as they round the bases, past the living and the dead, heading at top speed for home (262).

Many contemporary works present the theme of the reality of the spiritual or the contrast between reality and illusion. For example, in Robert Siegel's *Alpha Centauri*, when in the world of the centaurs, Becky feels a "great joy she couldn't explain. Everything, every leaf and blade of grass, seemed much stiller, much more *there* than it had been. Lights and colors and fragrances from the wood were more intense. Time moved slowly, more distinctly" (63).

John White's books emphasize the theme of reality versus illusion. In *The Tower of Geburah* Chocma tells the children, "There are realities beyond those your eyes see." As a prisoner in the castle, Lisa does not know who Gaal is but wonders why, if he were so powerful, King Kardia had not been kept from the evil sorcerer: "Who was he, anyway? Perhaps he didn't even exist. Perhaps it was all a fairy story?" The sorcerer grants her all the things she wishes for—food, bath, and her Uncle John—but they turn out to be illusions because "Gaal is the only source of real things." Lisa begins to think, "Nothing is real . . . nothing is real . . . perhaps I'm not real . . . perhaps there is no me. . . . Someone said the only real things come from Gaal?. . . is Gaal real?" In the throne room of the witch, Kardia also begins to doubt if Gaal is real: "It was as though Gaal had never existed. 'It was, after all, only a dream,' he murmured, 'While this is real, most horribly real, and I am undone.' " When Gaal sends a pigeon to guide the children, Kurt and Inkleth the dwarf cannot see it because of their unbelief. Later, Inkleth tries to convince Kurt Gaal is just a delusion. However, later Kurt can see the pigeon when he begins to believe in Gaal.

In *The Sword Bearer*, because of his dreams and visions of future events, John is confused by what is real and what is a dream. Lord Lunacy tries to convince him that the Changer is only a dream: "The Changer not real? What was real?" But in a vision John is told that mortal eyes rarely see what the Changer is doing. The angelic world is also invisible until John's eyes are opened: "A legion of angelic beings, flaming blue and armed with swords and whips of light" descend with "claps of thunder." They confront ominous dark brown clouds that take the shape of mythological creatures, serpents, and animals: "Behind them in a glory of blue light the angelic hosts were driving them, lashing them with awesome whips of light."

The starvation of the people of Anthropos results from their refusal to go to Gaal for food: "They could not see this food, Lisa," says Gaal. "Their eyes are blind to it, and their tongues cannot taste it." Finally, life after death is portrayed as more real than our world. In Gaal's land, the Bayith of Yayin, which is said to be "everywhere," Gaal tells the children he has conquered death. When he commands the dead King Kardia to arise, Kardia springs up through his satin pall, "more real and more solid than he had ever been."

In her trilogy, Madeleine L'Engle, by means of space-time travel and
size changes, can show their relativity and explore the question, "What
is real?" One of the key lessons of *A Wind in the Door* is the reality of
the invisible spiritual world and the limitations of intellect. In the recent
"sequel" to the trilogy, *Many Waters*, Sandy and Dennys, who are usually
rational and only believe in what can be seen, must broaden their perceptions of reality. They tamper with their parents' experiment with
virtual particles, which flicker in and out of being. When they travel
back in time, the boys encounter virtual unicorns, who, like virtual
particles, must be believed in in order for them to appear.

One of the main purposes of fantasy is to overcome abstraction by
making it vivid and concrete and help us catch a glimpse of reality.
Harvey Cox observes that since Christianity "is anchored both in the
world of fact and in the world of fantasy," i.e., the real world outside
that of the factual, it "has developed images that facilitate fantasy and
the channels by which the fantasy world and the factual world can touch
each other" (*The Feast of Fools*, 80). Some writers illustrate that since
spiritual reality is ignored in our world, by restructuring it a writer can
give it credence and value. Also, since spiritual truths are profound, we
must constantly change the ways we describe them to avoid the limits
of any one description. Robert Siegel declares that in fantasy

we may discover something that can be represented in no other way, that
otherwise would remain unseen. Fantasy ought to be important to Christians
because we are concerned with the unseen world. A novel presents the visible
world, the world that we see, quite literally. But there is no way directly to
present the unseen world, whether it's the world of the spirit, or the world of
our own psyches, except through symbolic images. And fantasy does just that.
It provides us with the images, the symbols, the archetypes to grasp what's
going on within us psychologically and spiritually. Without the ability to imagine
the unseen, our spiritual lives are impoverished (Miller and Miller, 2).

Revelation, for example, illustrates how images can depict spiritual
phenomena by mixing the earthly and supernatural. Frequent allusions
are made to such symbols as the trumpet, tree of life, sacrificial lamb,
and Mt. Zion. Christ is associated with images of hard textures (minerals
and jewels) or brilliant light to convey the transcendent and permanent,
while God's splendor is associated with jasper, carnelian, emerald (Rev.
4:3), rainbow (Ezekiel 1:27–28), and encircling brightness (Ryken, *Literature*, 345, 347). These images are often intentionally vague. Lewis
argues that when we try to convert Biblical images to abstract thought
we fail, because "our abstract thinking is itself a tissue of analogies."
Are these likely to be more adequate, he asks, "than the sensours,
organic, and personal images of Scripture—light and darkness, river and
well, seed and harvest, master and servant, hen and chickens, father

and child? The footprints of the Divine are more visible in that rich soil than across rocks or slagheaps" (*Malcolm*, 52).

The Bible is thus the source of many of the images used in fantasy, where the supernatural world in fantasy is similarly portrayed by using concrete images and mingling the familiar and unfamiliar. Examples of archetypal symbols used in fantasy are blood, dragons and beasts, light and darkness, sun, water, sea, river and fountain, gold, the city, birds, garden, tree, purifying fire, sinister forest, music, and cave. In addition, the inner world is made real and personal by giving it concrete form through characters and action. Lewis asserts, "Persons and events which in themselves are local, immediate, and material can reveal transcendent glories and convey that glory into the most ordinary aspects of our lives" (Williams and Lewis, *Taliessin through Logres, The Region of the Summer, Stars, Arthurian Torso*, 8).

## REALITY OF GOD

Lewis emphasizes that like heaven, God has become "unreal'— like a "gas diffused in space," "vaporous, vague, indefinable, shadowy." Although we associate spirit with ghosts and shadows, spirit should be presented as even "*heavier* than matter" because Reality finds its center in a concrete but non-material Almighty, who is concrete Fact (*Miracles*, 95). Thus language about God must use metaphor and imagery to convey His reality and concreteness. Poetic language is powerful because it can "convey to us the quality of experiences which we have not had, or perhaps can never have, to use factors within our experience so that they become pointers to something outside our experience" (*Christian Reflections*, 133). Even if the images are wrong, the belief behind them is not.

Ryken calls the use of images we can understand to describe God the "principle of accommodation" (*Literature*, 18). Although images and symbols are "less precise and more elusive than propositional language," they "preserve a sense of mystery appropriate to a work that depicts spiritual realities that transcend ordinary reality" (340–341). Donald Richardson distinguishes between symbolizing various aspects of Christ's character rather than painting a picture of him: "Symbolic writing . . . does not paint pictures. It is not pictographic but ideographic. . . . The fish, the lamb, and the lion are all symbols of Christ, but never to be taken as pictures of him . . . the symbol is a code word and does not paint a picture" (*The Revelation of Jesus Christ: An Interpretation*, 16).

Analogy is another means of talking about something we have not experienced; to describe God we use comparisons to things we know such as King or Father. For example, in *The Mind of the Maker*, Dorothy Sayers explains the trinity by comparing it to writing a book. Madeleine

L'Engle affirms that we "learn through analogy, through story. A distinguished writer friend of mine said that Jesus was not a theologian but God who told stories . . . . An analogy is something that opens the door or the window and gives us a glimpse of the truth that gives meaning to life" ("Allegorical," 15). Lewis notes that even the Scripture uses analogies to present God (such as God grieving). But we cannot get rid of the analogy to a literal truth, for we would only substitute a theological abstraction (*Malcolm*, 51).

While many fantasy works contain Christ with a different name but human, Robert Siegel's *Whalesong* is one of the few books to present both God and Christ in a different form. The creation story is retold as if God were a whale. The Spouter of Oceans is said to have "swam alone in the ocean of his being. So great was his bliss that he said to himself, 'I will share my joy with others, whom I will make like myself.' At that he took a great breath and spouted "every living thing into existence." Everything is "the vapor of his breath and will be so until he draws it in." The whales are creatures like him, formed to "swim forever in the Ocean of Light." One day man will live peacefully with other creatures because the Whale of Light had done "something among men to bring it to pass."

When Hruna the Whale takes the Deep Plunge to determine the direction of his life, he notices a great flaming Light too bright to look at. Even if it were to burn or kill him, Hruna wants to approach it. At first the Light sings to him, then stops and turns:

Somehow I could look upon that Brightness without burning. His face had the most beautiful smile on it and even something of laughter. He showed me . . . what I was meant to be . . . he turned and swam away in sport, beckoning me to follow. . . . I chased after him . . . he would dart away laughing (66).

When asked if he is the Spouter of Oceans, the whale simply smiles and Hruna sees "*that* before which all words drop away."

Another whale illustrates Christ's redemption and resurrection. After discovering he will be the new leader, Hruna decides to sacrifice himself for the others to divert harpooners. But the great white whale Hrakelena emerges from the deep, diverting attention from Hruna. With streaks of blood streaming from his side, he sings a death song:

By losing all things you will lead into life A pod in peril. They will find new power. Though the steel harpoon cut home to your heart, Your ransom will render new life to the remnant (134).

In a vision Hrakelena appears to Hruna looking just like the Whale of Light except he has his own features. Hrakelena says the Whale of Light promised that he had done something so that whales could live some day at peace with all creatures.

Christ's redemption and resurrection are successfully portrayed in Richard Adam's *Shardik* through a bear twice the normal size. While the religious parallels are obvious, the use of a magnificent animal conveys the power and danger associated with holiness, while the description of the bear's extreme suffering evokes our pity.

Adams creates a new civilization called the Beklan Empire. A cult on the island of Quiso led by Tuginda the priestess worships Lord Shardik, the incarnation of the Power of God: "he is from God—God is in him." Although Shardik used to dwell in the land, he was slain by a wandering slave-trader. But "He did not die. He passed from one bodily home to another." He has now returned "through fire and water." Kelderek Play-with-the-Children, an Orteglan hunter, is the first to spot him and feels dread, awe, and fear of being torn to pieces. The bear gives him a "trancelike sense of unreality . . . a sense of being magnified, of being elevated to a plane higher than that of his own everyday life. It was impossible that there should be such a bear—and yet it lay before him" (74). He has been chosen to find and serve Shardik as a "vessel" God will "shatter to fragments and then Himself fashion . . . again to His purpose."

By using chains and drugs to keep Shardik from escaping, the Orteg-lans defeat Bekla, and Kelderek becomes Crendrik the King. He is also the "Eye of God," a "magic and religious king concerned with the per-ception and interpretation of the divine will," mediator "to the people the power of the bear." Tuginda maintains, however, that the attack was not God's will but abuse of the bear, and that their acts have been blasphemy. When Shardik escapes, Kelderek follows, realizing he must determine Shardik's purpose on earth: "Something there was to be dis-covered, something attainable only at great cost, the one thing worth attaining. . . . This it was that would constitute Shardik's supreme gift to men" and would show men the meaning of their lives and how God wants them to live.

Along the way, Kelderek learns the significance of the Streels of Urtah, a place where retribution is brought upon the wicked. Once an evil-doer enters of his own will, he is killed and his body cast into the depths of the Streel. Rarely does a person return alive from the Streel, but when he does it is "a sign God has sanctified him and intends to make use of his death for some blessed and mysterious purpose of His own." Lord Shardik returned alive from the Streels, but his death is again "appointed by God, and it is certain." Yet he "has committed no evil."

After suffering "putrescent wounds," drugs, imprisonment, weary journeys, "misery, pain and loss," and abuse by men, he saves children from the slave-trader by dying in a final act of wrath that fills the earth and sky. "In spite of mankind and of all folly, Shardik had completed his work and returned to God." As Shardik lies on the funeral barge, Kelderek notices how unmajestic he now seems: "The poor, wounded face had been cleaned and tended, yet all . . . could not obliterate . . . the marks of Shardik's wounds and sufferings . . . less colossal he looked and . . . shrunken in the grip of death." The people are told "of his coming alive from the Streel; of his ordained suffering; and of the sacred death by which he had saved the . . . enslaved children from the power of evil." He was an "actual bear" who was also the Power of God "who made plain to us, by his sacred death, the truth we never understood."

In White's *The Sword Bearer*, God is referred to as the Changer, but he is only a voice like thunder surrounded by a blue light because he is not a man but a maker: "He is light, light that sees through a man yet makes him strong and joyful." The Changer promises to always be near John even though he cannot see him. In White's other books, Gaal is one of the few contemporary Christ figures who is developed and becomes personally involved with the children. One goal in creating a supernatural character is to make one to whom readers can respond in a personal way and, and at the same time, to still present some of the attributes of God and Christ.

Gaal is the Shepherd, Son of the High Emperor. The children decide that Gaal cannot belong just to the land of Anthropos: "He's too—too big . . . I've never heard of a Gaal in our world. . . . Perhaps he's not called Gaal in our world." As in Lewis' *The Lion, the Witch, and the Wardrobe*, Gaal was once stabbed by the Lady of the Night, a witch, in a cave where "he slew Death itself." Although he is vigorous and strong like a youth, his robe, hair, and beard are white. Lisa has trouble describing his face: "It was young yet it was old, very, very old. It was merry yet it spoke of untold sorrows. It was kind yet it was stern; tender yet incredibly tough; gentle yet as strong as steel" (White, *Tower*, 175). Like Lewis, who says he borrowed the images from the Grail legend, White associates his character with light and a sweet smell. While the witch gives off a foul odor like bad breath and scotch, Gaal has "a perfume about him, something like the smell of freshly sharpened cedarwood pencils."

Gaal can feel the pain and sorrow of each individual, be playful, or supply his or her needs. In *The Tower of Geburah*, Lisa crosses a channel to get to Gaal: "What she saw when she looked up she never forgot as long as she lived. The same strong face was smiling down at her as though she were the only person in the world. Tears spilled from his brown eyes and ran down his cheeks like a spring shower in the sun-shine" (180). After Mary McNab receives Gaal's blood on her, he scram-bles to his feet, pulls her up and "holding her by both hands burst into the merriest laughter. Then he twirled her in mad circles dancing and laughing with the laughter of deep heaven." Later he chases the children on the ship with playful movements that are "full of grace." At the end of their long journey from the Tower of Geburah, the children are startled to see Gaal standing in the cave offering them breakfast: "He had river trout frying in butter, fresh bread, milk, honey, cream and a pot of hot oatmeal. . . . It was the best sort of fire. . . . None of them had realized how much Gaal had meant to them."

Stephen Lawhead identifies the themes of his books as "God and His love, His care, His insistence on concerning Himself with human affairs, God's revealing Himself to man, and the many forms that takes" ("Stephen," 28). His supernatural character, the Most High, is a tall man with wide shoulders and "the stamp of a wise, seasoned leader." While he appears solid, his outline grows

fuzzy at the edges as if made of focused beams of living light or clothed in an aura of rainbowlike luminescence. . . . The Man of Light's eyes gleamed like hot coals and his face shined with the radiance of glowing bronze . . . the man's burning eyes . . . held his in a sort of lover's embrace: strong, yet gentle; commanding, yet yielding (*In*, 169).

The trinity is portrayed in Gregory Smith's *Captive Planet*. Planet Refuge is inhabited by Le-oin, tall, fur-covered creatures with heads like a deer's. Although they worship the Source and Power, "something bad happened and made the Source angry." Then "the Friend came and made them happy." Lam meets this Friend, who is "an older man, but strong. . . . He had a kind face but sand clung to his eyebrows and hair. His clothes were worn and dirty as if he had traveled a long way in the desert" (143). When man says, "I have always been near you," Lam feels as though he recognizes this "unknown friend" who "seemed to know everything about him."

Even when the supernatural figure is invisible, he promises to be near. In *Tales of the Kingdom* by David and Karen Mains, Christ appears in a number of forms, including that of a beggar, peasant, young man, and King. On Sighting Day, children try to find him in the Great Park. Mercie explains, "It is a huge game of seek-the-King. He appears in disguises." Hero cannot understand why he cannot see the King, while his brother can. The King, in the form of a beggar, explains, "You must see me with your brother's eyes. . . . You must see me as he sees me." The "moral" of the story is that this game "must be played with a child's heart, which believes and is always prepared to be surprised, because a King can wear many diguises." Mercie tells Dirty a secret that everyone in the Kingdom learns first: "The King does not have to come in order for us to see him. He is always present." Similarly, in Muriel Leeson's *The Path of the Promise Keeper*, Promise Keeper says he won't leave the children but at times he will be invisible, and at those times they must remember and obey his instructions. "I'm always with you," he assures them. "It's just that there are times when you can't see me. But I'll be there as you travel . . . the Dark Ones will try to make you feel you are alone."

Finally, in Ruth Nichols' *The Marrow of the World*, a Christ figure appears in two forms. Although he says he has "many names," Kyril Tessarion is both the great king and wizard in the "different world" the children are brought to by a "Power." Kyril fought many years "to win this land from the evil things that held it." Like Aslan in Lewis' Narnia tales, he drove out a beautiful witch named Morgan "by power stronger than her own." In the form of a wizard Kyril is called Leo. All the lines of his face "swept upward, from the black brows to the corners of the thin, laughing mouth. His skin was very dark. Beneath their lids his eyes were green as emerald. Kindness, sternness, and nobility all were written in the face." Before the children return to their world, Kyril closes his fingers around their wrists, creating a "cool burning sensation, like a bracelet of white fire." When he releases them, their wrists bear this mark: "I have set my mark on you. Because of it, you will never be wholly severed from us, and in a time of great need . . . we shall meet again . . . you will always see more deeply than others."

## SUPERNATURAL CREATURES

Supernatural creatures are another aspect of the spiritual world religious fantasy shows to be real. Lewis explains that because we want to be united with beauty and receive it, "we have peopled air and earth and water with gods and goddesses and nymphs and elves—that, though we cannot, yet these projections can, enjoy in themselves that beauty, grace, and power of which Nature is the image" (Lewis, *The Weight of Glory and Other Addresses*, 13). Such creatures also present to us an old reality we have forgotten and help us see nature and man in a visionary way. Drawn from Medieval concepts of the universe, they illustrate the idea of hierarchy and cosmic order.

In the Bible, spiritual beings are often presented figuratively. According to Lewis, "Creatures higher in the natural order than ourselves, either incorporeal or animating bodies of a sort we cannot experience, must be represented symbolically if they are to be represented at all," and they are usually human because that is the only rational creature we know (Lewis, *The Screwtape Letters*, viii). In the Bible, angels are portrayed as glorious beings greater than man that can be visible or invisible, travel at inconceivable speed, protect the saved, and deliver from peril. They also reveal God's purposes and provide guidance. Their glory is associated with "brightness, splendor and luminosity" (*Weight*,

12), just as in the Bible God and heaven are associated with light (I John 1:5, I Tim. 6:16).

To portray such beings, then, contemporary writers most often use the image of light and solidity. For example, in Harry Blamires' *The Devil's Hunting Grounds*, where angels are portrayed as solid and visible, the narrator's guardian angel chastises him for picturing angels as "transparent wraiths." In *Alpha Centauri* light around centaurs called the Old Ones is described as having "a weight, a palpable texture, as in old paintings. It brought clarity and a sense of great calm. . . . Even the feeling of rock or grass underfoot was a source of joy" (178). Similarly, in Douglas Livingston's *Journey to Aldairoon*, one of the lesser gods, called the Old Ones, is "of the light, robed with light, and though he became distinct from the light, yet he stood only in it. His hair was the white of light. His skin burned bright, white-golden," and his voice "sounded like spoken light."

Harold Myra describes his telora in *Escape From the Twisted Planet* as balls of "brilliant, burning," golden light, "terrible" in countenance but in human form. They are spirit beings who rule the planets, guide, and observe and rejoice in all. This concept is derived from the neoplatonic idea of angels as ruling intelligences of the heavenly bodies. The telora's bodies are invisible, "real enough in their dimension, yet so different that they're beyond our perception."

A different type of supernatural creature is portrayed in Madeleine L'Engle's *A Wrinkle in Time*. On the planet Ixchel, the creatures are tall, gray, fur-covered, have four arms, tentacles on each hand, and unhuman faces. Not only must they teach Meg to not view them as monsters, but they give her a sense of security because of their "delicate, springlike smell." They have only indentations for eyes because they do not see; rather they know what things *are*. Thus they teach Meg the limits of the senses, to "look not at the things which are what you would call seen, but at the things which are not seen. For the things which are seen are temporal. But the things which are not seen are eternal" (169).

Three other supernatural characters, Mrs. Who, Which, and Whatsit, are called guardian angels, messengers from God. Mrs. Whatsit was once a star but now appears in various forms: "The complete, the true Mrs. Whatsit . . . was beyond human understanding." These stars battle the Black Thing and give up their lives in so doing. Similar sacrifice is illustrated in *A Wind in the Door*. The cherubim Proginoskes (which means "to know in advance") is reminiscent of the one in Ezekiel's vision, for he is wings and eyes, flames and smoke. First, he teaches Meg that things are real even though we cannot see them. Then, to avoid being Xed or annihilated by the Echthroi, Progo chooses to X himself. It is also the only way to show his love because love "isn't how you feel. It's what you do." Earthlings do not have this choice. However, the children know Progo still exists in spirit form when the wind blows the door shut at the end of the story.

In L'Engle's most recent book, *Many Waters*, the nephilim are winged creatures who slept with the daughters of men, as described in Genesis 6:1–4. Some believe that unlike fallen angels, demons are spirits of giants produced by angelic "sons of God" who came to earth and married the "daughters of men." The fallen angels took on human bodies. The result of the unholy union was a mongrel race, neither angelic nor human. L'Engle parallels the 12 evil nephilim with 12 good seraphim, and each takes on the form of an earthly host. Seraphs and nephilim are brothers but went separate ways: "The seraphim have chosen to stay close to the Presence." The tall, winged Nephilim came from El (God) like falling stars. Thus evil creatures are usually a perversion of good.

## EVIL

Although good beings are important, depicting hell and evil helps us visualize their reality. The predominant plot of religious fantasy is the war between good and evil, as described in Ephesians 6:11–12:

Put on all the armour which God provides, so that you may be able to stand firm against the devices of the devil. For our fight is not against human foes, but against cosmic powers, against the authorities and potentates of this dark world, against the superhuman forces of evil in the heavens (New English Bible).

However, in Christian fantasy, good always wins out. Writers, avoiding the Manichaean heresy, are thus saying that the power of evil is limited; although it may seem omnipotent at first, the power of God is absolute. Usually, evil in fantasy is depicted as not originally bad but a perversion, mockery, or an absence of good.

By portraying evil, fantasy exposes a reader to the inevitability of sin and death. Tolkien believes that evil in fantasy teaches us that we have an eternal element and allows us to "experience" evil without actually having it affect us spiritually (*Letters*, 106). In addition, it can teach us about ourselves. Lewis' purpose in *The Screwtape Letters*, for example, was not to speculate about the diabolical life but to throw light from a new angle on the life of men (xii).

The Biblical conflict between God and Satan is portrayed as a war in heaven between Christ the Lamb and his angels, and Satan the Dragon and his demons. While the battle is spiritual rather than physical, the physical is used in both fantasy and the Bible as a symbol for the spiritual conflict. In Rev. 12:9, Satan is symbolized as a great red dragon of epic stature who attempts to destroy Christ. The Battle of Armageddon results in the final defeat of evil (Rev. 20:1–2), the restoration of Christ as King, and the establishment of His Kingdom.

Lin Carter suggests that evil be presented as "tenacious," "strong, not easily banished, not without great effort uprooted or slain," and "something tremendously solid and alive and vigorous" (122). He believes Lewis was successful in portraying evil as the "Real Thing," whereas Tolkien's was too shadowy, flimsy, and two-dimensional. Evil is usually associated with blackness and the inability to create, cooperate, and trust. It is also often portrayed as deceptive and difficult to discern because it appears in many disguises. While dragons and snakes are popular forms for the devil, it is sometimes an alluring female. This rebel has henchmen and followers, or works through humans and other creatures.

The main theme of John Bibee's *The Magic Bicycle* is the reality of the invisible world of evil beings. John finds a Spirit Flyer, the magic bicycle, in a dump. A gift of Magic from the Kings, it has the power to fly or save him from evil. But when he wants to use it in anger or revenge, it refuses to work. John gets into trouble when he refuses to trust it: " 'Let me go!' John commanded. 'I can do this without your help.' "

Evil is portrayed as a black snake with red eyes and fangs and a white circled X on its chest. It wants to get the Spirit Flyer away from John because he might use it to break the chains that make a person the slaves of evil. When the Order of the Chains is complete, Treason will rule the Deeper world forever. Even if the chains are broken, the Daimones can put the chains back on: "A person can still act like a slave, even though the locks are broken. The Daimones try to put broken chains back on their assigned people. They shadow them hard and whisper dead thoughts. Soon a person can believe he's a slave again when he isn't" (205).

John learns that he only sees "one shadow, that of a horrible snake. But that's only a tiny part of the whole Deeper World." John's Spirit Flyer goggles allow him to see this Deeper World, "an invisible world that holds our world together; it touches our flesh and bones, as well as our thoughts and dreams." Things in this world really aren't invisible but "deeper." The shadows are real, "so strong you can touch the darkness as if it were hard, like a brick."

When John's family is X-removed by the Daimones, he must rescue them by staying on the Spirit Flyer, obeying, and not trying to fight, because its "not the object, but the power behind the object" that is important. He also must be equipped with the light, horn, mirror, and a slingshot which "make the Magic more complete. These instruments appear junky and broken "because they *had* to be broken. And they had to be broken because *we* are broken. . . . Can you imagine how hard it would be if these things *weren't* broken but new? . . . You'd be blown away in the wind, burned up by the heat" (203). In addition, "you can't fight the battles of the Deeper World with the weapons of our lesser world. You need Magic to stop Tragic."

Each person has a Daimone assigned to him, and John uses the slingshot to kill a giant Daimone that looks like his friend Barry, who succumbed to Sweet Temptations. This candy works especially well on greedy boys: "The red part was good, but the black part was too bitter, even making his stomach ache a bit. The strong sweet flavors almost covered the bitterness." When you eat two, the flavor increases.

The murder creates a path of light through which his family escapes, but their eyes are still closed. As a key from the Three Kings fills the room with music and light, they awaken, the locks break, and their chains fall to the floor: "For one deep Magic moment, all six saw the wonders of the Kingdom of the Three Magical Kings." The light comes from the Kingson. John's Uncle Bill, who had refused to believe in the magic of the Spirit Flyer, now has his eyes and ears "open to the Deeper World." When those chains fell off, he became free in "more ways than one."

As with John's Spirit Flyer Goggles, a number of objects in other books give the ability to see the invisible, spiritual world of evil. The pendant in White's *The Tower of Geburah*, for example, makes evil visible, while the Mashal stone (Hebrew for "rule or dominion") helps one see a creature who may appear harmless for what it is. The stone thus helps you judge the true nature of things. For example, John recognizes Lord Lunacy, one of the many forms of the Mystery of Abomination, as a Dragon and what he tells him as lies. He appears one time as a massive human head with a skin film spread over it like wax:

Blank, colorless eyes stared blindly down at him over a massive nose. . . . The lips . . . were thick, wide enough if they opened to swallow John, the couch and the table all at once. . . . The eyes suddenly opened to reveal bright and luminously yellow orbs. . . . It was like a death mask come to life (155).

Yet John asks why the Changer does not simply get rid of him, Mab says he does not know, thus implying a greater purpose for evil. The stone also makes one invisible, feel ashamed and guilty, and gives off a blue light that gives courage. But it is only powerful in all of these ways if the wearer is following Gaal's laws.

Writer Walter Wangerin believes that evil must be portrayed as greater than ourselves so that we are forced to seek "some thing, some pattern, some ritual, some person, some deity, something else to enlist on our side" ("Of Books," 7). In White's *The Sword Bearer*, for example, another stone, the Proseo Comai (Greek for "prayer"), gives one the desires of his heart. At time's beginning the Changer created a mountain of these stones and blew them like bubbles throughout all ages and universes "so that whoever might wish to call on him for mercy and aid could do so." The stones themselves have no power but they put one "in touch with the power of the Changer. We are encouraged to express our distresses to him by means of them." In Wangerin's *The Book of the Dun Cow* and *The Book of Sorrows*, the evil Wyrm, a great serpent who leaves beneath the earth, attacks the hearts of the animals and makes the Keepers fight among themselves. He transforms himself into thousands of worms that infest the rooster Chaunticleer and can thus work through him.

Nimrood the Necromancer in Stephen Lawhead's Dragon King trilogy, whose name is perhaps derived from the Babylonian rebel Nimrod in the Bible, is a mortal man but can become a powerful black snake that can be beaten. His face is twisted and cruel: "Two piercing eyes burned out from under a heavy menacing brow." His face is creased with interwoven wrinkles, each crevice representing an evil its owner had contemplated: "So bent was the black soul which inhabited that body, it twisted all it touched. The face was a mask of hate." But he never seems powerful or frightening, simply cackling, "Blow, wind! Thunder, roar. Lightning, rend the heavens! I, Nimrood, command it! Ha, ha, ha!"

Current children's fantasy that depicts the theme of the battle with evil are Muriel Leeson's Promise-Keeper books, Robert Siegel's *Alpha Centauri*, and Madeleine L'Engle's trilogy. Promise-Keeper's world is said to be at war. The children imagine how "neat" the land would be with all the Dark Ones killed: "You know how he said, 'We always win'? Maybe someday we'll win for the last time, and they'll be gone." Another theme is that good will come out of evil, as in Siegel's *Alpha Centauri*. Becky is told that sometimes "the Shaper may take what the Warper has twisted and make from it a thing more beautiful than before. Sometimes good is better for having overcome evil. But finally, only the Shaper knows the 'why,' and finally only he shapes good out of all" (194).

Madeleine L'Engle states that her books deal "overtly with the problem of evil" (*A Circle of Quiet*, 32). *A Wrinkle in Time* is her rebuttal to the German theologians and her "affirmation of a universe in which I could take note of all the evil and unfairness and horror, and yet believe in a loving God" (*Circle*, 118). In *Wrinkle*, the Powers of Darkness that are taking over the planets appear as shadows or smokey hazes. A battle with these powers is being fought all over the cosmos. On the planet Camazotz, for example, darkness is the Black Thing. Portrayed as a "devouring cold" that wants to "eat and digest," the Thing is similar to Lewis' portrayal of evil in *The Screwtape Letters* as digesting and hungering. It is also tangible, "like some enormous malignant beast of prey." A disembodied brain called "IT" controls the planet and has taught everyone to submit, creating total uniformity. In L'Engle's books, therefore, sameness is evil, while uniqueness is what makes something real.

Because IT makes Meg hate, the only weapon against IT is her love for her brother, Charles Wallace. This same weapon against evil is used in *L'Engle's A Wind in the Door*. Here, the evil Echthroi are described as nothingness. In the New Testament, "echthroi" is the Greek word for the hater, enemy, opponent, death, and devil. L'Engle describes what they do as Xing: annihilating, negating, destroying, extinguishing. The only way to defeat them is to fill the void they create by loving or through self-sacrifice.

Evil can also be beautiful, illustrating the allurement and deceptiveness of temptation. Like Lewis' Jadis the witch, John White's Mirshaath (Hebrew for "wicked" or "criminal"), the witch in *The Iron Sceptre*, is tall and beautiful with a white face. According to Anthropos' history, some rebelled against Gaal, including Mirshaath, who studied evil and used magic to slay the priests of dark spirits. She became bride of the Spirit of the North, slew and devoured him, then took on his power. Sometimes, however, she appears as an ugly witch with wrinkled skin, matted hair, rags, sores, and rotten yellow teeth, or appears in the form of a dragon. She has made the country of Anthropos exist in perpetual winter, draught, and famine, and the kings and queens are frozen into statues. But the children throw Gaal's blood before her throne to destroy her and bring the frozen statues back to life.

In *The Sword Bearer* White sets up contrasting images of good and evil: two magicians, one who performs the Changer's miracles and one who uses power for himself; two towers, the Tower of the Garden Room and the Tower of Darkest Night; and the good blue light of the Changer and the red light of evil. Qadar are "scourers of the night skies," or bat-like creatures on which a tall figure stands. Evil creates boiling bitumen, swamps, a foul stench, and leaves a black emptiness: "It's not as if something black was there, but as if everything else had been taken away and only darkness left."

An objection to the evil in such stories is that it may frighten certain readers, especially if the books vividly portray battles and wicked characters. David Holbrook, for example, objects to the fighting in the Narnia books even though he realizes it symbolizes a moral struggle. He argues that the books show aggression, fear, sadism, and hate; since readers identify with the protagonists, they identify with such attitudes. But Lewis contends that we should not protect children from the knowledge that there is death, violence, and evil in the world. Rather, such protection may breed shallow escapism. Since children will inevitably meet enemies, they should at least know that brave knights, heroes, comforters, and protectors exist, heroic courage is possible, and that good will win: "Let there be wicked kings and beheadings, battles and dungeons, giants and dragons, and let villains be soundly killed at the end of the book" (*On*, 39–40). L'Engle agrees that the responsibility of the writer is to give children a weapon against evil through laughter and help them prepare for it (*Circle*, 181).

According to G. K. Chesterton, fairy tales do not produce fear in a child or the idea of evil or the ugly: "The fear does not come from the fairy tales, the fear comes from the universe of the soul" (*Tremendous Trifles*, 85–86). These things are in the child already because they are in the world. But they do give the child a clear idea of the possible defeat of evil, a Saint George to kill the dragon he has already had in his imagination (86). When the child sees brave heroes, he learns that terrors have a limit, shapeless enemies have enemies, and "that there is something in the universe more mystical than darkness, and stronger than strong fear." The heroes may be traditional, Christ-like superheroes, but more often they are children. Through identification with such protagonists, the reader, in turn, learns moral values, as will be examined next.

# Chapter 2

# The "Fairyland of the Soul": Heroes and their Spiritual Journeys

...how I have wandered into the deeper fairyland of the soul (MacDonald, *Phantastes*).

## MORAL IMPACT

Writers agree that while a story may contain a different world or creatures, the morals must remain the same as in our world, thus encouraging a moral response in the reader. George MacDonald, for example, believed that there should be "no Invention" by the author in the moral aspects of the created world ("Fantastic," 14). Since fantasy maintains the same moral laws, it must show man as fallen: "Men have 'fallen'—any legends put in the form of supposed ancient history of this actual world of ours must accept that" (Tolkien, *Letters*, 203). Since all legends and myths present aspects of the truth and keep reappearing, all stories are about the fall, says Tolkien. Chesterton agrees that every "deep or delicate treatment of the magical theme . . . will always be found to imply an indirect relation to the ancient blessing and cursing," and the work must be moral, not moralizing (*Sidelights*, 260).

In modern science fiction stories, Lewis observes, alien species usually accept science but are devoid of moral standards. The implication is that scientific thought is objective and universal, but morality is not (*Christian*, 61). Popular thought tends to distinguish between scientific and moral or metaphysical thought. The former is believed to "put us in touch with reality," whereas the latter does not. Religious fantasy thus reverses this tradition. Elliot Miller insists that imaginary worlds are valid if they correspond to the biblical world view, that of "absolute moral standards based upon a transcendent God" (Scheer, "Malice in Wonderland?", 32).

Tolkien identifies one goal of a writer as encouragement of good morals. By embodying them in unfamiliar ways, he can "bring them home" (*Letters*, 194). For instance, if the reader identifies with good characters, he can learn through their lessons and experiences. Madeleine L'Engle, who calls her fantasy novels her "theology," agrees that fantasy's purpose includes a moral response to the world around us. She also thinks that "right doctrine is far more often taught in stories than in direct dogma" ("Allegorical Fantasy," 15, 18). This fact is exemplified by the letter the New York C. S. Lewis Society received from a monk. He wrote that he had read the Narnia tales three times in three years because they were "about the most spiritual books I have read in my 16 years as a monk."

This letter illustrates that a story may make a more lasting impact than a theoretical presentation of principles (Kilby, *Images of Salvation in the Fiction of C. S. Lewis*, 7). It can also convey theological insights by "showing" rather than explaining, although most books unfortunately rely on the latter. Fantasy can potentially be a mode for presenting moral or spiritual values and doctrines which cannot be presented in realistic fiction. Typical moral values include "high things" such as majesty, courtesy, nobility, purity, courage, goodness, sacrifice, and splendor. The story form helps the reader remember the spiritual message: "Good fiction aims at the heart and soul, while non-fiction aims only at the head" (Scheer, 31). In discussing MacDonald's works, for example, Hein observes,

The reader is required . . . to suspend his disbelief concerning curious psychic and material phenomena—asking only self consistency in these areas—and to depend for his bearing upon his grasp of moral laws alone. When he does so he takes a firmer hold upon his knowledge of moral principles (87).

Fantasy is a particularly effective vehicle for presenting moral and spiritual ideas and creating belief in a reader because it encourages the reader to align with a certain character. For example, Walter Wangerin explains, "I wanted to tell a story that was worth telling, that was exciting, and yet drew the feelings of the reader so that they would identify with or feel commitment to these characters. The reader would care about relationships and be moved" ("Of," 6). Since characters undergo a quest or tests, the reader experiences the same things, thus making him act or choose: "A splendidly created character or set of circumstances, by drawing us into its own world, allows us not simply to evaluate but actually to experience, to stand in the very shoes of hero or villain" (Kilby, *Images*, 7–8). The story then works on the reader the same way as it works on the main character. Since clear-cut contrasts also force the reader to take sides, the writer can manipulate the reader's response as sympathy or disdain.

For example, Murphy notes that because C. S. Lewis' fantasy poem, *Dymer*, is in the form of a "hesitation fantasy," the reader is made to undergo Dymer's experience. As Dymer suffers illusions, daydreams, delusions, and fancies, "the reader hesitates and dreams false dreams along with Dymer" (7). But the poem's structure as a hesitation fantasy encourages this response and should thus not be compared with prose fantasy. Walter Hooper observes that Lewis wrote prose because of public taste rather than the difference in the possibilities of the two genres (Preface, *Narrative Poems*, xi).

Usually, the character goes to another world to learn about it, then returns to earth for a time, as in *The Promise Keeper* and *Tales of the Kingdom*. In Leeson's books, the children learn they are citizens of Promise-Keeper's kingdom but must live in the real world. Some day they will return permanently. They are confused about how "two worlds can go on at the same time." But with their own "saucers," they can "come and go as they please—for ever and ever! And the Dark Ones would not be able to drive them out or make them forget where they had been." Likewise, in *Tales of the Kingdom* Scarboy must return to the Enchanted City as the "King's man," because "one goes into the Inmost Circle in order to come out again. Entrance is only the beginning of the quest."

The basic plot is that of an ordinary hero who undergoes adventures in a strange landscape, has a goal or quest such as a foe to overcome or a person to be found, undergoes a series of tests or obstacles, and eventually restores order. Physical strength, courage, resourcefulness, and morality may be tested, while negative characters may need to be converted or expelled.

## SUPERHEROES

In *The American Monomyth*, Robert Jewett and John Lawrence trace how this same storyline is found throughout American popular culture as a secular version of the Christian story. The monomyth begins and ends in Eden, with the United States seen as the site of the millenium. First, a chosen people is under seige:

A community in a harmonious paradise is threatened by evil: normal institutions fail to contend with this threat: a selfless superhero emerges to renounce temptations and carry out the redemptive task: aided by fate, his decisive victory restores the community to its paradisal condition: the superhero then recedes into obscurity (xx).

While the classical monomyth was based on rites of initiation (the hero leaves, undergoes trials, and is integrated into society), they believe the American monomyth derives from tales of redemption and the Judeo-Christian tradition. Although every culture has invented a figure who would put things right, America, with its religious heritage, has more of a redeemer myth, despite displacement and secularization. The superhuman powers of God and angels are transferred to an ordinary citizen who becomes a superhero. People still hope for divine and redemptive powers, even though science has made them less credible.

Robert Short believes science fiction can be religious when it tries to help people find ultimate meaning in their lives: "But even when this fiction *doesn't* understand Christ as the fulfillment of these needs, it can still bear an unintentional, unconscious, almost predictable resemblance to Christ" (15). A good example is *ET*. Although there are analogies to Christ in the book and film, the scriptwriter and cinematographer did not realize the similarities until during the filming (Kotzwinkle, *E. T. The Extra-Terrestrial*, 65).

ET comes from heaven to a lowly place, is loving, compassionate, and has healing powers. Like a disciple, Elliott is a chosen one, linked to ET telepathically. He "knew this thing had been handed to him from the stars, and he had to follow or—or die. . . . He couldn't know that a cosmic law had touched him, gyrating him in a new direction: he only knew he felt better than he'd ever felt before" (Kotzwinkle, 64–65). Several times, the story mentions the necessity of childlike faith. Hunted by authorities, ET eventually dies, leaving the equipment flickering and the house and valley trembling. But he is resurrected and appears only to trusted friends. When the authorities search for the body, they find an empty van. Finally, when ET ascends in his spaceship to return home, Elliott looks up at the ship: "It was ET multiplied a millionfold, the greatest heart light the world had ever seen. Its mysteries shone into him, and messages of love and wonder ran up and down his body." "I'll be right here," ET says, "with fingertip glowing over Elliott's chest."

*Superman* has similar biblical echoes, as discussed in books such as *The Man From Krypton*, *The Gospel According to Superman*, and *The American Monomyth*. Because the planet Krypton is about to disintegrate, Superman's parents wrap him in red, white, and blue clothes and lay him in a box sent to earth. Jor-El, the father, says, "All that I have I bequeath you, my son. You'll carry me inside you all the days of your life. You will see my life through yours, and yours through mine. The son becomes the father and the father the son" (Short, *The Gospel from Outer Space*, 40).

The baby reaches earth at a carefully chosen place and is taken in by adoptive parents. At 18, he must go to an Arctic wasteland where he enters an "impenetrable secret sanctuary" in the Forest of Solitude. He spends years there "mastering his super-powers and communing with the image of his father in preparation for his lifelong war against evil" (*Superman—the Movie—the Magazine*, 14). The voice of his father says, "They only need the light to show them the way. For this reason, and this reason only, I have sent you, my only son." When he reaches 30, Superman returns to the city "to fight for truth, justice, and the American way."

## CHILD HEROES

Reader identification is effective when the protagonists are not superheroes but rather common people like ourselves—searching, questioning, and changing. Lewis advises that the more "unusual" the scenes and events, the more "ordinary" and "typical" the characters should be. One of the most important themes in fantasy, then, is that of the common individual as hero. In describing *Lord of the Rings*, for example, Lewis points out that Tolkien wanted to show the "mythical and heroic quality" of man:

Much that in a realistic work would be done by "character delineation" is here done simply by making the character an elf, a dwarf, or a hobbit. The imagined beings have their insides on the outside; they are visible souls. And Man as a whole, Man pitted against the universe, have we seen him at all till we see that he is like a hero in a fairy tale? (*On*, 89)

Such creatures convey a positive view of man and show that the most insignificant person can be a hero. One of the main purposes of the plot is also the hero's transformation to the status of king, reflecting a spiritual change as well.

Madeleine L'Engle agrees that man is not common; anyone can be a hero, performing tasks required of him (*Circle*, 211–212). Thus a trend in her own and other recent fantasy is to have more female, group, and child heroes. For example, in Calvin Miller's Singreale chronicles, a female Graygill and Star Rider save the unfallen Edenlike village from evil by secretly planning their own attack, devising a trap, learning to use fire-glass swords, and then fighting the perpetrator of evil themselves. Similarly, in many of the children's books, the child characters are surprised to find that they have been "called" to another world for a purpose, fulfill ancient prophecies, and have the ability to fight battles and use weapons. Often, they feel unable to perform the tasks, yet they change and develop qualities they never knew they had. They are always provided supernatural help through animal or human guides and counsels, provisions, and special gifts. Although aids—usually an old man or woman—suggest direction, they may at first appear ominous and speak in riddles. In a number of books, the heroes receive special clothes or weapons reminiscent of spiritual gifts or the armor of God which equip each person to perform his role.

In *The Promise Keeper* and *The Path of the Promise Keeper*, Muriel Leeson uses both child heroes and Biblical imagery such as the cross and treasures of the Kingdom to convey Biblical principles. In the first book, a UFO appears on earth with "Small Ones" lead by a tiny man called Promise-Keeper. The children visit their land and learn that to avoid attacks by the Dark Ones, they must obey Promise-Keeper's instructions. In the sequel, the children return to the land to search for treasure in the Golden Cave. On their journey, they are attacked by the Dark Ones and learn to stay on the path, follow instructions, and use their special weapons.

When earth was created, and there were no Dark Ones in Promise-Keeper's land, people were able to travel back and forth between the two lands as citizens of both worlds. However, one of the Small Ones who rebelled was exiled by the One-Who-Lives-Forever. Now called the Dark Leader, the rebel changed some Small Ones into Dark Ones who ruined people's minds. In fact, they succeeded in affecting everyone born. But a "day is coming" when every Dark One will be cast out from this land into a place prepared for him."

*The Path of the Promise Keeper* uses a number of Biblical images. The children travel by spaceship to the land of the Promise-Keeper to search for the treasure in the Golden Cave. But to reach it, they must cross a huge, evil lake that appears to be black, oozing slime full of Dark Ones. However, a stick magically appears that they use to test the depth of the water. Unsure whether the stick is from the Promise-Keeper or Dark Ones, they examine it. Suddenly, it takes the shape of a cross, and as they begin to plunge it into the black slime, the goo changes to gold. Promise-Keeper explains that "those who attempt to cross without using the stick, fail."

Both books illustrate that children can be heroes and must learn obedience. In the Promise-Keeper's land, a girl can fly a spaceship like a boy, handle a shield, and throw stones as straight as a boy. This is "the only place where being the youngest means you get to do important things." They will also receive help with their tasks. When Bill asks Promise-Keeper if he is really sure they can handle the trip alone with unfamiliar weapons, Promise-Keeper replies, "Do you think I would set you a task you had no hope of doing?" All their needs are provided: bags of white rocks, water that suddenly appears when they need it and disappears when they are finished, and a resting place that begins to fade like an out-of-focus TV picture. "You will always find what you need," Promise-Keeper promises. Against the Dark Ones, the children use two aids. One is white, rectangular stones with writing on them that are thrown at the enemy. They also have the ability to test whether one is a Dark One if he leaves a black stain where the stone is touched. The other weapon is the Abilon shield, which no arrows can penetrate.

As the children journey to Promise-Keeper's land to discover what is in the Golden Cave, they must stay on the path and do exactly what Promise-Keeper says. Harold observes, "I think as long as we do *exactly* as Promise-Keeper says, it'll be all right." Bill learns from experience that when Promise-Keeper gives instructions, "he mean[s] them to be obeyed," even when he is invisible. But the Dark Ones have set up snares: "If they can't get you to walk on a path deliberately, they try to catch you through accidents." If they don't make you forget the rules, they trick you, or the arrows and Dark Mist of the Dark Ones make you forget about Promise-Keeper and his world. Promise-Keeper warns that

the Dark Ones will never stop trying to discourage you from discovering all the joys of this land. They will attempt to block you every step of the way on your trip to the Golden Cave. But you are not without protection. Just remember my instructions. Stay on our path, unless I tell you to leave it to follow my special markers. Never be without your shield and pouch of white stones. The Dark Ones know our rules. They will be watching for you to forget or deliberately break them (*Path*, 23).

The children are given new golden tunics so that they can be linked together firmly by a small silver chain. Thus if a Dark One tries to seize any one of them, the others will be alerted and can help; he will also be too heavy to carry off. This image seems to symbolize the way all believers are related to one another. On earth, they will still wear these tunics, though invisible: "Only true citizens like yourselves will know that you have them. The rest of your Earth people will not believe they even exist. . . . On Earth, you will benefit from the chain and tunics, but they will be things you experience, rather than touch or hold" (109).

In the Cave the children find a Great Mirror that shows them that some day they will look like Promise-Keeper, and a key to open the door to their treasures. Each child receives a different treasure: a Pearl, a chest of jewels, and a golden cube. But every gift reveals a vision of the child telling a friend about Promise-Keeper's world. The treasures can also contract so they can be taken back to earth and shared. Finally, the children learn that this cave is only like an entrance hall; the realms beyond it can be explored only after they leave earth permanently.

In John White's books the children are called to Anthropos whenever there is trouble. Wesley is told, "You were drawn here for a purpose." Each child, even the most unheroic, is thus important: "Gaal seldom uses powerful people. Neither knights or kings." Kurt, however, cannot understand why Gaal should use someone like his obnoxious cousin,

Mary McNab. But Gaal says, "The greatest wars are not won by generals or mighty warriors but by weak and little people who have the courage to obey." Once in Anthropos, the children are also assured that Gaal will guide them. King Kardia tells Lisa, "I doubt not that he who sent you hither will guide your steps," and "somewhere deep in her mind she began to feel, not that she had been here before, but that she was meant to be here."

The children also have specific tasks to perform, often believing they are unable to carry them out. Wesley never does understand what happened to him as he faced a seven-headed ogre:

One part of him was terrified. Yet he seemed to possess a strength and speed he had never before known in his life. . . . As two large hands reached out to seize Wesley, he swung the oar first one way, then the other. To his amazement he seemed to have smashed through both of them. It was as though his arms were moving by themselves (*Tower*, 254).

His brother Kurt is depressed because he realizes that each child has done his part, but he has yet to perform his dreaded task of slaying a giant rooster who guards Poseidon's kingdom: "Why did Gaal have to choose something so impossibly hard?" He thinks he is being punished or that maybe Gaal has never truly forgiven him. While he is afraid of the rooster at first, when he remembers the words, "He whom Gaal pardons is pardoned indeed," they give him a sudden strength: "I'm a servant of Gaal," he screams. "Listen, you dumb bird--*he pardoned me!*" The huge rooster then becomes funny rather than threatening.

In the final book, John Wilson, the first boy to visit Anthropos, learns that he is the Sword Bearer who must slay the Goblin Prince so the Mystery of Abomination will leave Anthropos. Unconfident in himself, he nevertheless speaks against evil in a sudden burst of courage. He "never knew what made him say it, but suddenly the words came with surprising firmness and clarity . . . he found himself talking, wondering where the impressive words came from." John has a pain in his shoulder from a wound inflicted by his neighbor, Nicholas Slapfoot. The pain grows stronger when evil is near but disappears when he is in the Changer's presence. John becomes aware that "the power of Old Nick was the power of an evil he must now destroy. . . . 'You're not just *outside* me, but *inside* me.' " When he finally kills Nick it is with "terrible power, power that was never his," and he feels "free and cleaner than he had ever felt in his life. All the pain had gone from his shoulder."

Finally, the children learn that if they obey, Gaal will help them. Lisa, for example, must pass through the tunnels and follow the pigeon and blue light Gaal sends. Whenever she strays from the path or is fooled by fake food, she runs into trouble. Inkleth and Kurt go to the lake their own way and have trouble, unlike Wesley and Lisa who follow Gaal's path. Food represents Gaal's manna-like provision. In *The Iron Sceptre*, the children are provided each day with bread and fish in the Cave of Gaal. The loaf grows no smaller when taken, and fish are somehow cooked. Similarly, in the final book of the trilogy, the dwarves receive a magnificent feast each day from the eagles, and a canopy of fireflies gives both light and protection.

In L'Engle's *A Wrinkle in Time* Charles Wallace must be rescued from IT, but his sister Meg is the only one who can do it. Mrs. Who tells her, "God hath chosen the weak things of the world to confound the things which are mighty." Yet she is not forced to act. Mrs. Whatsit uses the sonnet as an analogy for free will. While the sonnet has a strict rhythm and meter, the poem has complete freedom within it. Likewise, you are "given the form, but you have to write the sonnet yourself." In the sequel, *A Wind in the Door*, she must save him from death. "This is too much responsibility! I'm still only a child! I didn't ask for any of this," she protests. Again, she learns that size does not matter because it "is not always on the great or the important that the balance of the universe depends." Rather, "one child, one man, can swing the balance of the universe."

Quentin, in Stephen Lawhead's Dragon King trilogy, is portrayed as a humble youth, lacking heroic qualities, who eventually becomes king. He feels he can make no difference: "I am no one. No one at all." But an elder at Dekra tells him that "there is more to you than meets the eye." Quentin feels compelled to go on his mission by something outside himself: "I felt something was pulling me. Like I was *supposed* to go." A greater, higher, wiser god who knows Quentin is calling and has "special plans" for him: "God grants to every pure heart a blessing in kind, and the strength to carry out his purpose. In so doing you will find your own happiness and fulfillment." Each person is given "a special task in life, and a blessing to carry it out." The god has chosen Quentin: " He was caught up in the swiftly running stream of history . . . moved by an unseen hand toward an unknown destiny." He fulfills a prophecy that as king he will usher in an age of Light and be called Lotheneil, the Waymaker, because he "will lead men's minds toward Winoek, the God Most High."

His sword Zhaligkeer, the Shining One, is forged in the lost mines out of lanthanil, a healing metal. But he must trust God to help him find the lanthanil to forge the sword: "The Most High will show us aright. We must remember that it is he who guides us to his own purpose. We need not fret ourselves over much about the things we cannot foresee." The artisan, Inchkeith, who is afraid to touch it at first, is cured of his deformity, and it makes him feel "more alive and whole and at peace" than he ever had been in his life. Zhaligkeer is possessed of the "holy power" of the Most High, and its flame is the symbol of the god's presence with the King. As an instrument of judgement, it can only be raised in righteousness, not anger.

Children are heroes in other contemporary works. In Chris Spencer's *Starforce: Red Alert*, Zak and Eve must rescue their father and fly a spaceship to another planet: "Here they were being commissioned by the greatest powers in the western world to fulfill" the role of saving him and "would do so with all the mighty resources of the Starforce system to back them up!" Similarly, in Jeanne Norweb's *The Forbidden Door*, the children are considered heroes because they rescue a baby dragon, Nimeon, who later becomes King. When they devise a plan to rescue some baby dragons, Nimeon thunders, "No!. . . This is not a task for children." But the Master of Wisdom quietly replies, "It may be they were sent back for this very reason. . . . True, they are children, but there are times when the small and the weak may do what the great and the strong cannot." The children also act differently when they return home: they are more polite and quicker to admit when they are wrong. Thus one's experiences in the other world can produce an inward, spiritual change.

**SPIRITUAL JOURNEY**

While Tolkien calls the physical journey a technical device, a thread to string things together, the quest is also symbolic of an inner journey (*Letters*, 239). This spiritual quest is usually one's search for God or the self. Religious fantasy thus shows characters gaining self-understanding as a result of experiences that force them to examine their spiritual natures. Ursula LeGuin believes that fantasy "is the natural, the appropriate language for recounting of the spiritual journey, the struggle of good and evil in the soul" (59). In contemporary fantasy, pools, mirrors, and names are the most common images used to show a person discovering his true identity.

Douglas Livingston's *Journey to Aldairoon* is the best example of a physical journey symbolizing an inner quest. The orphan Rafe is raised by Shamar the priest, who found him on his doorstep. While Rafe wants to be a priest too, he wants to find his identity, for he feels unlike others in his land and questions the gods: "Did the gods watch his every move? Did they listen to all his questions? . . . Why didn't they show themselves to him? . . . He remembered how he had always been filled with more questions than there seemed answers for" (16). Shamar assures him that when the "Old Ones" want to give him an answer they will.

Three dreams—of a panther, a lady and a unicorn, and a phoenix—inspire him to become Rafe the Seeker, bound for the Forbidden Mountains. A man in the panther dream beckons him to follow him to Aldairoon. Rafe believes these dreams are "messages from the Old Ones" calling him to a quest. Along his journey, the panther and unicorn, called Protectors, as well as a mysterious Presence, watch him and show him the way. This Presence is "stronger than himself. It was not frightening . . . but it filled him with a certain dread, as though he were inadequate to meet the Presence, and if meet it he did, he did not know whether he would run away in terror or fall helplessly at its feet" (20).

A Hermit tells him only the One, "the God of gods," knows who he is. All other gods are sent to point to him. Thus Rafe determines to seek and serve him "with my whole life, with all I am and all he can make of me." Rafe learns he is Rafael the Healer, who will become Tor or King of Galorr. Every Tor must take a journey, "a quest for one's self," before he comes into his kingdom. During this journey the gods reveal his special gift of service for the kingdom. Galorr needs a Healer to bind its wounds; restore dignity, freedom and prosperity; and cause a "Restoration." As Healer, Rafe is "called to belong only to others, to heal, to serve." In him will also

lie the Word that releases the power in us all to do what is required of each. . . . For only in every person's freedom, to be all that he or she can be in each's choosing the Light over Darkness . . . can this great Evil be cast down and driven from the land (125).

Aldairoon is "the journey all men and women must make who would be fully themselves." It is a pool into which Rafe must look to learn his name. Each person must find his own way to Aldairoon because "the true Aldairoon lies within each of us." Here a person also learns his name, "which is the beginning of finding his own place among men." In learning his name, Rafe has begun to be himself, and when he learns what it means, he will become fully himself.

Finding one's true name is another method of self discovery. "Naming" in tradition is associated with incarnating, creating order, affirming, and creating by calling into existence. A name is the incarnation of a being by God's word, thus affirming his identity and allowing him to know who he is. If you know someone's name, you also know his true essence and significance and can be in full relationship with him. In *Alpha Centauri*, this idea is used when a centaur undergoes her "Dreaming." Here she comes to know "her hidden name, a name she kept secret for the rest of her life" and known only to herself and Shaper.

In John White's *The Tower of Geburah* the Pool of Truth "reveals true things," gives the characters the "true form" they should possess in Anthropos, and heals ills caused by deception. In *The Iron Sceptre*, a mirror reflects one's ugliness, an image of sin. Fat and pimply Mary McNab eats the gigantic dish of ice cream from the Circle of Enchantment of Bodily Yearnings. When she vomits it up, what comes out becomes a mirror which shows her swollen. Then the witch appears: "You mustn't look into a mirror that came from inside you. You will never be beautiful that way. Come to my palace and let me give you a *magic* mirror, a magic mirror far better than your blue one. . . . I will give you my kind of beauty" (87). The witch promises that if she had darkness in her heart, she could look as beautiful as the witch. But first she must pass a test, by getting Kardia's sceptre. When Mary does, she becomes beautiful, but her face is "in some strange way proud and hungry" and filled with hate. This beauty also wears off.

Gaal tells her she must choose to trust him or the witch because there "is only one beauty, Mary, not two." He offers to let her have his beauty in her: "Beauty comes from joy, Mary. I've already given you some of my beauty." As she looks at her reflection in a pool, "she saw herself still fat but with glory on her face, a glory that made her gasp. Her face glowed as though a light were shining beneath her skin while her body and limbs were alive with grace." Princess Tiqvah notices, "You wore an enchanted beauty before, but now there is the light of joy and peace on your countenance" and "gentleness and happiness about your own face that is warmer and clearer."

In *Tales of the Kingdom*, the Sacred Flames show a person as he truly is. The main character's name is Scarboy because he refuses to be branded by the evil Enchanter and is burned accidently on the cheek. This scar makes him self-conscious, and because he always holds one hand over it to hide it, it prohibits him from working effectively. But he finds out that he is not truly ugly but has only seen himself that way: "We see without real sight. All things seem ugly—most of all, ourselves." Scarboy will recognize the King in the Enchanted City because he too has a scar.

Scarboy, also called Hero, must face his greatest enemy in combat. This enemy turns out to be himself, for we must face ourselves before we can make any other quests: "The boy learned that quests can be a journey inward as well as a journey outward. There is a kingdom within that must first be conquered before one comes brave enough to challenge the world without." He knows that he must walk through the Sacred Flames to meet the King or else his quest will not be over. In the Deepest Forest the Great Celebration takes place. Subjects of the King gather in the Inmost Circle, surrounded by the Sacred Flames where they "become as they really are." The old and funny looking Caretaker becomes a tall and broad-shouldered Ranger Commander—"not what he seemed." When the King takes a Crippled Girl through them, she is healed.

Throughout Madeleine L'Engle's space-time trilogy, Meg changes from a girl who dislikes the way she looks and cannot adapt at school to a mature, confident expectant mother. In *A Wind in the Door*, a name is said to make a person unique and know who he is, as love does. In contrast, Echthroi are Unnamers. When people are named, all the Echthroi will be vanquished. But when a person is not named, he is open to either being Xed or named. Because Meg is a Namer, her three tasks are to Name Mr. Jenkins, get Sporos to Deepen, and fill the void created by the Echthroi. Sporos is a farandola inside a mitochondrion who refuses to "deepen" (root, mature) because of pride: "The temptation for farandola or for man or for star is to stay an immature pleasure-seeker. When we seek our own pleasure as the ultimate good we place ourselves as the center of the universe." He believes that if he forms roots he will not be able to move and become "a prince among Echthroi." Thus Meg's three tasks illustrate the stages an individual must go through to mature: assert and accept his identity, renounce the self and mature, and love others.

Finally, Walter Wangerin's *The Book of the Dun Cow* uses both naming and the mirror, which reveals the self. After Chaunticleer chooses good over evil, he sings a compline to comfort the animals and calm their fears of the enemy. Then he names each one, as well as the enemy, in an attempt to clarify and create order. In addition, the evil rooster Cockatrice, who is covered with scales and has a serpent's tale and a red eye, is a mirror for Chaunticleer. The mirror or speculum is a medieval literary device illustrating the idea of seeing oneself better. Thus Cockatrice shows that Chaunticleer must fight the hate, despair, and lack of faith within himself. To be a proper leader of the coop and defeat Wyrm, he must change within.

## CONVERSIONS

One of the most important results of the spiritual journey is an *inner* change in the characters and, in turn, the reader. One of the key purposes of religious fantasy is to put a person "on the road to God." Most writers feel that even if a reader misses the point or does not associate the story with religion at all, he may be put on the right track. In *Out of the Silent Planet*, Ransom decides to publish his experiences on Malacandra in the form of fiction because it "would certainly not be listened to as fact." Rather, it would prepare people for the Gospel: "What we need for the moment is not so much a body of belief as a body of people familiarized with certain ideas." Chad Walsh says that when he read Lewis' *Perelandra*, he found his "imagination being baptized":

At that time I was slowly thinking, feeling and fumbling my way towards the Christian faith, and had reached a point where I was more than half convinced that it was true. This conviction, however, was a thing more of the mind than of the imagination and heart. In *Perelandra* I got the taste and smell of Christian truth. My senses as well as my soul were baptized. It was as though an intellectual abstraction or speculation had become flesh and dwelt in its solid bodily glory among us (107).

To achieve this effect, a common technique is to have the main character become converted. However, to be successful the work must allow the reader to be inside the character's thoughts long enough so that the change is believable. In Myra's *Escape From the Twisted Planet*, David encourages his wife Charlotte, an undeveloped character, "to let the Aelor-force flow through you, and control you." There is no insight into her thoughts and no struggle.

In contrast, in *The Tower of Geburah*, food, cleansing, salvation, and magic images are combined to show Lisa's conversion. In the dungeon where she is held prisoner, Lisa is brought food by the evil jinn, but his magic can only produce fake food. The more she eats, the more she craves. When she tries to bathe her sticky hands and face, she cannot get clean because the soap and water are also illusions. The jinn admits that "real cleansing can only be carried out by Gaal. For our part we're not prejudiced about the things Gaal's people call dirt. Really there's no such thing as dirt."

In the tunnels, Lisa must also cross a chasm, and Gaal explains that to get across she must cross the bridge. At the end of the bridge is a bar resting in a slot: "The rough bridge was a T shape, with the crosspiece at the T at the far end." She must trust Gaal to catch her if she falls. As Lisa wipes her palm on the sleeve of his robe, it makes it burn. But she is cleaner, and the sleeve remains pure white because "Gaal was not just clean. He was cleanness itself." Gaal leads her to his Fountain of Dam so she can become totally cleansed:

For a moment she caught her breath with the cool shock, but almost at once she felt like swimming hard. . . . Putting one hand up to feel the back of her hair, she found to her surprise that the filthy stuff that had clung to her was gone. She stared at both her hands to find they too were clean (*Tower*, 201–202).

Lisa tells Gaal, "You made me clean inside as well as outside." Gaal then presents her with new clothes and gifts. Her shoes of "basar" will never wear out and will let her run swiftly on errands, while a red sash of "qosht" turns blue in the dark to show things as they really are. A crown of "tiqvah," which helps her never lose heart, is made of "Zabach" stones from "living purity, crushed between rock and fire." The light shield of "aman" deflects weapons. Finally, the Book of Wisdom, when read aloud, makes goblin shadows visible, emits a light, and is used in battle to dispel evil.

In Lawhead's *In the Hall of the Dragon King*, Quentin, an acolyte at the temple of the old gods, undergoes an inner journey to be free of the old gods he used to serve with fear and superstition in the temple. While once he had believed that the gods do not care for men's lives, he learns that there is a nameless god—"the One"— who is above all others and cares. An elder of the Curatak in the city of Dekra leads him underground to their library. In this room the young Auga receive a blessing from the Most High God: "The Blessing is the gift of god. All that is required is a true heart and a desire to receive it." From this point on, Quentin's friend Toli notices the change in Quentin, while Quentin is amazed that this god is powerful enough to change his followers.

To receive the god's blessing, all he needs to do is desire to receive it. He is given a drink from a fountain, then the priest touches his forehead with it: "Water is the symbol of life; all living things need water to live. And so it is the symbol of the Creator of Life, Whist Orren." In a vision in which Quentin encounters the Most High, the god tells Quentin his touch will cleanse him and give him the blessing he seeks. A similar vision in *The Warlords of Nin* shows Quentin a river of Truth and water of Peace. The river gives life to all who seek it, but evil defiles and poisons it.

While minor characters also become converted, they seem extraneous to the story and make the evangelistic intent blatant. A young, wounded, dying soldier, for instance, asks Durwin about death. Durwin replies that he must choose between two paths, one into darkness, the other to a wonderful city where a "loving king" eternally reigns. All he needs to do is simply believe in God the King. Similarly, in *The Sword and the Flame*, Durwin tells Esme, who seeks hope like his, that it comes from believing in the One True God: "Seek him and you will find him." He wants all of her, including her "love and worship, everything." Eventually, in admiration for a god who really "walks among his people," she prays, "Most High, if you will receive me I will follow you." By the "rising sensation" in her soul, she knows her prayer has been answered.

In his *Empyrion* books, Stephen Lawhead has the two main characters gradually become believers and uses the mist image as an effective image of spiritual rebirth. As Treet and his companions travel to the land of the Fierri, they pass through a blue mist like an "immense curtain." As a result, they become covered with angry, raised, itchy blisters, and eventually covered with a three centimeter thick crust which is like a "cocoon." After days of fever and nightmares, Treet eventually cracks his way out of it, breaking off huge chunks, and realizes that his skin has not only completely healed but is smooth, moist, supple, and without blemish: "He had emerged whole and unspotted." Aware that a "miracle" has taken place, he becomes "overwhelmed with giddiness— an intense, nonsensical desire to dance and sing, to prance and cavort and abandon himself to sweet, reckless joy. . . . I am reborn!"

Still, Treet has "little use for religion, tending to see it merely as something to keep the dim, cold unknown from becoming too frightening. He wasn't easily frightened, so relegated religion to the dustbin of outmoded ideas" (*Empyrion: The Search for Fierra*, 166). But "the Infinite Presence" chooses him for the task of preventing Dome from attacking the Fierri. In a torture tank he is protected from succumbing by awareness of an "entity," an "alien presence":

If consciousness were pictured as a great miasmic sphere inside which self-awareness dwelt, then a portion of Treet's sphere had been gently interfused with the alien entity's sphere. . . . He felt centered: a runaway planet that had been captured, stabilized, and pulled into useful orbit around a life-giving sun . . . he knew that his life would be forever changed. (*Empyrion II: The Siege of Dome*, 163)

Treet's girlfriend, Yarden, is similarly converted. By being around the Fieri, Yarden hears them explain how "the creation of the cosmos had cost the Infinite Father something; He had paid a tremendous toll to bring His beloved into existence. He had labored, and suffered the pain of His laboring. In this suffering, love itself was born" (*II*, 229). Love, she learns, is "taking the pain of another as your own." Eventually, the inner voice of the Infinite tells her to surrender control: "Come to Me, Yarden. Give Me the gift of yourself, and I will give a gift far greater than you can imagine. Yarden, trust me and believe. . . . Yes, I'll trust You, she thought. *Yes!*" (331).

In Lawhead's science fiction novel *Dream Thief*, Spence Reston's conversion takes even more time. On Mars, where inhabitants worship Da Elna, the All Being, Spence confronts his true nature for the first time and examines what he has done with his life. As a scientist he trusts only "what he could see and examine" and considers religion "harmless do-goodism" that weaker minds turn to when frightened. "And yet, he had prayed . . . to this same Supreme Being in his own moment of doubt and pain." Spence is still not willing to admit that God exists or will help him. But when a dark "mind of utter chaos and depravity" tries to absorb him, Spence calls to God to save him. A voice tells him to come into the light, which begins to shine down upon him like a pool:

With a terrific roar the darkness dissolved and ran away and a brilliant white light, brighter than ten thousand suns, blazed. He felt its power and its vibrant, living energy as it danced over him, tingling every pore, every square centimeter of his skin. Now it was inside him, penetrating his flesh and bones and burning into the fibers of his soul. He could feel it like fire—consuming all impurities, devouring any remaining shreds of darkness which clung to his inner self, cleansing the very atoms of his being. Spence then knew that he and the light were one: it had done its work in him and he was transformed into a living beam of light (279).

But Spence is not yet totally converted. When he prays for a small Indian boy to be saved, for example, Spence believes it is no use: "God did not intervene in his creation anymore . . . 'I almost believed'. . . . 'God! Why?' " But as if in response, the boy miraculously comes to life.

Spence is told that he will be able to stand up to the Dream Thief because "the light that is in . . . us . . . is greater than all the darkness in the universe. God is working in you, Spence." People believe that the Dream Thief is a god of the Himalayas who sneaks into people's dreams, replacing them with madness. But Spence asks, "What difference does it make if I believe in him or not?" "Belief has the power to shape reality," his Indian friend replies. "God is meeting you at every turn . . . Back there in the camp you prayed for a little boy who died and he lived again. . . . And you insist you cannot see it?" (307). Spence recognizes he is fighting not to believe because it will change him and his "tattered naturalistic world view."

On a mountainside, Spence finally feels certainty, something as a scientist he had ceased to believe was possible. "That the immutable absolute might be the Divine Being had never occurred to him," yet he feels it approaching him in the shape of a "fiery, ferocious" tiger. When he drinks Essilia during a ceremony that allows him to fully commune with the Martian Kyr, he has contact "with the God he had long denied, but could deny no longer." His calling is to now do something higher than his ambitions, to help the Martians implement their abilities on earth.

The central character of Smith's *Captive Planet* also becomes converted. Lam, a pirate, becomes interested in the faith of those of the Way of Tsu because it seems so real to them. Padu assures him the Power is at work in him: "If you put your trust in Him, He will become more real to you than the world you can see." Similarly, the Le-in, strange creatures on the Planet Refuge, follow the Source. When Lam attempts to understand their language, he becomes "aware of a desire within himself to feel the joy these people" feel. But he does not "understand how to receive it." At last he meets the Friend, who knows everything evil he has done. "I am a man like you," says the Friend, who is also the Source and Power. The remedy for Lam's life is to believe that he is Lam's Friend. Lam realizes that his "haunting dreams, the strange feelings, the longings, they had all been for the Friend. . . . For the first time in his life he felt he was not alone." Excited that the Friend has accepted him, Lam has a "new feeling of freedom."

M-stones made of Monobarite are symbolic of the Power's guidance and an expression of one's faith. It glows with a blue-white light, especially when near other stones. It can also "give warmth; it can bring light; and it can make you think further. It is the way the Source helps us." It does this by amplifying energy (light, movement, thought) applied to it when one needs power. Lam, for example, receives amplified emotional and physical energy to fight Kurdon as the promise "I will never fail you" goes through his mind.

Another aid is prayer, which the rebel forces of the Way of Tsu use to seek help in fighting. Meline, the King's daughter, tells Lam, "You've begun to notice that things happen when we pray. . . . I've been praying that you would." Even though Lam does not know how to pray, he follows the example of the others: "The Friend looked back at him gently but with a strength that seemed to radiate from inside. Lam forgot that he was just imagining and felt he should confess his fear to the Friend." For the first time in his life he feels he has "hope, and a reason to live."

The book also contrasts the types of sacrifices required in two religions. The evil Doomen of the Dominion have a different form of worship than the Way of Tsu. Their altar has "hideous carvings" in its black stone:

A monstrous serpent with powerful wings and talons twisted in one part tyrannized the central carving. Beneath its atrocious form a strange procession of smaller creatures was pictured as carrying dead bodies to the serpent. Nearby were carved scenes of torture and torment, some of them lewd and sadistic (25).

*Tales of the Kingdom* uses both the imagery of dirt for sin and cleansing flames for salvation. A girl named Dirty lives among the pigs. After she meets the King, who appears as a beggar and invites her to join him in the Sacred Flames, she tries to wash herself: "I've washed and washed, but I'm still dirty. I'm all pig inside. The King will never love me." When she attends the Great Celebration, she is disappointed that the King, the only one who can make her clean, is not there. But, she is told, "The King does not have to come in order for us to see him. He is always present." Hearing him speak to her, she goes through the Sacred Flames and becomes Cleone, the clean one.

Some books contain other striking redemption images to convey the meaning of salvation to a character. In Calvin Miller's *War of the Moon-rhymes*, Old Sammuron gives his life in exchange for Jendai's: "Your blood is mine. / Your hurt grows here upon my ancient skin— / As I take your wounds!" First, they lie down beside one another. Then a lesion begins to bleed from Old Sam's shoulder while the lesion on Jendai's closes. Jendai cannot understand why "he felt as if he had just been born. His newness made him look inward with shame upon all that he had been before."

A more unusual image is found in the short story "Mother and the Flying Saucer" by Mary McDermott Schideler (Melrose, 33–43). Flying saucers from Uranus visit earth to learn about death because the aliens there are unified and do not know the complexity and division humans experience. Mother has an auto accident but lives when one of the

Saucers dies for her: "The Saucer had not merely died for her, it had died instead of her. Its love had enabled it to take into itself that death that reached for her, and so it was that she lived. It had died her death."

## UNBELIEVERS

Because many readers might align with an unbeliever, some books contain one or more skeptics who are more resistant to change. Fantasy can thus create the possibility of belief in a skeptic or lead an unbeliever toward belief. Clyde Kilby reports that many people have been converted by reading the Narnia chronicles ("How," 31). A person who tends not to take religious faith seriously might see it as plausible when it is part of the plot of a fantasy or science fiction format or takes place in a secondary world.

In John White's *The Tower of Geburah*, while some of the Friesen children believe right away in Gaal the Shepherd, Kurt refuses to go on the path Gaal tells the children to take and becomes increasingly surly and disagreeable as they near the tower. Kurt awakens Shagah the Sleeper, an evil sorcerer, who promises to make Kurt a great magician if he uses his power to destroy the tower. Like Edmund in Lewis' Narnia tales, Kurt thinks to himself,

Now he would show Lisa and Wesley! In his mind he pictured their admiration and envy. He would be able to say to them, 'See, I understood what the real truth was right from the start!' They would look up to him and be grateful to him. He could go back to their own world with . . . power (290).

Only after almost ruining the mission does Kurt realize that he has been used by Shagah and must confront Gaal:

Kurt never told anybody what went on between Gaal and himself. . . . They spent a long time together. Sometimes they sat and sometimes they walked . . . when Kurt came back, he was no longer afraid. You could see he'd been crying, yet you could sense that he was at peace with himself (311).

In White's *The Sword Bearer*, John Wilson is a runaway and apparent orphan. Lord Lunacy tries to convince him that because he hates his father for deserting him and thinks he is better than the other children, he is evil: "John was gripped with a wild exhilaration. He was evil. It was a new sensation to him, a sensation he had never before dared to let himself feel. He was different" (57). John thus becomes resentful, sulky, humiliated, and bitter because he cannot use the sword that will impress the Matmon and prove he has power. So he joins a group of dwarves who do not drink of the "wine of free pardon."

One must partake of this drink before he can enter the Master's service: "Those who absorb it and do not reject it are changed. They know evil and good. And they reject the evil." While some scowl after drinking it, John notices its effects on others. One dwarf's upturned face seems "almost to shine while from his eyes tears streamed. . . . the look on his face was not a look of pain, but of joy, as he gazed at something he alone could see." He tells John he is crying because he is happy: "Such kindness. Such great kindness." Others similarly have "their faces transformed by joy" and sing and dance. But Lord Lunacy says because John is to be ruler of Anthropos, he must drink the wine he gives him so he can be filled with dark power. John begins to swell with "a fierce and exultant pride."

When John tries to drink the wine of free pardon, he is disgusted and spits it out, then flings the contents out. John is told that no one can make him drink it; he must want to. He is ready to drink only when he realizes that he must to use the sword effectively and to make the Tower of Darkest Night sink:

His shame and guilt at first seemed to be crushing him, but as the fires inside him burned on he knew he was being set free. Tears flowed from his eyes, and he let them flow. His arms and legs were shaking. The shame and guilt were evaporating, leaving in their place a huge contentment that swept over him in waves of fire and light. He closed his eyes and let his whole body tremble. It was a wonderful trembling. He wanted it to go on forever. He felt as though all his fears and angers and bitternesses were being shaken out of his bones. Something powerful was happening to him, powerful but gentle (163).

A dragon, Telgan, is the unbeliever in *The Forbidden Door*. Wondering what is on the other side of the Forbidden Door, he disobeys the laws of the Great One by opening it, despite the disaster that will come to his country. He hates Nimeon, Crown Prince of Dragonland, even though he saves his life at the Door, because Nimeon is what he "should have been." Their country of kind Green Dragons must fight evil Dark Dragons, who have contempt for "the Great One, the King." As Telgan becomes more disagreeable and sulky, the King warns him to turn "back from that path before it is too late or else you will bring much evil on yourself. And in the end you may even forget the Great One and then you will have nothing left except darkness and misery" (Norweb, 56).

Telgan eventually chooses the side of the Dark Dragons. At first they give him "power and praise." But when he is injured they throw him out to die because they have no pity on the old and sick. Since he can "never quite forget the Blue Road"—a symbol of eternal life—he returns to ask Nimeon's mercy and permission to lie near the Blue Road until he dies and is taken Home.

A different technique is used in the short story "Certain Distant Suns" by Joanne Greenberg (Melrose, 59–76), where the logical consequences of unbelief are carried to absurdity. Bessie first gives up belief in God, then banks, germs, electricity, and gravity. In each case, when she stops believing in them, they no longer exist for her. "Foolish woman," she is told, "a soul goes in and out of belief a hundred times a day. Belief is too fragile to weigh a minute on. You stopped running after Him, looking for Him, struggling with Him. Even his laws you turned from!" (76).

In conclusion, conversion of a character is one of the most commonly used techniques of contemporary religious fantasy writers. But the conversion must be integral to the story, not existing in isolated spots unrelated to the action or produced suddenly in minor characters who exist in the story solely to be saved. Otherwise, the didactic intent of the story becomes obvious, when it can be more effectively conveyed through images. Believability, then, is an important quality of the character's change, as well as one of the most important elements of the fantasy world itself.

# Chapter 3

# "Walking the Tightrope": Qualities of Good Fantasy

[Explaining] what Christianity means to me . . . is very difficult. It's walking the tightrope between art and propaganda (Stephen Lawhead, Interview in *Axis*).

## BELIEVABILITY

Lewis gives advice on how to write about other worlds. First, the secondary world must not be a backdrop for a story that could have been told in another way. Rather, the purpose of the secondary world is to create wonder, serve as a metaphor for our world, and catch the reader unaware. This other world must be different enough from our world to make it worth going to faerie for, and something must happen once you get there. Finally, the writer must not break the spell and bring the reader back to earth (*Letters*, 278–279).

A key quality of this other world is thus believability. It is important to emphasize that it is the meaning that is true; the other world is not to be taken at face value. Tolkien insists that it should be presented as true, with an inner consistency of reality, an internal logic, and laws that make things explainable. As sub-creator, the fantasy writer creates a Secondary World the reader's mind can enter that must be convincing, self-consistent, detailed, and not an illusion: "The moment disbelief arises, the spell is broken; the magic, or rather the art has failed" ("On Fairy," 37). He says the writer cannot just say "green sun" but must make a world in which this will be credible. Thus good fantasy is difficult to write because it is an art that uses "enchantment" rather than "magic." Enchantment produces a secondary world we can enter, while magic is a technique that only alters the primary world and seeks power. Fantasy's goal is enrichment, delight, and the satisfaction of human desire;

it is not an end in itself ("On Fairy," 13, 52). Lewis, on the other hand, says the writer needs to put only enough science in the story to create a "willing suspension of disbelief."

However, it is important to establish the reality of the supernatural; adequate history and background must also be included or the work will fail to convince. Dorothy Sayers suggests, "If you want the reader not only to follow but to accept and believe a tale of marvels, you can do it best by the accumulation of precise and even prosaic detail," which she calls the "trick of particularity" (*Further Papers on Dante*, 7). Not only can description and other details make the world believable, but the characters must also be transported in and out effectively.

### Description

Because Tolkien thought the reader should be free to picture scenes, he avoids specific description. An "essential power of Faerie is . . . the power of making immediately effective by the will the visions of 'fantasy' " ("On Fairy," 22). By use of the adjective one becomes an enchanter and creates a new form, turning "grey lead into yellow gold." According to Lewis, if a reader wants "egoistic castle building" he will demand realism and dislike the fantastic because he won't like the fact that events cannot really happen (*Experiment*, 56). He thus distinguishes between realism of presentation (detail, close-ups, description, minor characters) versus realism of content (trueness to life). Realism of presentation involves making the story vivid by "palpable" and "sharp" detail such as the "dragon sniffling along the stone" in *Beowulf* (*Christian*, 134). The writer, Lewis suggests, must not rely on adjectives or adverbs but rather must *make* the reader feel. The art lies in "making us believe we have imagined the unimaginable" (*The Discarded Image*, 207).

In *A Preface to Paradise Lost*, Lewis describes Milton's use of images to arouse the reader's imagination rather than simply describe his own. He uses language to control what already exists in our mind. Similarly, through detailed and often sensual description, religious fantasy helps us visualize heaven's future glory through using forms of beauty and pleasure that convey future apocalyptic splendor. In Lewis' *Voyage of the Dawn Treader*, near the End of the World, the light grows brighter and brighter, the sea smoother and white with lilies, and the water clear and luminous like "drinkable light."

In "The Cosmic Trilogy of C. S. Lewis," Wayne Shumaker suggests that description can be used to present meaning while avoiding rational explanation. He cites the example of Wither, head of N.I.C.E. in Lewis' *That Hideous Strength*. He interprets the man's white hair to mean that "evil has been active in Earthly affairs since the Fall." The large face shows "evil is everywhere," the watery eyes indicate that "evil can't stand the light," and his lack of attention to others reflects how "evil is self-centered" (61).

Lewis' books themselves were initially conceived as images such as the floating islands or a faun carrying an umbrella. Details of setting and atmosphere are important, serving often as religious images. For example, some see the vertical Malacandran landscape as an image of spiritual aspiration. Similarly, the floating islands versus the Fixed Land of Perelandra suggest to Clyde Kilby the difference between obedience and conformity or adherence to rules without conviction (*Images*, 31). In John White's *The Iron Sceptre*, a map depicts the Kingdom of Darkness as a series of concentric circles, each one representing a different temptation. In other fantasy, sensory impressions often become metaphoric and show or suggest rather than explain ideas. Water, for instance, is often a baptismal or cleansing symbol; dark forests, fog, ice and snow are associated with evil. Setting, then, functions as more than just a backdrop, because it is a "spiritual landscape in which even the least element might carry a moral meaning" (Wolfe, 201).

Often the landscape parallels the inner spiritual quest. In *Journey to Aldairoon*, the Forbidden Mountains symbolize Rafe's search for identity. As he nears the top, a strange dark fog overtakes him "as though some spiteful Power was searching for him." When he calls out for help from the "One who has divided light from Darkness," he finds himself in a column or chimney of clear air that moves with him and is surrounded by the menacing, boiling fog. Eventually, darkness closes "tightly around his heart," and he begins to doubt, "overwhelmed by fear and desolation." But "when the black despair pushed deeper into him, probing for his center, it came face to face with a fire that even Rafe had never suspected burned within him."

Similarly, in Richard Ford's *Quest for the Faradawn*, Nab must climb the Mount of Ivett to meet Asgaraoth, the Lord of Good. But a thick, damp mist so envelops him that he cannot see, and dips and hollows make his steps difficult. Every time he regains confidence, he begins to go downhill. Suddenly, the weight of his responsibility comes to him: "The mist seemed to be growing thicker all the time and his body was so damp and cold that he began to shiver uncontrollably. He sat down on the ground and, burying his face in his hands, allowed despair to take him over" (292). Yet through the mist he senses the warm light of Asgaroth and feels like he is floating on the mist, "no longer tired or miserable or afraid; he was suddenly invincible. He could have gone on for ever, such was the power and strength that surged through his body even to his fingertips" (292).

Other details that encourage believability include geography, maps, history, literature, and invented names. Unfortunately, few contemporary writers create detailed secondary worlds, certainly none with the completeness of Tolkien's books. However, Tolkien's primary goal was to create a world in which his languages could exist and present it as history. Because the goal of contemporary writers is to convey religious ideas, the imaginary lands are usually left vague as in traditional fairy tales, or the names suggest allegory, such as Anthropos (man), Terran (earth), Ekklesia (church), or Adamlanda.

Lewis recommends that names be "beautiful, suggestive, and strange." He invented new words by connecting syllables for their emotional suggestiveness (*Letters*, 284). Proper names should not be chosen only for sound but "because they are the names of splendid, remote, terrible, voluptuous, or celebrated things" (*Preface*, 40–41). In Lawhead's Empyrion books the names and terms are too unusual: Turdy, Piipo, Yos, kraam, bhuj, and Asquith Pizzle. Other contemporary writers such as L'Engle and John White use names from Latin, Greek, or Hebrew, but only a reader armed with the right dictionary would know their meaning. This techique also contributes toward making a character "represent" something.

### Entering and Exiting

The writer must also get the characters in and out of the secondary world effectively and credibly. The other world often represents the real but invisible spiritual world which a character must learn exists even when he is not present or to which he will return after death. In John White's books, Anthropos is not connected with the real world but is said to be "another *kind* of universe in another age." To enter, the children see pictures on the TV sets in their uncle's attic come alive: "It almost looks like 3-D . . . almost like a tiny theater stage with no glass in front." As Lisa starts to touch the screen, she is suddenly kneeling inside the frame and then inside the picture: "Everything in the picture was swiftly growing larger and wrapping itself round her." Her brothers Wes and Kurt push their hands into the TV screen and compare the sensation to "coming up and breaking the surface of the water after a dive in the swimming pool," except their heads push up through a soft forest floor. You cannot get back into the land by the same route, and "the magic only seems to work when Gaal wants it to." King Kardia explains that she has come through a Proseo comai stone through which "come the desires of one's heart." In *The Iron Sceptre*, as Mary McNab lies in her bed, she begins to feel like she is floating. Suddenly, she is in a snowy other world.

The children return home a different way. For example, at the end of *The Tower of Geburah*, they are on an empty stage with a wall of black glass at the back which becomes the attic back home. At the end of *The Iron Sceptre*, Gaal leads the children to an alcove above which is a trapezoidal opening that slopes inward to meet the ceiling of their attic. When she sees Gaal, their Aunt Felicia screams, "Let me out of here!"

In most books, no time has passed on earth while the characters are in the secondary world. Lewis believed other worlds might have time with "thicknesses" and "thinnesses," not linear time like ours, and other writers use this same concept. When the children are called back to Anthropos for their second adventure, for example, 31 years have passed there, yet when they return home only a few earth hours have passed. An interesting image in White is the Cave of Gaal where Gaal was murdered and slew Death. At the top of the steps is a "hole where time is no more." The children's voices change as though they are coming "across a vast stretch of time." All three see things they are unable to describe—visions of various events apparently from Anthropos' past.

Other books make passage between the worlds easy. In *The Promise Keeper* the children are told, "Our time here is not the same as earth time. You can stay here as long as you like, and when you return to your planet it will be the same time as when you left." Each child is given his own space ship he can use to travel alone to Promise-Keeper's land whenever he wants to, and no one misses him. In *Alpha Centauri* Becky passes through the Eye of the Fog into Britain thousands of years back in time, to the Old Stone Age when Britain was not an island. She returns by riding into the same woods: "She'd spent months among the centaurs, and yet it seemed she'd returned to Canters a few hours after she left."

In *The Forbidden Door*, Laura and David come upon a small dragon, Nimeon, in Smuggler's Cove. He is crying because he needs their help opening a door that leads back to his country. Dragonland is not much different from their home, but the air is clearer and the colors brighter. There are "forests of huge trees, winding rivers flowing in and out of odd-shaped lakes, and broad meadows bright with spring flowers." "Whoever has power over the Door knows . . . the time and place and reason for opening the Door," the children are told. The door is only in the cave when there is a reason. No matter how long they remain, when they return home it is the same moment as when they left. Their grandfather asks them, "Why shouldn't there be other times and other worlds? It seems to me to be both pretty foolish and pretty arrogant to think this world and we in it are the beginning and end of everything, as though no other world could possibly have been created." After their third and final visit to Dragonland, they see a large bolt on the Door: "It swung shut behind them and they heard the bolt fall into place." They know it means they cannot return.

## "ALTERNATIVE THEOLOGY"

The characters are called in and out of the other world for a reason: for adventure, to perform a task, and to learn through their experiences values that may be applied in the "real" world. First, to attract both young and adult readers, the fantasy work must simply be a good story— a straightforward adventure. Lewis and Tolkien agreed that although fantasy must reflect truth, the action must be compelling, believable, pleasing, exciting, moving, and relevant. Like all good literature, the story must be interesting and pleasurable rather than exist solely to present truth or philosophy. Otherwise, art is being used as a means to an end. Contemporary writer Stephen Lawhead finds writing his fantasy and science fiction like "walking the tightrope between art and propaganda" ("Stephen," 24).

Yet Lewis considered the plot "a net whereby to catch something else . . . like a state or quality" such as "giantship, otherness, the desolation of space" and the numinous (*On*, 17). A good work, he argues, is more than just what happened, because a reader can re-read it and still be moved. Because it can present theological principles, one might call Christian fantasy "alternative theology," a phrase Chesterton used to describe George MacDonald's works. Madeleine L'Engle thinks "that right doctrine is far more often taught in stories than in direct dogma" ("Allegorical Fantasy," 15, 18). Unfortunately, there is a fine line between conveying ideas such as these and using obvious allegory.

Tolkien considers Lewis' *Out of the Silent Planet* successful because there are "a great number of philosophical and mythical implications that enormously enhanced without detracting from the surface 'adventure'." The "blend of *vera historia* with *mythos*" was "irresistible" (*Letters*, 33). Ideally, then, the story itself conveys the message. But it is difficult to integrate idea and effect so that the meaning emerges without didacticism. For example, fairy tales and children's literature of the Victorian period are noted for their moralizing. Charles Kingsley's *The Water Babies* (1863), one of the forerunners of contemporary religious fantasy, includes sermons in the narrative. Tom, a chimney sweep, turns into a river creature and learns moral lessons through characters such as Mrs. Bedonebyasyoudid. Kingsley tried to make both children and adults recognize the "miraculous and divine element underlying all physical nature" and "wrapped up" his "parable in seeming Tom-fooleries" to "get the pill swallowed" (Blount, *Animal Land: The Creatures of Children's Fiction*, 55).

For the moral to be one with the story, the theology must be presented through narrative action and embodied in situations so the work has a dramatic quality. For instance, Rolland Hein believes that George MacDonald's fairy stories are successful because he carefully integrates the moral with the aesthetic structure "so that the effect is seldom preachy" (139). The little discussed story "The Light Princess" uses Biblical images but because of the humor may only remind a reader of redemption. The nameless princess has no gravity (she floats in the air and is never serious). She loves swimming because it gives her weight. But the witch has one of her White Snakes of Darkness drain the water from the beloved lake. At the bottom a plaque says, "Death alone from death can save / Love is death. . . . The only way to fill the hole is with "the body of a living man" who "must give himself of his own will." A young prince who has fallen in love with the princess offers to give his life. Before he drowns, the princess feels love and pity for him and saves him, thus breaking the spell.

It is also desirable that spiritual qualities be shown working through people rather than using characters as personifications. Good and evil can also be illustrated by the characters' behavior, and their moral growth should be convincing. Furthermore, each episode should be related to the whole. If the theme is not presented believably and consistently maintained in the context of the secondary world, it will be made unbelievable whenever there are momentary lapses into realism or sermonizing.

Too often, however, religious fantasy tends to use exposition, preachy dialogue, explanation, argument, Biblical terminology that "explains" the book's mythology, statements that attempt to drive home the point, or characters and events that have no real relation to the plot convey religious ideas. Most important, the mythopoeic appeal may be sacrificed whenever ideas are set forth solely through speculation or conversation.

Preferable are statements that encourage interpretation such as Ransom's statement in *Out of the Silent Planet* that he drank life because death—the hnakra—was in the pool. Clyde Kilby says this statement suggests that "a safe journey through a dangerous world is better than a mindless trek in a perfectly safe one and that where peril is great the potential for joy is greater" (*Images*, 25). In *Perelandra*, Lewis suggests that the root of all evil may be the itch to have things over again, like eating the same fruit, hearing the same symphony twice in one day, or desiring what "might be." Such ideas encourage the reader to reflect and interpret, but unfortunately this technique is rare in other writers. Lewis says that you can read a good book a number of times and find more in it, as well as continued delight. This quality is often achieved when there are deeper levels of meaning to be found in statements, action, images, and so forth.

Lewis, Tolkien, L'Engle, and others believe that a good work should also not be written for one audience because only poor stories are enjoyed just by children. Lewis states, "No book is really worth reading at the age of ten which is not equally (and often far more) worth reading at the age of fifty—except, of course, books of information" (*On*, 14). Tolkien agrees: "If a fairy story is worth reading at all it is worthy to be written for and read by adults" ("On Fairy," 45). He calls the association of fairy tales with children an accident. Such stories were relegated to the nursery like old furniture because adults didn't want them ("On Fairy" 34). Lewis admits, "When I was ten, I read fairy tales in secret and would have been ashamed if I had been found doing so. Now that I am fifty I read them openly. When I became a man I put away childishness and the desire to be very grown up" (*On*, 34).

To achieve this universal quality, a writer should not talk down to the reader and should use the same rules to write for either adults or younger audiences. Most writers, in fact, claim that they write for both audiences. George MacDonald, for example, wrote not for children but rather for the "childlike, whether of five, or fifty, or seventy-five" ("Fantastic," 25). Similarly, Lewis explains that when his imagination led him to write the Narnia tales, he did not begin by first asking what children want and then trying to dish it out to them or by treating them like a distinct and inferior race (*On*, 51). John White wrote his trilogy for children "with an eye on adults reading" to them. Thus he tried to "write at a level that would hold an adult and at the same time be appealing to the child" ("Fantasy," 8–9). Ironically, Madeleine L'Engle says if she wants to deal with something too difficult for adults, she puts it in a children's book, because children do not fear the unknown and are familiar with the language of myth. Children understand concepts such as the "thinness" and "non-ness" in *A Wrinkle in Time*, whereas adults are afraid of the book (*Circle*, 231).

Since fantasy should be read primarily for pleasure and not edification, what any reader gets out of it will depend on his spiritual background. Tolkien believes the reader will not perceive any religious feeling unless it is in him also (*Letters*, 413). According to Lewis, the moral should arise from the "cast" of the author's mind, as well as "whatever spiritual roots you have succeeded in striking during the whole course of your life. But if they don't show you any moral, don't put one in" (*On*, 41–42). The goal is to convey meaning without rational explanation so that the message or religious echoes wake up things already in the reader. Like a picture, says Lewis, the story should trigger the reader's imagination and emotion and, instead of fixing attention on itself, stimulate activity (*Experiment*, 16). For fantasy to function sacramentally, MacDonald similarly recommends that a person read for pleasure, not edification. Incidents may or may not convey moral or spiritual truths, depending on the reader's spiritual state and needs: "Everyone . . . who feels the story, will read its meaning after his own nature and development: one man will read one meaning in it, another will read another" ("Fantastic," 25). The meaning is there not to be conveyed but, in MacDonald's words, to "wake a meaning": "The best things you can do for your fellow, next to rousing his conscience, is not to give him things to think about, but to wake up things that are in him . . . or . . . to make him think things for himself" ("Fantastic," 27).

Like nature, the work should be "mood-engendering and thought-provoking." If the reader cannot get the meaning, one should not tell him what it means. In fact, there is not just "one" meaning. MacDonald points out that although a fairy tale cannot help but have meaning, everyone will get different meanings out of it depending upon his nature and development. Since the writer only recombines God's elements in his works, there may even be more meanings than the author knows: "A man may well himself discover truth in what he wrote; for he was dealing all the time with things that came from thoughts beyond his own" ("Fantastic," 27). Since it is impossible to ever know all the meaning in our works, "the meaning we never intended may be the best and truest one," Lewis suggests.

These varied responses in readers may be achieved through imagery and anagogue. In *Images of Salvation in the Fiction of C. S. Lewis* Clyde Kilby defines an image as a "concept or idea whose meaning carries over from one context to another" (9). Since an image draws on several referrents at once, carrying simultaneously several levels of meaning, it can communicate different meanings to different readers. John Timmerman uses the term "anagogic insight" to describe "an immediate apprehension of spiritual patterns which has been stimulated by certain literary figures, symbols, or devices." The fantasy writer suggests such anagogues by carefully writing the story:

By repetition of pointing signals, or symbols, the author constructs a pattern which guides the interpretation. But in no sense does the writer force the pattern upon the reader. The reader, by following the pattern, claims the anagogic insight as his own. The story becomes his own story to the extent that his imagination interpenetrates the framework of the story and lives for a time in the world of the story. The insights thereby disclosed to one reader may vary from those disclosed to another reader by virtue of the degree of interpenetration. One symbol may affect one reader more powerfully than it would another reader. Similarly, one reader may take from the story insights not apparent to another reader. Thus the pattern is dynamic and varying (*Other Worlds*, 8).

In *Anatomy of Criticism* Frye notes, "The anagogic view . . . leads to the conception of literature as existing in its own universe, no longer a commentary on life or reality, but containing life and reality in a system of verbal relationships" (122). Madeleine L'Engle calls the anagogical level, which she believes is discernible in the best fantasy, science fiction, and apocalyptic literature, the level "which breaks the bounds of time and space and gives us a glimpse of the truth" (*Circle*, 82).

Frye distinguishes between "a 'concrete' approach to symbols which begins with images of actual things and works outward to ideas and propositions, and an 'abstract' approach which begins with the idea and then tries to find a concrete image to represent it" (89). George Mac-

Donald is perhaps one Christian writer who uses this technique the most. His purpose in writing was not direct instruction or entertainment but "by symbolic suggestion to penetrate eternal reality" (Hein, x). His symbols, images, and scenes suggest truths about experience because truth itself is hard to describe. Hein observes,

The symbol does not—it cannot—capture or imprison the insight so as to define it precisely and hence exhaust its meaning. For instance, the image of a fire burning in the shape of beautiful roses, as does the great-great-grandmother's fire in *The Princess and the Goblin*, tells us something otherwise unstateable about the nature of the holiness of God that loves into purity. Art may function this way, helping us glimpse what the mind has not otherwise discerned, and, when the glimpse is momentarily in focus, arousing a profound intuitive response deep within us (xvi-xvii).

## ALLEGORY

Lewis distinguishes between imagery and allegory. While images are "instruments for discovery," allegory is a "convenient illustration" (Williams, *Taliessin through Logres, the Region of the Summer, Stars, Arthurian Torso*, 7). Allegory is also different from symbol:

The allegorist leaves the given—his own passions—to talk of that which is confessedly less real, which is a fiction. The symbolist leaves the given to find that which is more real. To put the difference in another way, for the symbolist it is we who are the allegory. We are the 'frigid personifications'; the heavens above us are the 'shadowy abstractions'; the world which we mistake for reality is the flat outline of that which elsewhere veritably is in all the round of its unimaginable dimension (Lewis, *The Allegory of Love*, 45).

Religious fantasy has been called "symbolic fantasy," and this is perhaps one of its most important aspects because symbols present abstract ideas by pointing beyond themselves to the eternal. However, if the writer consciously seeks symbols, he risks lapsing into allegory, a story in which there is a one-to-one correlation between characters or events and a single abstract meaning such as psychological or spiritual experiences that they represent. The author intentionally plans these correspondences between the real and the immaterial or intangible. In addition, Lewis and Tolkien warn that if there are obvious Biblical parallels the work will become allegorical.

Throughout his letters, Tolkien adamantly describes his work as "applicability" because he disliked "conscious and intentional allegory." He contends that while not only myth and fairy tale but all art must reflect and contain elements of moral and religious truth, it must not be explicit as in the "real" world. While any worthwhile tale has a moral, this quality does not make it allegory. So even though his characters are individuals and "contain universals," they "never represent them as such."

According to Tolkien, the "imaginative man" in him made him embody his beliefs in symbolic or mythopoeic form. Fairy tales have a different and more powerful way of reflecting truth than allegory or realism. He did not consciously try to present his vision of truth, but rather his beliefs and ideas "came through." Because a writer cannot make a narrative out of nothing and finds it impossible to "rearrange the primary matter in secondary patterns without indicating feelings and opinions about one's material," the writer's own reflections inevitably will get worked in (*Letters*, 298). In fact, when asked his motive, Tolkien replied, "I am a Christian and of course what I write will be from that essential viewpoint" (Kilby, "Mythic," 9).

*Lord of the Rings*, he maintains, was based on certain religious ideas, but not an allegory of them. He once showed Clyde Kilby an unpublished paper by a British professor, which said that many misunderstood *Lord of the Rings* and did not see Christ's redemption of the world in it. Tolkien remarked that this was true except that this "schema" was not consciously in his mind before or while he wrote (Kilby, "Mythic," 9). Instead, his aim was to unite religion and myth so that Christianity would come to the reader as "shock" or "romance."

He describes *Lord of the Rings* as a "fundamentally religious and Catholic work," but it only became such in the revision because the religion was "absorbed" in the symbolism (*On*, 172). In addition, he did not feel obligated to fit his story to formal Christianity but rather "consonant with Christian thought and belief" (*Letters*, 355). He feared Christian ideas could be turned into allegory and thus propaganda. Objecting to a critic's description of him as a "believer in moral didacticism," he firmly replied, "I neither preach nor teach" (*Letters*, 414). Yet he was annoyed when critics wrote that *Lord of the Rings* has no religion.

Clyde Kilby, who worked with Tolkien on *The Silmarillion*, says Tolkien's work is not allegory, a "statement," or a "system" but myth: "It is a story to be enjoyed, not a sermon to be preached" ("Mythic," 10). At the same time, it "suggests the sadness of a paradise lost and the glory of one that can be regained." His characters endure journeys that are spiritual, as well as physical, undergo sacrifice, resist temptation, and display moral values. There is a Force and divine plan behind events, as well as supernatural figures such as the One (God), Valar (angels), Elbereth (Virgin Mary), and Gandalf, who becomes resurrected. In addition, Edenic allusions can be found in Valinor, the Blessed Realm, and Lothlorien.

In comparison to his own works, Tolkien thought the Christian meaning in the Narnia books was too obvious. Similarly, in writing about all of Lewis' fantasy works, Gunnar Urang emphasizes the tension that must exist between a story's controlling idea and the vehicle:

If the tension between the fiction and the idea collapses, then a heavier burden falls on belief. Unless the reader can implicitly accept the fiction's commitment to the values of the hypothetical world which the writer has constructed, he will begin to examine Lewis' ideas in their own right. If he finds them unbelievable, he will find the novel unbearable (28).

Because sometimes the Christian allusion in Lewis' books becomes too didactic, he is noted for making his fiction a formal apology for Christianity. For example, although Lewis says "all the human characters in this book are purely fictitious and none of them is allegorical," *Perelandra* makes explicit Christian references, particularly to the fall in Eden, and there are statements such as Ransom's "I'm a Christian." Because Ransom doubts, we are drawn into many apologetic arguments. Dennis Quinn thus argues that in Lewis' Narnia books, "spectacles, scenes, and images" convey ideas in lieu of action where heroes defeat foes. Since the human actions exist only for the symbolism, they are "at best rhetoric, at worst propaganda" (114).

Ironically, Lewis claims that in writing his Narnia tales he never consciously started with the moral or didactic purpose of conveying Christian principles nor first asked what children needed to hear:

Some people seem to think that I began asking how I could say something about Christianity to children; then fixed on the fairy tale as an instrument; then collected information about child-psychology and decided what age-group I'd write for; then drew up a list of basic Christian truths and hammered out "allegories" to embody them. This is all pure Moonshine. Rather, the Christian element pushed itself in of its own accord (*On*, 46).

Instead, religious elements may come unconsciously from the author's own mind. He never started from a "message or moral" because the "story itself should force its moral upon you." In a letter to Mrs. Donnelly, Lewis advises,

We needn't all write patently moral or theological work. Indeed, work whose Christianity is latent may do quite as much good and reach some of whom the more obvious religious work would scare away.... Don't try to "bring in" specifically Christian bits . . . none of my stories began with a Christian message. I always start from a mental picture ("Letter").

But he grants that any story can be interpreted allegorically if the reader tries hard enough.

According to Lewis, he was not exactly representing the real Christian story in symbols but rather things in his books are "like" Biblical ones or may "remind" us of them (Hooper, *Past Watchful Dragons*, 109–110). Consequently, one will not find a one-to-one relationship between stories and the Bible because he did not intend for us to. Walter Hooper warns that trying to explain stories such as the Narnia chronicles as one would decipher a code destroys their very purpose, so we should not search for analogies too closely or expect to find them. Instead, they "were written to give pleasure and (I think) as an unconscious preparation of the imagination" (*Past*, 99). Lewis himself gives advice on the dangers of trying to find parallels: "Within a given story any object, person, or place is neither more nor less than what that story effectively shows it to be. The ingredients of one story cannot 'be' anything in another story, for they are not in it at all" (*Studies*, 39–40).

The Narnia tales cannot be taught as a kind of systematic theology because there are not exact parallels between the Bible and Narnia, although "it is true that 'disguise' of a sort was part of Lewis' intention" (*Past* 106). Hooper points out that Aslan is not the son of God incarnate as a Lion. Also, there is no doctrine of Atonement in Narnia because Aslan is sacrificed for only one boy. Sometimes it is not until later that the two worlds are joined in the mind, or the reader may not recognize the source of the ingredients at all because they are used in a different way. Pauline Baynes, for example, told Hooper that she was moved by Aslan's sacrifice but did not realize who he was meant to be until after she had illustrated *The Lion, the Witch and the Wardrobe*.

Hooper contends such parallels and biblical echoes are not what the Narnia books are about or what makes them Christian, rather the moral themes that are part of the narrative (114). Charles Huttar outlines many other similarities and differences between the Narnia tales and earth. He similarly suggests that "indirect relationships" exist between the two worlds in the area of universal truths and values. But the events are not equal and only resemble or echo ours (130).

Although religious fantasy is clearly related to beliefs, it should not be allegory or sugar-coating for a sermon because some readers may be repelled. George MacDonald writes, "He must be an artist indeed who can, in any mode, produce a strict allegory that is not a weariness to the spirit" ("Fantastic," 25–26). Recently, there have been growing concerns about using allegory to present the message; such literature has been labeled "deceptive," and accused of hiding something "under its coat" or implying the truth is repugnant: "In it some see the symptoms of an apostate church hesitant to proclaim openly the name of Jesus, or the specter of worldliness in which Christians capitalize on the popularity of secular fantasy books" (Scheer, 31).

While some people believe that "allegory is a disguise, a way of saying obscurely what could have been said more clearly," argues Lewis, "in fact all good allegory exists not to hide but to reveal; to make the inner world more palpable by giving it an (imagined) concrete embodiment" (*The Pilgrim's Regress*, 13). In his "Apology" for *Pilgrim's Progress*, Bunyan lists several defenses for using allegory: it is like a fisherman's bait; Bible writers use Bible types, symbols and metaphors; its aim is to convert, not entertain; and, unlike sermons and lectures, stories are like "burrs" that stick with us. Lewis believes allegory is best when "it approaches myth, which must be grasped with the imagination, not with the intellect." His *The Pilgrim's Regress* was an attempt to explain his own conversion to Christianity, although he says not everything is autobiographical. It is "concerned solely with Christianity as against unbelief," although he believed it contained "needless obscurity," especially because of the private meaning given to Romanticism.

In *The Allegory of Love*, Lewis traces the history of allegory. Once there were two worlds from which the artist could create his work: the actual world (nature) or religion (supernature). But the rise of literary allegory introduced the "other world" of "pure fancy" (82). When religion was an integral part of the universe, literature presented the universe as a unified whole. Although people believed that the Bible speaks literally of sacred history, they also felt it describes events within man's soul. As a result, fictional forms became used to express spiritual ideas allegorically. For example, Spenser's *Faerie Queen* uses the symbolism of Revelation to describe the incarnation and the inward quest of all Christians. Redcrosse knight must rescue Una, who stands for Truth or True Church, from oppression by a great dragon. This poem, says Lewis, was a fusion of medieval allegory and romantic epic—an ideal form for presenting a "Platonized Protestantism" (*English*, 380). But, Lewis adds, the use of pictorial images was also important. Spenser is more interested in an inner state of a character than the outward story or action. The narrative story, then, is the surface expression of the inner life (*Spenser's*, 97, 124).

As man became aware of an inner conflict, he naturally looked for a literary mode to express it. When these inner forces were personified and dramatized, they took the form of "psychomachia," or a soul battle between virtues and vices. Allegory's "aim and method are to dramatize a psychological experience so as to make it more vivid and more comprehensible," explains Sayers (*Whimsical*, 207). Parable and fable often do the same thing: "Each of them tells a literal story that is complete in itself, but which also presents a likeness to some spiritual or psychological experience" (207).

A contemporary example of allegory is John White's trilogy, *The Tower of Geburah*, *The Iron Sceptre*, and *The Sword Bearer*. In the second novel, the characters must travel through three Circles of Enchantment: Bodily

Yearnings, that which Dazzles the Eye, and Blasphemy. Fortunately, the seriousness of the allegory is alleviated by the humor. For Mary McNab the first circle is a giant dish of ice cream, while for King Kardia it is a giant fenfinch pie. There also appear characters such as the Goblin of Hatred (horse-sized beetle), the Spirit of Greed (a yellow bird), and the Sprite of Envy (green snake).

For a reader familiar with Hebrew or Greek, however, it becomes apparent that White intended the entire series to be allegory. For example, the children find themselves in the country of Anthropos (Greek for "man/person"), which is controlled by the evil sorcerer Hocoino (Greek for "devil" or "defiler"). The true king Kardia (Greek for "heart") has been imprisoned, while the witch Mirmah (Hebrew for "deceit" or "treachery") has gained control of the capital city, Nephesh (Hebrew for "soul" or "spirit"). The children must retrieve a special book, key, and jeweled orb from the Tower of Geburah (Hebrew for "strength"). Lisa meets a girl named Suneidesis (Greek for "conscience"). Finally, the delivering Christ figure is called Gaal (Hebrew for "redeemer") (Edwards, "Letter," 5).

A totally different form and purpose are illustrated by *Tales of the Kingdom* by David and Karen Mains. This series of related stories uses elements of both allegory and parable to teach children, although the style and meaning are sophisticated. Karen Mains calls them allegory, the purpose of which is to teach ("Fantasy"). They might also be called parables because each tale teaches a different Biblical principle, with the moral appearing in italics at the end. For example, in one story the main character discovers "that the kingdom was for outcasts, and one must become an outcast in order to follow the King." In "The Baker Who Loved Bread," when the Baker beats a stranger trying to steal his bread, he learns it was the King in a different form. When one of the King's children is hungry, the King suffers. Thus the Baker is told to feed the King's people. This story, then, illustrates Jesus' teaching in Matt. 25:37–45.

The history behind the entire book, however, is allegory. A great King, "Son of the Emperor of All," once ruled the City. But the Enchanter deceived the people, put a spell on it, then exiled the King. The Enchanter now rules the Enchanted City with fire. He brands people with a hot poker to show they belong to him. But the King will some day bring about the Restoration of the Kingdom, although his Kingdom is "Anyplace Where the King Rules." Scarboy, an Orphan and Outcast, runs away and comes to the Great Park where he is renamed "Hero." Princess Amanda, loving a forbidden thing, keeps a small dragon's egg, even though Dragons are not permitted. The dragon grows and starts fires, thus beginning the War of Fire because of her disobedience. The Great Park is now vulnerable to Burners, who spread "fires of destruction, and "Naysayers, who freeze people's minds by saying "no" in their hearts.

Karen Mains compares fantasy to signing for the deaf. Fantasy explains the Bible to audiences who need to understand concepts in their own terms, just as missionaries explain concepts by using examples from another country's culture. In every culture, as illustrated in Richardson's *Peace Child*, there are redemptive analogies that can be used to interpret the Word to their world. "When Christ became a man he put on our metaphor," concludes Mains, so we become Christlike when we use symbol and metaphor.

Often, if allegory is used in a work, not every detail has a corresponding meaning. Works also differ with respect to the extent they use allegory. Northrop Frye classifies literature on a sliding scale from explicit allegory to anti-allegorical. *Pilgrim's Progress* and *The Faerie Queen* are examples of the former. Works like *Paradise Lost* have a major doctrinal interest. In the center are stories with suggestive imagery and only explicit relation to ideas and events (91). The latter might be exemplified by Hein's interpretation of MacDonald's fantasies. He warns the reader against "hunting for precise meanings when meaning is suggested only in the general pattern and occasional elements of the story" (145).

While the traditional writers of fantasy have debated about the use of allegory, contemporary writers have explored other options. Two of the most commonly used methods involve presenting unfallen worlds, the Biblical story of creation, and the falls of Satan and man in a new form, as described in the next chapter.

# Chapter 4

# "Past Watchful Dragons": Supposition and Re-mythologizing

But supposing that by casting all these things into an imaginary world, stripping them of their stained-glass and Sunday school associations, one could . . . steal past those watchful dragons (C. S. Lewis, *On Stories*, 47).

## SUPPOSITION

Lewis distinguishes allegory from "supposition." Each mixes the real and unreal in a different way. For example, in Bunyan, the giant represents despair. But this is fact, not supposition, and allegory existing only for the meaning. In contrast, when ideas are "supposed" in fictional terms, we can see them in new ways, and the story exists even if we remove the theological elements (*Letters*, 283). Lewis claims he was not exactly representing the real Christian story in symbols but rather things in his books are "like" biblical ones or "remind" us of them. He points out, "It would be rather a tall order to have a story strictly about God (beginning 'One day God decided'. . .) but to imagine what God might be supposed to have done in other worlds does not seem to be wrong" (*Letters*, 261).

What would Christ be like in a different world? Aslan is Lewis' answer to the question "what might Christ become like, if there really were a world like Narnia and He chose to be incarnate and die and rise again in *that* world as He actually has done in ours" (*Letters*, 283). In a letter to a little girl, Lewis wrote,

I'm not exactly "representing" the real (Christian) story in symbols. I'm more saying "Suppose there were a world like Narnia and it needed rescuing and the

Son of God (or the Great Emperor Oversea) went to redeem *it*, as He came to redeem ours, what might, in that world, all have been like?" (Hooper, *Past*, 109)

Lewis admitted it is hard to draw interesting, convincing, good characters like the King and Queen in *Perelandra* or Aslan, who are better than yourself (Letter to Jenkins). To see a person inferior to yourself, all you have to do is to stop doing something, such as being vain, greedy, cruel, or envious. But Lewis says to portray a better person involves imagining and prolonging the very best moments you have had. Since we regretfully do not know what it feels like to be good, such characters usually end up like puppets and uninteresting because they are not individuals. Thus Lewis thought it was almost impossible to write about a person like the Green Lady, who had to be both a virgin and pagan goddess. But if he could only partially succeed, he believed it worth doing, for we have forgotten about man's potential and perhaps see most people as worse than ordinary.

In the form of a Lion, Aslan can portray certain qualities of Christ: he is awesome, solemn, stern, and compassionate, a "terrible good." This technique leads us to a clearer knowledge and understanding of Christ. Aslan says the reason they were brought to Narnia is "that by knowing me here for a little, you may know me better" in England. Ironically, most children who wrote to him knew who Aslan really was, whereas most adults never saw the Biblical connection.

Another supposition in fantasy literature is questioning what an unfallen race would be like and how we would affect it. Lewis feared that if humans were to meet aliens, we would infect them with slavery, deceit, and corruption. Thus one reason he decided to write science fiction was that while traditional writers made humans good and the aliens monsters, he did the opposite (*Christian*, 173). He enjoyed speculating about whether there are other races, and whether they are good, evil, or have a redemption of their own. In *Perelandra* Lewis shows the Bent Oyarsa's tactics in great detail, thus expanding on the Genesis account of the temptation. *Perelandra* was thus the first science fiction work to present an unfallen paradise, working out the supposition, "Suppose, even now, in some other planet there were a first couple undergoing the same that Adam and Eve underwent here, but successfully" (*Letters*, 283).

James Blish's classic novel, *A Case of Conscience*, uses an unfallen planet to pose the question of whether the Devil is creative. The Edenic Lithia is inhabited by reptilian creatures who have only powers of reason and conform without force to the "highest ethical code we have evolved on Earth." This situation poses for the scientist and Jesuit priest, Ruiz-Sanchez, a "problem in theology." He wonders if, being free from the "terrible burden of original sin," they are also free from Adam's curse.

In addition, guilty of the Manichaean heresy, he believes the Devil has created this race to show humans that perfection is possible without God.

Gordon Harris' *Apostle from Space* similarly raises the question of whether unfallen races exist on other planets. An alien from the planet Elon appears to Reverend Jonathan Winkler, an Episcopal priest, during the 1970's. The alien, whom Winkler names Peter, has been sent to determine the motives behind earth's space exploration. Inhabitants of Elon believe in Christianity. Christ's sacrifice, it seems, was universal— "for all creatures here, on Elon and other planets . . . and others we have never seen." They are more technologically and telekinetically advanced than earth because of their obedience to God's laws. They also have no organized church because God directly reveals himself to them. Peter returns to Elon, concluding, "We cannot believe you are ready to join other peoples of His universe. I came in His name. I leave with a prayer that you will come to accept His will. When you do, we will return to help" (182–183).

In many other contemporary novels there is an Edenlike secondary world or part of that world. According to Leland Ryken, the longing for such a paradise comes from the undeveloped Biblical description of Eden that is left to our imagination. Imaginative literature reflects people's longing for the lost paradise and restoration of the Garden (*Literature*, 37–38,40). There is thus a spiritual need to create secondary worlds. The Genesis Eden was lush with vegetation and a place of freedom and communion with God. In addition, the Eden story contains the "conditional if," which Chesterton believes lies at the heart of fairy tales: "In the fairy tale an incomprehensible happiness rests upon an incomprehensible condition. A Box is opened, and all evils fly out. . . . An apple is eaten, and the hope of God is gone" (*Chesterson, Orthodoxy*, 56).

### Contemporary Edens

Harold Myra's *The Choice* develops the story of Eve to include her creation, temptation, life after the Fall, and death. He uses various devices, such as describing their special abilities, portraying the supernatural, rephrasing actual verses from the Bible, and using dreams and images, to suppose what life was like in Eden. God is called Aaael, Eve is Risha, Adam is Kael, Cain is Onar, and Abel is Erlin. Before the fall, Kael and Risha have "empath sense," the ability to feel each others emotions. In addition, they commune with plants:

The tree was sentient. And not only the tree . . . but the grass and the vines and bushes. She detected a unique kind of intelligence; the tree could not reason, but it was aware of all its internal functions, and of all other vegetation (15).

They also communicate with angels such as Shia, who takes on flesh to be with Risha. Like light with substance radiating "blues and greens and golds," Shia has the beauty and curves of a female but great strength. "She felt solid under Risha's hands, but her flesh looked like a form of energy." Her face radiates joy and seems about to "fuse into colorful, musical light." Beings such as Shia from other worlds "sing the joy hymns of the universe. They take the form of colored "living stones" the size of birds but also transform into the shape of spires, towers, trees, and lightning. When Kael and Risha join their festivities, the stones cover their bodies, penetrating them with sensations, transporting them, and changing their frame of reference. One of the stones takes the form of a man, Mevorah, who tells them that thousands of invisible "Great Ones" such as these are at war with others who are no longer part of them.

Most important, before the Fall, the couple communes with Aaael, who is "so much more than a voice and a joy within us." When he takes on physical form, he appears as a man: "It was the mark of Aaael's ultimate grandeur that he could compress all of that [glory] into the form of a man—as if all the stars and novae had fused into one man-sized creature."

Risha also has an established relationship with the serpent before the temptation. Sight of him delights her more than any other creature in the Garden. He moves alertly and has the beauty of a butterfly, except his wings are even more glorious, "like thousands of colored dragonfly wings sealed together, translucent, affixed in a marvelous latticework." As in Lewis' *Perelandra*, Myra develops the temptation scene, making the serpent's various arguments and appeals take several days.

Dreams that portray "mysteries" and the "great challenges before them" foreshadow the Fall. For example, in one dream, the two stand before a platform on which sits a creature of light. Below are chanters with human faces and coverings of skin, fur, leaves, or serpent's wings. "Fists of light" descend from the platform and form crowns of light about an individual's head. When a bronze light settles about Kael, it leads him slowly to its pleasures: "I saw the alien look controlling your face," says Risha. "You and the light rose inexorably to the platform."

After the fall, cold shapes and shifting shadows stalk Risha: "skulls with meat on them, battered noses, low-slung jaws, penetrating eyes. Arrogance glowed from those eyes . . fixing upon her hungrily." Mevorah enters the Garden, holding a wooden cup into which "the specters were being forced, howling and spitting and wailing." Then he hands Risha the "cup she had brought to herself." But she cannot even lift it to her lips. Aaael, however, walks toward them with an "indescribable expression of love, holiness, grandeur" and suffering. He raises the cup to his own lips:

It seemed that he drank forever, drank all of it. She could smell the stench and see the slime at the corners of his mouth, but still he drank!. . . She felt she was pouring the filth into Aaael's mouth herself. . . . His eyes penetrated her spirit. Then he crushed the cup under his foot (69).

Predominantly through conversation and Risha's thoughts, Myra contrasts Risha's life after the Fall with the Edenic glory: "She found it an awful thing to be awake in the universe." Not only is she cut off from creation, especially the animals, but "her sense of Aaael's presence" is gone: "How she remembered Aaael's lips calling her name in the garden . . . and his face looking at her with approval. How she longed for that look now." Her "old communication with the trees had been cut off," and they "were screaming. Screaming against defilement." In addition, she grows apart from Kael as she grows "more tentative" in her faith. Finally, she must experience death for the first time as she discovers her murdered son Erlin. Then she must deal with Onar's banishment and exile.

Myra adds a second temptation as the devil takes the form of a man who appeals to her sensuality, but she resists. Shia explains that the evil angels "have always been sowing dissension among you. It's your own lusts and rebellion that respond. . . . They cannot destroy you unless you invite them to. . . . It was of Aaael that you withstood temptation" (116). Shia also tells her that while she cannot return to the garden, there is hope: "Through your seed shall come salvation."

Myra's novel *Escape From the Twisted Planet* also portrays unfallen worlds. David travels to a planet which he names Blue Eden, an all blue subterranean world with rectangular trees. The people know no fear, guilt, pain, or sense of time, and use 100% of their potential. Creatures seem to "evaporate" when they die. Here, serpents are still beautiful, with graceful necks and exquisite, colored, undulating skin. David feels tempted to teach the couple sent to develop and populate this planet about "guilt, fear, and rebellion."

Similarly, on another Edenic planet he realizes that if the inhabitants experienced guilt, they would understand it, but it would "produce a planet as twisted and tormented as Earth." Yet he feels a "deep inner struggle against the desire to make these people become like himself, to tear from their idyllic lives of unspoiled joy and dynamic." He also encounters unfallen humanoids called "the first," those born after Adam and Eve fell, whom he tells about Aelor's (Christ's) visit to earth. Their universe is what earth "could have been—trillions of families scattered to the distant stars, still multiplying happiness, still discovering, still innovating."

A 1984 science fiction novel for young people, *Starforce—Red Alert* by Chris Spencer, illustrates the use of this theme of an unfallen Eden for a younger audience. Children seeking their lost father on the planet Terran find they have been "called" there by the "Maker" to bring the Book of the Lamb so the people can learn from earth's mistakes. Earth's inhabitants are at war with one another and have forgotten about the Bible. Terran is a perfect, sinless world that must be warned about what happened on earth as a result of its own fall in Eden, as well as alerted to the enemy's tactics and the consequences of ignoring the Maker's commands.

Although Spencer does not describe this world in great detail, he draws a clear parallel to Eden: "All the scenic beauty of earth is here, but—well, it's somehow been rearranged. . . . This is somehow much better than earth. Like earth must have been before it was . . . spoilt." There is no violence, anger, pride, fear, jealousy, or enmity among the animals. The people, who have happy and untroubled faces with "shining eyes," never die and can walk through solid walls. In addition, there is no obvious source of illumination; "the light was simply there!" The city shines like gold, its buildings integrated with the landscape.

In the center of the city is The Maker, "the wonderful, invisible friend who met with his people morning and evening in the beautiful garden that he himself had planted." He also made a man and woman, Quintay and Shara, to enjoy it and keep him company. In the middle of the garden Maker stored great knowledge and learning in thousands of small "transparent, glowing cubes" small enough to fit in one's palm. By holding a cube, a person can obtain the knowledge in it. However, one more brightly glowing cube separated from the others is not to be touched.

One of the children from earth, Eve, is lured by Sath, Satan's agent on Terran. Sath tries to get the inhabitants of Terran to touch the cube: "You shall not die; the truth is that The Maker does not want you touching that cube because he knows that in the day you touch it your eyes will be opened. You shall be as gods." The near fall is averted when Sath turns into a hideous monster, while Micha (the archangel Michael) transforms into a warring angel. Flying over the monster's head, he glows with a blinding light, holds a huge, flaming sword, then turns into the shape of a red cross. As Micha shouts, "The blood of the Lamb," Sath falls in torment and is banished from the garden.

Eventually, Spencer explains the Biblical parallels by telling the story of Christ's death and sacrifice on earth. When Zak notices that what is happening "on Terran is Eden all over again," his father replies that "Terra means earth." The only differences are that "on Terran the enemy had waited much longer before slithering into the garden with his deceptions and lies." The Maker restrained him until the spacecraft could come from earth. Thus "the ending of *this* Eden story had been left to" the children. While explaining the Biblical parallels seems to destroy the purpose of creating a "new Eden," Spencer may have thought it was necessary because of the younger audience for whom this is written.

In another youth fantasy, *The Forbidden Door*, while there are Green Dragons and Dark Dragons in Dragonland, there is little evil. The children do not know whether it is "because most of them did not know how to do evil" or whether "they know and choose not to." The dragons are forbidden to open the door in a cave connecting their world and ours. But Telgan, a dragon who has turned evil, opens the door, thus permitting the children to enter their land.

Robert Siegel's *Alpha Centauri* discusses a centaur paradise where men have not fallen. The centaurs call it their true home, "though we were born in this one. It is a world where men have never gone the twisted way. . . . In that world there is no killing. One may live forever in forests where birds are as big as centaurs and trees rise higher than mountains" (71). One centaur finds it hard to describe the "blue trees that soar like cliffs in which hang houses with floors of grass and walls of flowers; water that falls for hundreds of miles. . . . There, the First Ones never yearned for the Thing That Is Not." Before the Fall the Singing stones allowed the Forbidden Ones to pass back and forth between worlds. After Kalendos desired the Thing That is Not, Shaper blocked the door so evil would not spread.

In White's *The Sword Bearer* the Regents are clearly reminders of Adam and Eve. They used to walk with Changer daily until they failed to believe what he told them. Then they fled from his presence. Yet he clothed them in fur and appointed them to rule the kingdom from the Scunning Stones made at the dawn of time. Anyone else who sits on them dies instantly. The Regents will rule for ages to come until Gaal comes. This descendent of the Regents will be "the Victorious One, the Vanquisher of Death and Destroyer of the Mystery of Abomination" whom he will slay.

Two contrasting towers depict this conflict. The Tower of Darkest Night is a thin, white imitation of the Changer's Tower built by the Mystery of Abomination. From there he controls the planets and will bring them to a standstill, and darkness will cover the land. Contrasting this is the Tower of the Garden Room, from which the Regents emerge. Solid and built of rock, it contains a garden inside the tower with no evidence of a room, and an unsupported door leading into it.

### The Singreale Trilogy

Similar but more subtle use of unfallen worlds can be found in the Singreale trilogy of Calvin Miller, a pastor. These are the only recent fantasy books that use a developed and detailed other world, the planet Estermann, with different beings and its own history. The trilogy develops the history of the two rebels, Parsky and Thanevial, and their attempts to turn others to evil. The main theme of the trilogy is the spread of evil on the entire planet: "There are worlds unspoiled in the deepening sky, / Where the riders of night have not flown. / But here there is red where the animals bled, / And tastes, once forbidden, are known."

There are three Edenic worlds. First, "Estermann is a perfect world built perfectly," for there is no evil, disease, suspicion, or burglary, and even the largest creatures are friendly. It is described as a "poster color world" where everything is "more so than on earth." Miller develops this world in detail. There are, for example, new animals such as congrels, centicorns, dragon-like catterlobs, grumblebeaks, and kamdrammels. The snake is a symbol of good, one of the guardians of the Singreale diamond: "How long we've feared the scales and fangs, / And the grinning head where the forked tongue ran. / But the deep black slits in the yellow eyes / Once gazed in love when time began" (*Guardians of the Singreale*, 16). The red foliage includes candolet and ginjon trees and minion shrubs.

The inhabitants of the land of the Graygills have long pointed ears, live to be at least one thousand, have round houses, and like to sing and dance. The name "Graygills" not only describes the color of their sideburns and sidelocks but also symbolizes sinlessness. Although they are not permitted to murder or eat meat, one Blackgill, Parsky, causes his friend Raccoman to unknowingly eat congrel meat in a stew. As much as he despises the idea, Raccoman finds the stew delicious and cannot understand its lure; in fact, he is desperate to eat it. As a result, Raccoman's gray gills turn black. Parsky, the survivor of a race that in the past murdered animals for food, soon causes others to eat. War breaks out among meat eaters, non-eaters, and the animals who begin to murder in revenge. In the first book, the Graygills try to defend themselves against these attacks.

In *Star Riders of Ren*, Rensland, another continent, is also threatened by evil. This is the land of noble Star Riders twice the size of the Graygills. A rebel, Thanevial, and his beast followers, the Drogs, attack the land of King Ren which was once at peace. Thanevial, the best knight, asked King Ren to build him his own city. When the king refused, Thanevial betrayed Ren and bathed in the red fluid pits because he craved power. Miller tells us these pits represent one's power to choose. Thanevial was lured by "the intrigue of now knowing the full taste of his evil alter-ego. He seemed to hunger for power, and the red pits, which soon became known as the forming pits, lured him into the fierce possibilities of all he later became" (19). Thus he became a hideous monster:

He was the first to see his handsome form become grievous and his face and body become scaly and grotesque. . . . His body showed the consequences of his rebellion. Talons replaced his hands and feet, his fair skin cracked and broke, his facial structure grew grotesque as his hair fell out, and his eyes softened into shapeless spheres of milk-white horror (19).

He lured other knights whom the pits change into hideous monsters with scaly faces and bodies, claws, and white, shapeless, bulging eyes; they eat live flesh. In addition, "their natures and desires, even all their allegiances, change. They will do anything their evil lord suggests." For example, the knight Congaard lies down naked in the red spring: "Velissa and Raccoman watched in horror as the red liquid of the spring boiled over his white body. The stained skin grew dark in the inky fountains as the scarlet hues turned to venomous black and bubbled around the changing form" (32). Thanevial built a Tower Altar from which he longs to rule all of Esterman.

Although Thanevial and his drogs are stopped, they head toward the land of the Graygills through a system of underground tunnels. In the final book, Raccoman, his wife Velissa, and two titans return to Canby to protect their land. Yet another Eden is discovered, the valley of the Sundals. While Velissa and the titan Raenna protect this land from Parsky, the others use Selendrenni, huge, fire-breathing salamanders, to defeat Thanevial and his drogs.

The Singreale is called a symbol of the power of a non-human being: "He is a spirit that swells from galaxies to Nebulae. He is the essence of all living things and passes every breath of being through his own spirit, and all of it burns like a beam of radiance through his universe and settles in splendor in the diamond" (*War*, 121). The diamond is called "the pure fire of being . . . the radiance of the ideal, the source of life as it should be." If its fire is trusted, "the light will change your lives. Walk in the light and you will know life and peace." The diamond can dispel darkness, can help one discern evil, and gives an inner light, "the power of truth in the face of evil." It also can take on different forms, such as the creature Grendelynden.

Most important, the diamond is used as an image of salvation. When Raccoman desires to have his black gills gray once more, he goes to a cavern before which is a sign that says "The Path of Pain and Hope" to undergo the Ordeal of Singreale. His fiance Velissa tells him black can never be white except for pain. By chaining himself to the walls of the cavern, Raccoman painfully receives the light of Singreale in his face "until all the inner black is gone." Similarly, King Ren strips himself naked and rides away with the Singreale: "I must go away and take the Singreale with me, and here in the lightless night, I shall be born again." Later, he says when he laid the diamond over his breast and pressed it, "it passed into my own being and flooded every window of my soul. Then my form dwindled and became that of the naked ally whose treasure was an inner light" which he used to save those who did not follow Thanevial.

## RE-MYTHOLOGIZING

One of the most commonly used techniques in current religious fantasy is to "disguise" the parallels by presenting the Christian cosmology in a different way. This effect is achieved by creating a new "mythology" as either the basis of the entire story or simply as background mentioned only briefly. In most books it is what some might consider simply an allegorical presentation of Biblical ideas, but the parallels may or may not be obvious depending on the intended audience level. The writer's aim is usually to present these concepts in new ways.

Before Lewis became converted to Christianity, he found certain expressions silly or shocking. Yet he did not mind the same ideas in story or mythic form because he was prepared to feel the myth as "profound and suggestive of meaning beyond [his] grasp" (Hooper, *They Stand Together*, 427). Although we often feel we ought to feel a certain way about God, "obligation to feel can freeze feelings." Thus Lewis' goal was to strip the Christian message of its "stained-glass and Sunday school associations" and give it new form and meaning by putting all these things into an imaginary world (*On*, 47). By stealing past inhibitions and traditional religious concepts and terminology, he could make them, for the first time, "appear in their real potency." In "The Fantastic Imagination," George MacDonald describes fantasy as giving new embodiment to old truths, thereby translating or "transfiguring" Christianity into a wholly new form.

A goal of re-mythologizing, then, is to present Biblical truth in a more understandable and palatable form. Some writers feel that young people in particular are cynical, turned off by traditional religious terms they consider boring, and overfamiliar with certain values, emotions, and situations. Robert Hughes, author of the Pelmen trilogy, finds fantasy "a good genre for putting ideas forward, especially Christian ideas that are ... eternally true, but begin to sound boring when encrusted in theological language. In fantasy, the images aren't frozen in layers of interpretive material" (Melrose, 177). Scott Pinzon defines a Christian fantasy writer as a person who knows God intimately enough to take everlasting truths, clothe them in completely new symbols and events, and proclaim them with heart-stirring originality" (7).

Francis Molson uses the terms "displacement" or "translation" to describe "ethical" fantasy's ability to take human situations, emotions, and ideas and put them in new contexts to avoid this cynicism and overfamiliarity (Molson, 98). Since this type of writing "avoids conventional theological" language and allusions, readers will not avoid, misunderstand, or associate it with religion. It can even "talk about" good and evil and belief in God and encourage "faith in transcendence" without "irritating" certain readers because it does so "obliquely." In addition, if the religion in the story is presented in a different form, the reader may be caught unaware. Lewis is convinced that any amount of theology can be smuggled into people's minds "under the cover of romance" without their knowing it.

The Bible itself uses indirect methods to refer to events such as Satan's rebellion. For example, Isa. 14:12–14 refers not only to the king of Babylon but also to Satan:

How you are fallen from heaven, 0 Lucifer, son of the morning! How you are cut down to the ground, you who weakened the nations! For you have said in your heart: "I will ascend into heaven, I will exalt my throne above the stars of God; I will also sit on the mount of the congregation on the farthest sides of the north; I will ascend above the heights of the clouds, I will be like the Most High."

Similarly, Ezek. 28:12–15, in referring to an earthly king, speaks indirectly of Satan. In Rev. 12:4, John refers to a red dragon pulling down "a third of the stars of heaven," which may refer to fallen angels, with his tail. The Biblical conflict between Christ and Satan is portrayed as a war in heaven between the Lamb and the Dragon. While the battle is spiritual rather than physical, the physical is as a symbol for the spiritual. In depicting this conflict, many of the archetypes and images of fantasy are used.

Chesterton says we do not know why certain images and metaphors are accepted by our imagination before "reason can reject it; or why such correspondences seem really to correspond to something in the soul" (*Everlasting*, 121). But fatigue has affected Christianity; it is "almost impossible to make the facts vivid, because the facts are familiar." He is "convinced that if we could tell the supernatural story of Christ . . . as of a Chinese hero, call him the Son of Heaven instead of the Son of God, and trace his rayed nimbus in the gold thread of Chinese embroideries," we would accept it better than we do concepts such as the atonement. We would "admire the chivalry of the Chinese conception of a god who fell from the sky to fight the dragons and save the wicked from being devoured by their own fault and folly" (*Everlasting*, 20). Lewis says what some call "demythologising" Christianity can "easily be 're-mytholgising' it—and substituting a poorer mythology for a richer" (*Malcolm*, 52). This method and its effect are exactly what many current books attempt to achieve.

### Re-mythologizing in Lewis and Tolkien

In *Pilgrim's Regress* Lewis retells the story of the Fall in Eden using different terms. A Landlord once farmed land himself and had no tenants. Then he decided to make a farm in the center of the land and let a married couple care for it. He only forbade them to eat the mountain-apples. Then a Landowner came around who was one of our Landowner's own children but had quarreled with his father and "set up on his own." Because he persuaded the wife to eat an apple, an earthquake split the land in half.

Similarly, Lewis presents Biblical history in mythic form in the space trilogy. Maleldil lives with the Old One. The Oyarsa (ruling angelic spirit) of earth was one of the brightest and greatest of Oyeresu who wanted to become like Maleldil and thus rebelled. Desiring to destroy other worlds, he smote the moon and much of Malacandra (Mars) and now attempts to invade Perelandra (Venus). During the Great War, Maleldil drove him out of the heavens, confining him to the earth and region below the moon, where a number of eldila who followed him also reign. Some day the memory of this Black Oyarsa will be blotted out when Maleldil returns to earth in war. Lewis identifies this Bent One, as he is also called, as "Satan, the rebel angel." He also explicitly explains the connection between his mythology and our world by saying Maleldil might be God. In a personal letter to Miss Jacob, Lewis explains outright the "dark secret" to be found in the space trilogy:

You have the angels, the *eldila*. You have Maleldil "who lives with the Old One"—i.e., God the Father and God the Son. . . . He did and suffered terrible things in retrieving Thulcandra (i.e. was incarnate and crucified in Earth) fighting the Bent One, the *eldil* who had gone wrong (Satan, the rebel angel). The "confined and regimented" state of my mind is revealed in the story at every point."

However, according to Lewis, only two in sixty reviewers realized he is anyone other than a "mere invention."

In *The Silmarillion*, Tolkien tells the story of the creation, fall, redemption, and apocalypse with his own modifications. However, he still uses many of the themes of the Bible and echoes much of its wording. This "monotheistic but sub-creational mythology" has three Falls, that of Morgoth, Elves, and Men (*Letters*, 235). Although it is different in form than in the Bible, he maintains the fall of angels in his cosmogony contains elements of truth. One difference is that in the Bible the Fall of man is a consequence of the fall of the angels and evil brought into the world by Satan. But in his book, "the rebellion of created free-will precedes the creation of the World (Ea); and Ea has in it, subcreatively introduced, evil, rebellions, discordant elements of its own nature already when the *Let it Be* was spoken" (*Letters*, 286).

Paralleling the fall of Satan is that of Melkor or Morgoth, an angelic spirit, who revolts: "To Melkor among the Ainur had been given the greatest gifts of power and knowledge, and he had a share in all the gifts of this brethren. He had often gone alone into the void places seeking the Imperishable Flame" (*Silmarillion*, 16). He is thus expelled from Arda. Sauron, another angelic spirit, becomes his servant and later instigates a revolt in Numenor. He convinces the Numenoreans to ignore Valar's ban to cross forbidden waters and go to Aman the Blessed, thus becoming like the Valar and possessing everlasting life. As a result, Numenor sinks into the sea. With echoes of the Flood story, only the faithful are saved and allowed to sail to Middle Earth. Finally, while the Bible shows man was intended to live eternally but became mortal because of sin, Tolkien's elves are immortal and men mortal, although mortality is seen as a blessing.

### Re-mythologizing in Contemporary Fantasy

Contemporary writers use this same technique of retelling the story of creation, the Fall, redemption, and the future war in heaven. The most obvious allegory seems to be predominant in books written for younger readers and published by religious publishers. It is apparently difficult to avoid blatant Biblical parallels at the risk of offending certain audiences, and, at the same time, not make the allusions so subtle that they are missed altogether.

On the simplest level and most frequently, God is given another name: Da Elna, Elohim, The Great One, the One, the Maker, the Shaper, the Power, the Source, Aelor, and so on. In Lawhead's Empyrion books, the Supreme Being expresses himself in aspects such as Protector, Sustainer, Comforter, Seeker, and Teacher. In other books, the mythology is not developed, but God, Christ, and Satan are given other names. In John White's *The Tower of Geburah*, for example, God is the High Emperor and his son is Gaal the Shepherd; Satan is the Lord of Darkness. In Traylor's historical fantasy, *Noah*, Lucifer is called Angel of Light, Golden Orb, Great Governor of the Skies, Lightbearer, Master of the Air, Mentor of the Overseers, Orb of Wisdom, Oversoul, Prince of the Power of the Air, Prince of This World, the Serpent, Son of the Morning, Spirit of the Air, Sun, and Universal Spirit (11). Calvin Miller uses a free verse form to remythologize the Bible in his trilogy *The Singer*, *The Song*, and *The Finale*. In *The Finale*, a retelling of Revelation, Satan is called the Prince of Mirrors, World Hater, and Dark Prince; Christ is the Singer and Troubadour; the Holy Spirit is the Invader; anti-Christ is Elan; John is Dreamer; Christians are Singerians; Michael is Ansond or the Golden

Knight; heaven is Lifeland; and the old and new Earth are Terra 1 and 2.

In some books, as in Lewis' space trilogy, the purpose of using a "new mythology" is defeated because the author eventually spells what it means. In Harold Myra's *Escape From the Twisted Planet*, God is called Aelor and E*AHL*OUL, Christ is Aelor-ke, and the Aelor-force must flow through one who wants Aelor Power. The latter is described like an energy, "a flood of power from an immense Niagara Falls generator, but a power more personal, meaningful, exhilarating." The Twisted One, an evil telora or spirit being, rules the earth; other telora inhabit and guide inhabitants of other worlds. Yet in parts of the book, Myra uses Christian terminology and quotes long passages from the Bible.

A book for younger readers, *The Magic Bicycle* by John Bibee, retells the Biblical story of the Fall using different terms, although children may not see the parallels:

A long time ago, Magic filled the Deeper World and our world. Three Magical Kings ruled over all. Deep peace was in every heart. But then a powerful prince of the Aggeloi wanted more power and defied the kings, wishing to kill them. This Aggelo called himself Treason. Because he broke the Deeper Laws of the Kingdom of the Kings, his Magic died. Yet his deeper powers remained. But deeper powers without Magic are Tragic. . . . But then one of the kings, the King Prince, came to the lesser world to prove that Magic was stronger than the powers of Tragic. Magic returned with him to the lesser world for those who wished to be in the Kingdom of the Kings. The King Prince left to prepare a new Magic place in the Kingdom. When he returns he will put Treason and all his followers in a Deep Dungeon (161–162)

In Robert Siegel's *Alpha Centauri*, a secondary world fantasy written for a broader audience, the background is both developed and integral to the plot. The Christian "mythology" is presented as the history of the centaurs and by using totally new names, although the Christian parallels still seem obvious. While visiting a farm in England, Becky, through the "Eye of the Fog," is carried back through time to ancient Britain where the Rock Movers are trying to kill the centaurs. Alpha Centauri is still connected to Britain by a narrow piece of land but will eventually be cut off. Fulfilling a prophecy, Becky leads the centaurs to the Singing Stones so they can find the path to the stars leading to their home on Alpha Centauri and escape destruction by the Rock Movers.

God is called Shaper, a name that gives Becky "a curious prickly feeling at the back of her neck"; Satan is Warper. Once all people were at peace, and earth was a garden with talking creatures and rulers called The First Ones. However, Kalendos, cleverest of the First Ones, began to desire the Thing That is Not on top of the tallest mountain. Two groups then began to emerge: his followers, Rock Movers, who allayed their guilt by worshipping darkness; and the First People, beautiful and good but now becoming extinct. The Rock Movers illustrate the Old Testament need for sacrifice:

In their guilt, the man-slayers fell to the worship of darkness, trying to appease it with the blood of creatures, including blood of men and women. Eventually, their descendants became the Rock Movers, so named because they move huge stones hundred of miles to build temples to the stars (55).

They worship the statue Phogros, a spirit they believe first taught them how to count, divide, and "control [their] days."

After the "Fall," the world was changed. There were seasons, murders, and the people had to labor for food: "The very trees have soaked up the evil done there. . . . Thus have Rock Movers darkened every place where the First Ones danced with the woodland creatures." Kalendos' descendants, who hated nature and animals, are called the Divided Kind. In addition, "men are bent from their true nature." Although some day there will be a period of trouble on earth, a "greater good" will come:

In the last days the Shaper will send the Healer to earth. By a deed, a gift we cannot imagine, the Healer will begin mending the earth . . . the Warper will fail, and the Shaper . . . will work good out of this evil, and at last, in great triumph, heal the world completely (162).

Anyone marked by the Healer will be rejoined with heaven. Earth will be "remade as it was meant to be," with the centaurs returning to help in its renewal.

The form Siegel uses is effective for several reasons. First, the centaurs illustrate one of the themes of the book, the separation of man from nature. As half man and half horse, centaurs are an ideal symbol. According to Siegel,

The animals have always represented parts of us that we lost in the Fall, and that we will regain when we are renewed. . . . You can consider the beasts as the subconscious, the eight-ninths of our minds that are below the surface, the feeling and intuitive part. . . . In a rationalistic age there's a tendency among Christians to block out that whole aspect of themselves, to concentrate on rational belief and the will—which of course are very important—but to ignore the feeling and intuitive side of themselves. Yet God, being a jealous God, wants all of us (Fickett, 37).

Siegel also effectively illustrates the principle of self-sacrifice without becoming allegorical. Becky must travel alone to the First Ones and face trials, keeping on her journey even though she is tempted and encounters dangers. When her role is mentioned in a prophecy, she is stunned and confused by it: "The Shaper has worked to bring you at the hour of the centaurs' greatest need." Her power to work the Singing Stones is Shaper working through her, and she succeeds in opening the Path to the Stars only when she is filled with love for the Centaurs. The "Stone will open fully only for one who gives herself entirely for those who need to pass. She must forget herself—and all other things—for them." As she does,

Something larger than herself moved through her and was reflected from each face. It was a brightness and a pain—as if she herself were being torn apart— yet at the same time a suffering infinitely desirable. In it she noticed only the look of love on each face (242).

In an interview, Siegel said Becky sacrifices her whole self for the centaurs:

When she can forget herself, even her own fear of failure, and let something else work through her then she can completely identify with [the centaurs] in love and things open up. I think there is a spiritual principle operating here. This whole climactic scene is central to what I believe is going on in the book (Fickett, 37).

In *Captive Planet* Christ's sacrifice is retold through dream visions. The dreamers realize the "Source is telling them of the Friend, and they must tell the others." In the first dream, the moon splits to form two planets. After many years a comet hits one of the planets and it becomes dark; the other is knocked off its axis, causing earthquakes, devastations, and its death. As both planets shrink to the size of small stones, a man comes upon them "with pity in his eyes. He was a gentle, friendly looking man." After dipping the second planet in a stream, he breathes until the life becomes green, then spins it. Next, he breathes on the first until it is "clean and bright." But another comet stikes the man, "causing a terrible explosion. Flames leaped into space; sparks and lightning flashes convulsed around him." Although the man lies dead, his body suddenly begins to change: "It seemed to melt and glow, then form into a ball and become a sun. Both planets began to orbit this new sun."

In the second dream, as children play in a lake, an "immense arching back" with scales and fins swims toward them. A strange man suddenly comes to the shore and shouts at the children. Then he dives into the water and rescues several of them. When he sees others who are not saved, he splashes the water to attract the beast's attention. The children are able to reach shore, but the man is "torn apart by the great beast."

Although David Mason's *The Deep Gods* contains few other religious parallels, Satan's rebellion is retold as the story of a great whale. Daniel from the twentieth century is "dragged across time and space and thrust into a new body" to become Egon, who was killed in a boating accident. The Morra-Ayar, whales and gods of the deep, ask him to keep Narr's wall (Gibraltar) from being broken. If it is, the "oldest one" will swim free, and "man and sea-folk will dance no more together. . . . The bond will be broken." The oldest one who lives in the Locked Sea was once one of the Morra-Ayar. "He was one with us, wiser and older than all of us. But in one thing, he changed. He desired to go alone, into other seas, to sail in isolation and darkness while his mind sought deeper than ours could, for truth" (86). This "Lost One" causes death, destruction, burned ships, and war. Now imprisoned, the oldest one calls Daniel back in time to break the wall and set him free. But in so doing Daniel will no longer exist. Although Daniel's boat is destroyed like Egon's, Daniel becomes someone else, thus perpetuating his soul.

### Re-mythologizing in Joy Chant and Stephen Donaldson

The story of Satan's fall is also told in Joy Chant's *Red Moon and Black Mountain*, and successful redemption images are employed which are reminders rather than overt Biblical parallels. Also, her mythology is both developed and successfully integrated with the plot. While riding their bikes, Oliver, Nicholas, and Penelope Powell fall off a gate and find themselves in the land of Vandarei. There they are told, "You have been flung from your own world into ours, and I cannot yet tell why. But I sense a strong enchantment, and not without purpose." Many powers and gods exist in this land: Jr'nanh, Lord of Life who requires bloodless sacrifices; Iranani, Lord of wood and water; Star Enchanters; "and the masters of other powers, the Khentor magicians of the Wild Magic, earth witches, wielders of white witch-magic, and . . . sybils and seers and sages" (163).

The history is told as follows:

Long ago, the One created the Seven to be his servants, and the guides of his lesser creations. . . . the highest and greatest of them grew too proud, and rebelled, and fell. In your world also you must know of this. The power which he had was taken from him, and he was cast down and driven out. . . . Made to be a mighty servant was he, and even though Marenkalkon threw him down he is a mighty foe. He cannot make, only corrupt, and so he must work through others. The power that had been his now had to find other masters. Much of it was divided among the remaining Six. Of that which remains the Star Magic is a part (171).

The Children of the Stars or Star Enchanters alone can wield this Star Magic. These beings were created because the power was running wild on earth. Thus they were given charge of the "blood of the stars" which was placed in them. Fendarl, one of these Star Enchanters, became ruler of Bannoth and a servant of He Whose Name Is Taken Away and the Thrice Accurst. He "came to love knowledge and power more than honour, more than his virtue; and . . . dealt with powers which should have been his enemies . . . he practised the forbidden arts, and fell, and became a Black Enchanter" (43). Although he was bannished to the Mountains Beyond the Sea, he is now strong enough to return. Fendarl is unslayable by man, woman, or any creature of this land. If Fendarl wins, the people are lost, but if he is defeated, they still must fight the evil that exists.

Oliver is renamed Crowned Victor, and Li'vanh, the Chosen and Favored One. As the champion sent to slay Fendarl, he is right for the task because "someone who offers himself freely and without need, who has everything to lose and nothing to gain—he is immeasurably stronger" than Fendarl. There is power in "the given death—the royal sacrifice."

Using the Shield of Adamant and the Sword of Emneron, he fights Fendarl. At first he tries to pray "to the God whom he had refused to forsake, yet could not truly remember. . . . 'Oh help me God!' he cried suddenly, but silently." Fendarl attacks not by weapons "but by the air around him, which quivered and cracked. The world was buffeted, shaken; he was pulled and torn by the wizard's power, iron hooks dragged at his mind." He "could feel the enchanter's mind grappling for control of his, and knew he had not strength to resist that." But Li'vanh pierces him with a knife "against which all his power was naught."

There is an even higher Power, however, identified as Lucifer in our world, whom Li'vanh must now confront. His face is perfectly chiselled and pale, with silver hair and dark eyes. But there is "a pride, an egotism, an insufferable hauteur behind the cool detached face of such fearful beauty, an arrogance that demanded . . . worship . . . to swell his own glutted pride." Marenkalion, the Defender, covers Li'vanh with a shield, warning him he cannot prevail over this greater evil. In addition, after Li'vanh looks "upon the darkness in his own heart," he realizes he must now live "in the fear of himself" because he has shed another's blood. He must now "find his own way home" through self-sacrifice.

Every nine years, during the Autumn Feast, all tribes present a human sacrifice to the Dark Mother to bind Vir'Vachal, the Earth Witch. Li'vanh begins to wonder if a "freely offered sacrifice" would be stronger and prevent the need for so many deaths. Knowing he is not being "called" to do this, he nevertheless offers himself as the "one," "free" sacrifice. On the Holy Hill, he thus enters a cleft in the Cave of Offering that reaches to the deep places in the earth. As he follows Vir'Vachal, he plunges into darkness.

When he awakens, he is again Oliver. A young boy, the Keeper of the Fountain, tells him it is time to be Crowned Victor again: "All that you have lost shall be restored, and all that you have gained remain untouched." Oliver drinks from "the pool of Life and Death." "Those who drink bidden, drink blest, and drink life: but those who drink unbidden, drink death!" It also gives him "new life, and the heart to enjoy it." However, it will not give him eternal life because that takes more power and "more than water to do." Because he refuses to drink a liquid that will erase his memory of what happened, the boy tells him, "Then here lies your way. Go with gladness." As he walks around the tree, he is with his brother and sister back where they were with their bicycles.

In Stephen Donaldson's Chronicles of Thomas Covenant, the re-mythologizing is subtle and extensively developed. Thomas Covenant, a leper, finds himself transported to the Land, a different world. The Creator first built the Arch of Time "so that Time would be able to resist chaos and endure. Then within the arch he formed Earth" so that it would have a place to exist. He "made the world in all its beauty, so that no eye could behold it without joy" and created the myriads of inhabitants. But he discovered Despite, his brother and Enemy, "either within him or without," had marred the creation by "placing banes of surpassing evil deep within it."

Onto Earth Creator cast the Despiser—also known as Lord Foul, Corruption, Satansheart, Soulcrusher—and Earth became the Despiser's World to torment, afflict, and teach self-despite. Foul is depicted as essentially invisible, "though he cast an impenetrable blankness in the air . . . a shadow of absence rather than presence." The air around him reeks of both sulfur and attar, "the sweetness of the grave."

To give Earth hope, the Creator helped the Lord-Fatherer Berek create a Staff of Law out of the One Tree to wield Earthpower, the source of all the Land's power. This Law defends the Land and the natural order. Foul fights back by destroying the Staff of Law and desires white gold to destroy the Arch of Time and ruin the Land. Because the Law of Time preserves Lord Foul, if he destroys it he will be free again. The keystone of the Arch of Time is wild magic, the power of the white gold. White gold, as is found in Covenant's wedding ring, can unleash or control it: "It is the girding paradox of the Arch of Time, the undisciplined restraint of the Earth's creation." The white gold, however, is actually Thomas Covenant himself: "It was not a thing to be commanded . . . it was a part of him, an expression of himself. . . . it arose from his passion."

When the Law was destroyed, Foul destroyed the natural order and was able to gain new strength. The Sunbane arises from Foul's corruption of nature: "It was red and baleful, the color of pestilence. . . . like disease . . . it was an emanation from the ground, corrupted Earthpower radiating into the heavens. And that corruption sank deeper every day, working its way into the marrow of the Earth's bones" (*White*, 310). The Clave, the rulers of the Land, believe blood is the only power against the Sunbane, and thus begin to "preach the shedding of blood" and sacrifice many lives to draw away the Sunbane's power. Covenant walks into this Banefire but instead of dying emerges changed: "The fundamental alteration was internal. . . . Something important had been transformed or eradicated. . . . he had become new and pure and clean." His doubts and self-repudiation "had been reborn as certainty, clarity, acceptance." Foul's venom and his wild magic, despair and hope, have been fused in the Banefire and "made clean."

Not only does Donaldson echo the Biblical story of the Creation and Fall of Satan, but he also uses Biblical phrases associated with Christ to describe Amok, the ancient youth who is servant to ancient Lore. When asked who he is, he only replies, "I am who I am" and "I am the way and the door." Amok guides them to the Blood of the Earth, the "ichor" of the mountain rock where the Earthpower bleeds. Anyone who drinks of it gains the Power of Command to achieve any desired act over the Earth's creation.

The Land's Creator appears to Covenant in the real world as an "impossibly tall and healthy" but dirty old beggar with "long tattered hair and beard" and intense blue eyes. He chooses Thomas Covenant and Linda Avery to fight Foul. Since they come from outside the Land, they are not bound by Law and are powerful. The Creator is unable to help them because in so doing he would break the Arch. And if he or Foul tries to teach or help them, they will only be tools or extensions. Thus Donaldson introduces the theme of free will. "Only a free man could hope to stand against my enemy, hope to preserve the Earth," says the Creator. He does not manipulate his creations: "I elected you for the Land but did not compel you to serve my purpose." Covenant eventually realizes that "freedom doesn't mean you get to choose what happens to you. But you do get to choose how you react to it." To be effective against Foul "we have to make our own decisions. . . . Power depends on choice," he notes.

Covenant calls himself the Unbeliever because he does not believe the Land is real, only a dream or escape from his leprosy. Thus his name, Thomas, echoing "doubting" Thomas, is significant. Here again, a secondary fantasy world is used to parallel the inner spirit. He begins to believe that the "whole crisis is a struggle inside me. . . . I'm becoming my own enemy, my own Despiser." Thus he must work things out "subconsciously, so that when [he] wake[s] up [he]'ll be able to cope."

He tells Linda, "The darkness in us—the destructive side, the side we keep locked up all our lives—is alive here. . . . Here it's personified—externalized, the way things happen in dreams." He believes Lord Foul is "an externalized part" of one side of himself. The leprosy, too, parallels the diminishing health of the land.

Covenant not only refuses to believe in the Land but also that God can heal his soul, as he explains to Preacher Johnson in *The Power That Preserves*. Here Donaldson at last suggests the religious implications of the six novels. The Preacher reads from Leviticus, chapter 26, in which God warns that if Israel breaks his covenant, he will send plagues and pestilence: "Here in one short passage we hear the two great messages of the Bible, the Law and the Gospel, the Old Covenant and the New." Thus we learn the significance of Covenant's name and the breaking of the Staff of Law. The Biblical passage also explains the sickness of the land and Covenant himself: "[God] says, if you sin, if you break My Law, I will terrify you and make you sick. . . . The Old Covenant says to you . . . The leper who has the disease shall . . . cry, 'Unclean, unclean' " (17–18).

Under the Old Testament Covenant with Abraham, God promised the land which would be the center for Christ's future kingdom. To prepare the Israelites, God established the laws (Ten Commandments) and a system of animal sacrifices. If they obeyed the Law, they would be blessed; if they disobeyed, they would be cursed and scattered. However, he promises in Deuteronomy, chapter 30, eventually to bring them into the land so they can "possess it."

But the law "is only half of God's holy message," says the preacher. The other half is "chastening, heritage, forgiveness, healing," as exemplified by the crucifixion. Under the New Covenant, Israel will be regathered, will recognize and obey God, and the Kingdom of God will come after Israel is spiritually changed. Just as the Old Covenant was sealed in blood, the New Covenant was sealed and put into effect by Christ's sacrifice. During the Last Supper, Christ said, "This is my blood of the covenant, which is poured out for many for the forgiveness of sins" (Matt. 26:28 NIV). The preacher says all one must do is say, "I believe; help my unbelief."

There are many images of sacrifice and crucifixion, therefore, in the Chronicles. For example, Covenant's doctor remarks how a leper reminds him of statues of the crucified Christ from the Middle Ages. While the features are bland and sexless, the wounds are portrayed in such vivid detail that you think, "The artist crucified his model to get that kind of realism. 'Being a leper must be like that.' " In the hospital, Covenant's wrist is tied "so that he lay in the bed as if he had been crucified," and when he spews the fire of his wild magic at Foul, he stands "with his arms spread like a crucifixion."

When Covenant is severely wounded trying to pull the branch from the One Tree to forge a new Staff of Law, "he lay as if he had been crucified on the stone." But his greatest sacrifice comes when Foul strikes Covenant in order to get the ring, leaving a white flame spouting from his chest: "The wound bled argent: all his blood was ablaze. Fire fountained from his gaping hurt, spat gouts and plumes of numinous and incandescent deflagration." But when Foul tries to strike the Arch of Time, Covenant is resurrected within it and is able to withstand the bolts of Foul's power. When "it ended he had taken it all upon himself. Bravely he stood forth from the fire." The fact that he does not fight Foul makes him stronger and Foul weaker; in addition, Foul burns the venom within Covenant, leaving him free.

Linda Avery, as a physician, serves as a healer of the Land. She must "become the Land" by exposing herself to the Sunbane. But she too does not fight it. Instead, she "called it to herself, accepted it into her personal flesh. With white fire she absorbed the Land's corruption . . . the pain she had taken upon herself was swept from her—cured and cleansed, and sent spilling outward as pure Earthpower. With Law she healed herself" (*White*, 463–464).

Donaldson, the son of a medical missionary, says, "I consider fiction to be the only valid tool for theological inquiry. And I consider fantasy to be the most human and fundamental form of fiction. So it follows that I consider all really good fantasy to be religious fantasy on one level or another" (Melrose, 175). His use of redemption images and other Biblical echoes are successful because they are not blatant but a re-working of the theology.

### Re-mythologizing in Star Wars

In addition to the works mentioned, some writers such as Robert Short, Frank Allnutt, Robert Jewett, and John Lawrence maintain that certain "secular" fantasy works contain religious elements. The use of re-mythologizing, for example, can be seen in works such as the Star Wars trilogy, although the Biblical allusions might be considered less obvious.

The history begins before earth was created. Ages ago the Republic existed. The people worshipped a Deity called the Force who created the universe and was the source of supernatural power. The Force is described as an energy field generated by living things "and something more. . . . An aura that at once controls and obeys. It is a nothingness that can accomplish miracles." Yoda explains, "Life creates it and makes it grow. Its energy surrounds us and binds us. Luminous beings we are, not this crude matter." Because early man was unable to explain it, they sought a supernatural explanation. Thus it became a deity believed to control man's actions: "The force surrounds each and every one of us. Some men believe it directs our actions, and not the other way around. Knowledge of the force and how to manipulate it was what gave the Jedi his special power" (Lucas, *Star Wars*, 81). The Jedi knights were the most powerful, respected force in the galaxy who protected the empire, "guardians and guarantors of peace and justice in the Old Republic."

Although the Republic was a successful model, the people eventually drifted away from the Force and became materialistic, greedy, morally deteriorated, and corrupt. Governors turned on each other, and Senator Palpatine, who was elected President of the Republic, set himself up as Emperor. He was aided by Anakin Skywalker, a student of Obi-wan Kenobi, one of the Jedi knights. Anakin (Luke and Princess Leia's father), however, chose the dark side of the Force and became the Emperor's henchman. The Dark side of the Force is anger, fear, and aggression. If you choose one of these you become a servant of evil, but you must choose it of your own free will. A Jedi, on the other hand, must use the Force for Knowledge.

Anakin became Darth Vader (Dark Father), and his spiritual evil is reflected in his physical changes. The black mask he wears not only aids in his breathing and speaking but also conceals a skull-like, pasty-white, weak face. His goal is to kill the emperor and rule the universe with his son, Luke, whom he hopes to turn to the dark side. The Alliance, however, is composed of small groups, a religious remnant, who resist the Palpatine government and want to restore the Republic to its former greatness. In *Star Wars*, their secret rebel base on the planet Alderaan is threatened by the Death Star, a planet destroyer.

Luke Skywalker, who has been raised on the planet Tattoine by his aunt and uncle, is "called" to help in the Rebel cause by Obi-Wan (Ben) Kenobi, the last of the Jedi Knights. As in religious fantasy, there is a divine plan that determines Luke's destiny:

[Kenobi] suppressed a smile, aware that Luke's destiny had already been determined for him. It had been ordained five minutes before he had learned about the manner of his father's death. . . . Likely it had been finalized even before the boy was born. Not that Ben believed in predestination, but he did believe in heredity—and in the force (Lucas, 82).

When Luke attacks the Death Star, he no longer feels like "an individual, functioning solely to satisfy his personal needs. Something now bound him to every other man and woman in this hanger." Similarly, Han Solo changes from a selfish loner to one who is "part of the whole" and does things for other people.

Yoda, an aged teacher living on Dagobah, trains Luke to be the last

Jedi knight. Luke makes his way there somehow, "though he wasn't certain whether it was his hand alone that had guided his ship into this unexplained sector of space." Practicing with his light saber, he learns not trust in himself but rather the Force. Yoda explains that he fails because he does not believe. During this training, Luke battles with Darth Vader, knocking off his helmet and splitting it open to reveal Luke's own face. Luke does not know if this means he is fighting himself, has fallen prey to the dark side, or if it has an even darker meaning. Like Frodo and his Ring, Luke eventually becomes tempted to either follow his father, take his place by the Emperor's side, or rule the galaxy himself.

In *Star Wars*, Ben Kenobi undergoes a sacrificial death so Princess Leia and the others can escape. His body disappears, but he later resurrects as a spirit to give directions and guidance to Luke. Like the Holy Spirit, a "soothing spiritual presence . . . occasionally visited Luke in moments of stress or danger. . . . The presence . . . was sometimes like a familiar voice, an almost silent whisper that spoke directly to Luke's mind" (Glut, *The Empire Strikes Back*, 18). An afterlife is also implied when Luke believes some day he will be with Yoda and Ben "in the ethereal oneness of the Force."

### Role-Playing

Finally, a different form for fantasy that has generated some controversy but attempts to encourage participation is Dragon Raid, a role-playing game called "an allegorical simulation that portrays the Christian life." Again, the background is a fantasy version of the Biblical falls of Satan and man. The creators of the game define allegory as "the expression of spiritual truths by the use of fictional figures, or simply, a symbolic narrative . . . a familiar story told in a new and fresh way." The reason for using it is

because sometimes people have heard things about Jesus Christ (or about Christianity) to which they have developed very definite responses, both positive and negative. These learned responses may block any further input. By using allegory to retell those spiritual truths, the game provides a comfortable and non-threatening learning experience (Dragon Raid Manual).

The Adventure Master is warned to avoid "churchy" words like "salvation, which repel or bore some people."

The purpose of the allegorical story situation is to simulate trials in life. The participants role play as fictitious characters, allowing them to come closest to being on a real adventure. Thus by participating in the action, making decisions, and seeing and hearing through the imagination, they are prepared for challenges in real life. According to the creators, the game "uses the imagination to convey a biblical understanding of good and evil."

God is called Maker, Eternal Presence, High One; Christ is the OverLord of Many Names, Son of the High One, Judge of Evil, Rescuer, Second One in the One Almighty Spirit; Satan is the Evil One, The Deceiver, the Great Red Dragon, Abbadon. The mythological history is told, in part, in the instruction manual as follows: In the Dawn of Creation at the outer reaches of the universe, Eden Again was born from a large mass of intergalactic matter . . . with a Word, the planet Eden Again was forested and peopled." But the King of Evil, the Great Red Dragon, always existed. Created as a beautiful spiritual being, he nevertheless wanted to be served like the OverLord and initiated a rebellion. He and his followers were sent throughout the universe. Once one of the humans yielded to taking a gift not offered by the Eternal Spirit, they all craved a similar treasure. Separated from the OverLord, these people became dragon slaves.

The Maker thus sent the OverLord of Many Names to Eden Again on The Great Rescue. He drove the dragons and their followers North and a small nation of chosen people, the Called-Out-Ones, south. The OverLord "forfeited his own life" to help them escape a dragon attack by changing into a wall of turbulent water to weaken the dragon's fire. The Called-Out-Ones became known as the Twice Born who stay in the Liberated Land. But occasionally, the OverLord sends some called Light Raiders to the Dragon Lands on missions. A player role plays as one of these Light Raiders sent on dangerous missions against evil of all kinds in the Dragon Lands. Each character uses Character Strengths and Abilities; defensive armor and weapons, which illustrate various spiritual abilities and gifts; and WordRunes (Bible verses).

As illustrated by this game and the other works mentioned, the goal of supposition and re-mythologizing is to present the Bible in a different language. In some cases, the parallels border on allegory, while in others the religious elements are subtle, fully developed, and integrated with the story itself. Besides these methods, writers have explored other forms of fantasy, as will be examined in the next chapter.

*Chapter* **5**

# "The Tree of Tales": Other Forms of Fantasy

It is easy for the student to feel that with all his labour he is collecting only a few leaves . . . from the countless foliage of the Tree of Tales. . . . Each leaf, of oak and ash and thorn, is a unique embodiment of the pattern (J. R. R. Tolkien, "On Fairy Stories").

## FAIRY TALE

In *On Stories*, Lewis suggests that a writer chooses a certain Form, or "fictive analogue," for what he has to say, and this Form determines the shape or pattern of events and the effect of the work. He wanted a form that would bring the supernatural into the realm of experience, thus bridging the gap between the two. The "fairy tale was the ideal form," he writes, for the Narnia tales, and he even subtitled *That Hideous Strength* a "fairy tale for adults," although his space trilogy is considered science fiction. Tolkien, who complained that there were no fairy stories for adults, calls the fairy story "really an adult genre . . . for which a starving audience exists" (*Letters*, 209).

The fairy tale form, according to Lewis, has several distinct advantages: it can be brief, by both permitting and compelling the author to leave things out; requires a limited vocabulary, little description, and chapters of equal length; cannot be analyzed; cuts down on reflective, expository, digressive, and descriptive passages; concentrates on action and conversation; can be both general and concrete; makes experience palpable; gives new experiences; adds to life; and is flexible and traditional (*Letters*, 307; *On Stories*, 37, 46–48).

Because fantasy has developed from fairy tales, it usually portrays clear-cut good and evil, relying heavily on archetypes to set up patterns of opposites such as angel vs. demon, hero vs. villain, city vs. forest, and so on. Stephen Lawhead states,

The old archetypal images—the witch, the wizard, the king, the lost son, the father—those kinds of things reverberate not only in the Bible, but also in the world of myth. Archetypal characters and situations . . . can speak much more forcefully than if you were writing in what some people call "realistic style" (Scheer, 32).

Lawhead wants his readers to respond not only to the images but see what they point to: "a greater reality of God and how he works in people's lives."

Because traditional fairy tales deal with right and wrong, they often use the religious beliefs and symbols of the age in which they were written:

God figures and devil figures are often pitted against each other to symbolize the struggle between right and wrong, good and evil. In many respects, the religious ideas presented are quite fundamentalist in nature, with the devil seducing and the God-figure beckoning, and with vivid images of temptation and fall, punishment and despair, salvation and reward (Flatter, "Folktales: The Enchanted Lesson," 33).

But because contemporary readers live in a different religious context, they might not recognize the symbolism. Flatter gives the example of the devil dressed in dark green with a cloven hoof in "Bearskin, The Man Who Didn't Wash for Seven Years." The green and the cloven hoof were devil symbols at the time it was told. Bearskin resists the devil for seven years, symbolic of man's temptations. Flatter also believes the endless circle of the ring represents eternity.

Some object that fairy tales give children false impressions of the world. In *The Uses of Enchantment* Bruno Bettelheim defends fairy tales as beneficial for children because they teach them to learn what is right and wrong before they encounter the "real world." Lewis believes realistic stories are more confusing and improbable because the reader may expect life to be like that. They are "contrived to put across some social or ethical or religious or anti-religious 'comment on life' " (*Experiment*, 68). However, no reader expects life to be like fairy stories. Lewis adds,

Do you think I am trying to weave a spell? Perhaps I am; but remember your fairy tales. Spells are used for breaking enchantments as well as for inducing them. And you and I have need of the strongest spell that can be found to wake us from the evil enchantment of worldliness which has been laid upon us for nearly a hundred years (*Weight*, 5).

Chesterton agrees that "make-believe" is a misleading phrase. A child is not deceived or confused by words like "fact," "fable," and "falsehood" but knows the difference between reality and fiction: "This is the beginning of all sane art criticism. Wonder combined with the complete serenity of the conscience in the acceptance of such wonders" (*The Common Man*, 56–57). He feels children would make up such things for themselves even if they had no fairy tales.

An example of a contemporary fairy tale is Robert Siegel's *The Kingdom of Wundle*. While it uses a fairy tale format, Siegel presents the story through a wide range of images. But the "meaning" of the images is neither didactically superimposed on the story nor allegorical, only suggestive. Like a fairy tale, the story begins, "There was once a kingdom." This Edenlike kingdom, however, is so perfect and things go so smoothly that the King becomes bored and falls asleep constantly. Since others begin to follow his example, no one notices a Gryfuss enter the land. The Gryfuss is not a bad monster but causes kingdoms to virtually disappear, and the "sun shows weak and watery, if it shows at all." This effect becomes increasingly significant as one reads on because light and vivid colors become images of heaven and the ideal.

Prince Harold and his friend Gwendolyn are spared from the Gryfuss' effect, however, because they are in the tower telling stories of dragons and knights (later, we are told this is an important detail). Discovering what has happened, they go on a quest toward the mountains and ultimately the sea to find help. Eventually, they come to a golden land of no shadows lit by the Flower of the Golden Horn. An old man tells them that "Whoever looks into that flower achieves such clarity of vision that no mist nor shadow can remain long in his presence." However, shadows will try to reenter the land, prevent the Prince from looking into the Flower, and even try to destroy it.

Gwendolyn's task—the most difficult—is to remain with the old man and weave Harold's journey onto a tapestry. Harold's journey involves a series of significant images in which each solution is achieved for him. The first situation is a man sweeping gray ashes and filling the air so full of them that Harold's clothes become soiled. When the boy suggests leaving this desert, the man replies, "And show up in the light looking like *this*?" Ashamed, Harold beats at his clothes. After running for a long time, he plunges into a river which totally cleanses him.

Next, he encounters a huge red dragon which suddenly disappears when he turns his back on him: "Was the dragon there only when he looked at it, he wondered, or was it powerless to attack only while his eyes were fixed on the rising sun?" Finally, he reaches the Flower of the Golden Horn, which is "white and gold," "luminous," radiating energy: "The petals drew him in . . . toward an infinitely receding center while at the same time they grew from that center and published it abroad." On one petal, however, is a small beetle in which he sees a kaleidoscope of visions "mirroring all things he had ever desired or feared." Only when he sees a "light at the edge of his vision" is he able to pluck off the beetle. While he gazes happily into the Flower, he remembers his country which the Gryfuss had separated from the light. The old man then gives him a thin silver whistle, and Harold and Gwendolyn return home.

As they enter the Kingdom, everyone and everything awaken. They first go to the Gryfuss' cave, and Harold blows the whistle twice. The Gryfuss simply shuffles away to "attack" another kingdom. Each child begins to notice how the other has changed and grown. For example, Gwendolyn's eyes brighten the surrounding air: "The brightness grew more and more intense until the air crackled with clarity. Everyone around them saw more to look at" in the colors than in any other spring. Finally, Gwendolyn reveals the tapestry to the people. It shows all of the Prince's tasks on his journey in every color and in "living light." Then "the banquet hall filled with a million threads of unheard music weaving upon the air a tapestry of invisible gold." The story ends with their announcement of marriage.

A unique inversion of the fairy tale form is found in the writing of contemporary writer Tim Powers. He says his style is rooted in Chesterton's "theology of oddity." Says Powers,

> Essentially, I write topsy-turvey fairy tales. I'll exaggerate and caricature; I'll invert ethics; I'll transmutate the norm; I'll create ... oddity. ... The modern novel is generally but signification, while the fairy tale is semiosis. In the former, ethical patterns speak for themselves; in the latter, heterodoxy foils for orthodoxy (Grant, "Sacramentalism in the Speculative Fiction of Tim Powers," 3–4).

Tim Powers' *Dinner at Deviant's Palace* best exemplifies this method. The story takes place a generation after bombs have destroyed Los Angeles, and many seek solace in a cult religion formed by Norton Jaybush. Greg Rivas is hired to infiltrate the cult and rescue a woman he once loved in an act called a "redemption."

Jaybush's religion is an exact inversion of Christianity. It has its own sacrament, speaking in tongues, Sanctified Dancing, Prayer parlors, and produces Blood to be used as a drug. Jaybush, corpulent because he devours people, resides at Deviant's Palace, which has a "morbidly skeletal appearance," unsymmetrical windows and doors, and random arches. Here, one can be served poisonous food or enjoy explicit scenes and offensive sounds. Rivas successfully avoids the effects of the sacrament by inflicting pain on himself, while Jaybush becomes a crystal contained in a bottle.

## THE BIBLE AND FANTASY

Besides fairy tale, an important influence on the form, themes, and images of fantasy is the Bible itself. The Bible uses fairy tale motifs, especially in Revelation. Ryken believes the importance of these motifs is that "they give expression to man's longings and represent human wish fulfillment. Revelation transmutes this wish fulfillment into a spiritual mode and declares it to be a reality—to be, in fact, the ultimate reality" (*Literature*, 342). Revelation, chapters, 12–22, contains a lady in distress who gets rescued, exposure of a wicked witch, marriage of the hero to a bride, a wedding feast, and life forever after in a palace of jewels. Christ is the epic hero returning on a white horse to slay the dragon, Satan, defeat evil, and become King (Rev. 19:11–16). John, the narrator, is like the fantasy character who journeys to the supernatural realm, encounters spiritual beings, and returns to life renewed.

Both the Bible and fantasy literature, of course, illustrate the value of story. Tolkien and Lewis consider the very use of the story vehicle in the New Testament valuable for its beauty as a "concomitant of truth." In his sermons, Jesus illustrates the use of fiction as a good form for teaching. In addition, Biblical writers used narrative form rather than rational argument because using imagination helps readers envision spiritual truths in everyday events. Since thematic principles are not stated abstractly, they must be deduced from events or dialogue because they are one with the narrative. Also, because "narrative is a progression of events moving toward a goal, it is uniquely suited to depicting the dynamic, growing nature of religious experience" (Ryken, *Literature*, 77). John Shea, in *Stories of God: An Unauthorized Biography*, suggests that, ironically, "ethical fantasy" may be more Biblical than traditional religious stories.

As did Jesus, Christian fantasy writers to some degree use the parable form. A parable is a short story used to teach a truth, doctrine, or moral, or to convey a vision. Analogies or comparisons from real experience help the reader picture the supernatural, such as comparing the Kingdom of God to a banquet or wedding. However, parables use no fantasy elements such as marvels or talking animals. Lewis says parables also allow us to imagine parallels between the love and goodness of God and human relationships by analogy (*Miracles*, 95). The reader is made to judge characters in the story, then transfer his judgment to the spiritual level (Ryken, *How to Read the Bible as Literature*, 306). Ryken points out that parable is unlike allegory because parables may be interpreted several ways. Only some details may be symbolic, and they may have one or several themes (*How*, 151). John White writes that essentially "fantasy has the elements of parable in it. Jesus used it. The essence of parable, of fantasy, and of allegory is to use the medium to get across the truth in a way that is more compelling" ("Fantasy," 8).

John Aurelio, a diocesan priest, uses the parable form in *Story Sunday: Christian Fairy Tales for Young and Old Alike* and *The Beggar's Christmas*. "The Greatest Feat," for example, tells of four wizards who perform various feats of magic in response to the King of the Universe's promise to give his kingdom to the person who performs the greatest feat. One wizard gives the people all they ask for; one makes things change; one changes the speed of time; and one changes the world's colors. But, the King explains, these feats take the struggle, truth, meaning of time, and beauty out of life.

However, a young man whom the crowd had struck down is the winner: "There was one among you who rose from the dead . . . . anyone who finds him will share the kingdom with him forever." Aurelio, who uses these parables to preach to his congregation, says this story portrays in symbolism "the condition of modern man" and answers the question, "What would happen if Jesus were to come today?" (217)

## OTHER PRECURSORS OF RELIGIOUS FANTASY

Many other older works might be considered forerunners of Christian fantasy: medieval morality plays, *Beowulf*, the Arthurian legend, and so on. C. S. Lewis describes Dante's *Divine Comedy* as "a high, imaginative interpretation of spiritual life" and the father of Wells and Verne (*Preface*, 114). In the sixteenth and seventeenth centuries the sense of sin and inward crises also called for dramatic expression, with Bunyan thus emerging as one of the last great allegorists. After him symbolism was used as the predominant mode of expressing religious conflict.

Lewis points out that eventually nature was reduced to mathematical and mechanical elements by empiricism instead of being envisioned as genial and animistic (*English*, 3). When the rise of secular rationalism destroyed the belief that the supernatural was part of the real world, this idea was also rejected in fiction. Manlove writes, "Gradually fantastic worlds could rely on less and less of an element of prior belief in their possibility: nature ceased to be accepted as involved with supernature, and became what one experienced, where supernature was relegated simply to what one believed—or imagined" (259). Hence, when after a long time fantasy reappeared, it did so under the Romantic idea of the 'heterocosm,' the belief that the artist could create his own truth-system which need have no empirical connection with our own" (259).

With the rise of realism throughout the eighteenth and nineteenth centuries, only external, perceivable reality was considered important. The division of phenomena into natural and real versus the supernatural affected literature, giving rise to "sentimental" and speculative fiction.

The latter is a reaction against realism, treating the supernatural as real and establishing enough history and background to make the supernatural credible. The power of the supernatural, as has been emphasized, impels the story: "In the Primary World, the existence and activity of such powers are a matter of religious faith," whereas in "the fantasy's Secondary World, their existence and activity are subject to material proof" (Waggoner, *The Hills of Faraway*, 10).

There were other important precursors, especially in the nineteenth century. The spiritual "cleavage" caused by science was expressed again in allegorical fantasy such as Tennyson's *Idylls of the King*, which used characters of legend to symbolize Christian abstractions. The Kunstmarchen or art folktale was the product of German romantics who wanted to turn away from the rational. Writers such as E. T. A. Hoffman (1776–1822), Novalis (1772–1801), and Friedrich de la Motte Foque (1777–1843) strongly influenced George MacDonald, giving him the idea of using the fairy-tale form to express the mystical and supernatural. For example, in Fouque's *Undine* (1811), which MacDonald names as an example of what he means by a fairy tale, a selfish water nymph marries a human and receives a soul. But her husband rejects her, sending her back to the fairies. When her husband becomes unfaithful to her, she must, according to fairy law, kill him. Undine turns herself into a brook winding around his grave. Although she is remorseful for her sins, she is not redeemed. However, such works died out when they became more vehicles for philosophical ideas than simply tales.

George MacDonald was the first writer to blend holiness and magic. He saw fantasy's potential for showing the transcendent immanent in reality and how it requires moral behavior from man. Symbols and images present these theological insights, and instead of telling the message, MacDonald makes the moralizing part of the story, depicting spiritual qualities working in people (Hein, 114). By illustrating that fantasy could deal with religious questions, he became an important influence on C. S. Lewis.

In the nineteenth century, observes Marion Lockhead, there was a "renaissance of wonder." Up to this time childrens books had been seen as instructional and moral, whereas fairy tales were seen as foolish lies. Matthew Arnold was one of the earliest opponents of religious fairy tales and the writing of MacDonald in particular, calling for de-mythologization of literature and emphasis on conduct. Consequently, there was a need for the rise of fantasy in "de-mythologized" England, as Chesterton called it. Fantasy also seems to arise when there is insufficient cultural means to express oneself spiritually (Wolfe, 205). Thus the crisis of faith today may be similar to that in the Victorian period. Just as they turned then to medievalism for myth, so today writers turn to the past for other worlds.

## DREAM VOYAGE

One forerunner of modern fantasy is the dream voyage. Imaginary voyages such as *The Odyssey* involved the travels of heroes to various locations such as heaven or the underworld as a parallel to their spiritual, inward journeys. Imaginary voyages, Lewis notes, became valued when the great age of real exploration died out, because they maintained the wonder and glory of exploration. Dream voyage shows us truth veiled in allegory (Lewis, *Discarded*, 63). Tolkien, however, discounted the dream device as fantasy, which he felt "should be presented as 'true.' " If the writer tells you the tale has been imagined, "he cheats deliberately the primal desire at the heart of Faerie: the realization, independent of the conceiving mind, of imagined wonder" ("On Fairy," 14).

Lewis describes as fantasy his own *The Great Divorce*, in which passengers on a bus travel to heaven's outskirts, but he intended it to have a moral and "arouse factual curiosity about the details of the after-world" (*Great*, 8). He calls this description of the afterworld "an imaginary supposal" rather than a "guess or a speculation at what may actually await us." The most successful aspect is the image of heaven as "unbendable and unbreakable," an idea Lewis says he borrowed from a story in an American science fiction magazine.

A contemporary example of the dream voyage is Harry Blamires trilogy. Blamires explains,

I thought that readers ought to be softened up before I confronted them as a lay theologian. So I launched myself into the field of theological fiction because it would blend satire and seriousness. My aim was to contrast bad thinking with sound thinking in an amusing and ironic way. I started with this first-person record of a dream pilgrimage through the hereafter in which a guardian angel is often at hand to put the pilgrim's earthbound notions straight (*Devil's*, 7).

In *The Devil's Hunting Grounds* the narrator is taken before a celestial Selection Tribunal. Along with his guardian angel, Lamiel, he is sent to various places in Purgatory such as the College of Gnostics and the Backward Believer's Department. Blamires pokes fun at allegory, although he uses it. His guardian angel accuses him of

looking for some crude allegorical significance in the fact that Helicon is an isolated city which the main highways do not touch. . . . There are no allegorical significances here. Things do not stand for other things in that symbolic way. Things are what they are. . . . Helicon . . . is quite simply and unallegorically off the beaten track (109).

According to Blamires, while the emphasis in the first book is on the contrast between true Christian faith and "various forms of evasive pseudo-religion," the serious emphasis in *Cold War in Hell* is "upon the need for Christian obedience in the face of fashions and philosophies that ensnare with calls to self-centeredness and self-indulgence" (*Cold*, 8). The book is "concerned with what goes on in Hell's university, inside Hell's books, at a floor show in Hell, and even in its governing council chamber" (8). The narrator descends by elevator into Hell, which is much like a hotel, where he can observe the Cold War between Celestial and Infernal Powers. The devils illustrate the logical result of having total freedom of thought rather than accepting God's law. He also hears the arguments of various devils. Blamires comments, "Representation of life in Hell of course offers such opportunities for satire of contemporary anti-Christian ways of thinking. It also offers plenty of opportunity for pin-pointing where fashionable trends in contemporary life verge on the diabolical" (8).

In the final book, *Highway to Heaven*, the narrator takes a pilgrimage to the Borderlands of Heaven. Blamires can thus poke fun at various forms of worship and religions that emphasize selected doctrines. Blamires identifies the themes as the "nature of penitence, the mystery of faith, and the primacy of will over desire" (10).

The dream voyage technique allows the writer to present themes discussed in his "polemical" works through the arguments of various individuals the narrator meets, such as Logical Positivists. The problem with this form, however, is that action is sacrificed for many argumentative speeches, conversations, and type characters, the point of which might escape a modern reader unfamiliar with the various philosophies.

E. E. Y. Hales' *Chariot of Fire*, in contrast, presents voyages to heaven, limbo, and hell as real; the Publisher's Note in the introduction maintains this book is not science fiction. Hales bases his cosmology on the accounts of Dante, Milton, and the Bible. Henry Brock, the hero and writer of the account, "didn't visit worlds invented by writers but worlds revealed by the word of God." The publisher thus felt this more recent account should be published.

Because of his romantic lust, Brock is sent to the Circle of Romantic Passion in Hell, the second circle of nine. Upper Hell is "for the more superficial sinners," while Lower Hell is "for the real baddies, with a Limbo on top of Upper Hell for those who were not really sinners at all but good people who never knew Christianity." In the town of Angeli Caduti (Fallen Angels), there is "an oppressive, humid heat day and night," dust blown in from the street, a lack of twentieth century technology, and sex does not "seem to satisfy the way it had on Earth." In Hell, "You just do what you want to do. . . . Hell is where you are free to be yourself, and nothing but yourself." On the other hand, when he visits heaven briefly by mistake, he dislikes it because sexual desire is not permitted at all. Finally, Limbo, which he also visits, has "real peace,

not just idleness and squalor amidst a shabby out-of-date moderniza-
tion." There he meets the Woman of Samaria, who tells him about the
Jew who promised her living water. She is one of certain people in
Limbo who are given a second chance, the opportunity of Christian
baptism and redemption.

Cleopatra resides in Brock's circle but desires to become sovereign
over all of Upper Hell. However, Satan warns against it, calling on his
hosts of fallen angels and his cannons. When Michael comes on the
Chariot of Fire described by Milton, Brock senses the threat of Armageddon. He saves "the universe from war" by striking a deal in which
Cleopatra rules only in the Second Circle, so Brock is rewarded by being
permitted to go back to earth.

Returning with the Woman of Samaria, Brock helps her "find that
living water" so she can "go to Heaven, where the Jew is king." Brock
helps her understand that the Jew who spoke to her at the well is God:
"'God = His Son = your Jew . . . your Jew = God'." He goes on to answer
her questions about his birth, miracles, crucifixion, resurrection, and
ascension. After being given absolution and baptism, she dies of anemia.
Ironically, the flames of her belief rekindle his: "I didn't mean that to
happen but it has . . . I want to go to Purgatory, and from there—so help
me God!—I want one day to enter Heaven."

In the Postscript, the publisher surmises that Brock was trying to get
to Purgatory on one of the boats from the Tiber, as Dante described
them. Because it was 1975, the Holy Year of Papal Indulgence, Brock
was possibly permitted passage and threw the briefcase with this manuscript onto the grass.

Robert Heinlein's *Job: A Comedy of Justice* effectively uses travel in and
out of different worlds, including heaven and hell, to question God's
justice. Alex Hergensheimer, a fundamentalist minister and deputy director of the Churches United for Decency, walks through fire while on
vacation in Polynesia, only to find that he is Alec Graham in a different
world. He marries Alec's mistress, Margrethe, and together they
undergo various trials such as being hit by an iceberg, enduring a double
earthquake, and moving without warning into various times and places
which have lower moral standards than he is used to. The geography
is always the United States, and the history is the same up to 1890. But
"about a hundred years back something strange happened and the two
worlds split apart." For example, in one world William Jennings Bryan
was president from 1913–1926, in Alec's world Bryan was elected in
1896, and in Margrethe's world he was never president. They move as
far back in time to the horse and buggy era and forward to the rapture.

Alec believes that the problems they are undergoing are signs and
portents of the Second Coming—or else changes sent by the Devil to
deceive him. He begins to feel persecuted, paranoid that the world

around him is a conspiracy. Since Margrethe is not a Christian, he begins to worry about her soul going to heaven. He also tries to witness to those he encounters on his journeys. The situation therefore allows Alec to express the fundamentalist views about the authority of the Bible, cosmogony, the age of the earth, the date of Christ's birth, the time of the Second Millenium, Judgment Day, Armageddon, and the Rapture. Alec believes that "God so loves the world that even the damned may eventually be saved; no soul is utterly beyond redemption." But he also realizes that reconciling divine benevolence with divine justice is a "thorny" theological matter. Margrethe, on the other hand, believes Ragnarok is coming and that Loki, "the mischief maker" is working evil. At Ragnarok the world will be destroyed, "but over and over again the race of men gets another chance to do better than last time, ever and again without end." She dislikes the idea of the saved going to heaven and the damned going to eternal punishment.

During a Revival, they hear Brother Barnaby preach that "there may be other signs and portents, wonders of all sorts—but the greatest are tribulations, trials to test the souls of men the way Job was tested. Can there be a better word to describe the twentieth century than 'tribulations'?" (324). During the invitation, Alec and Margrethe go forward, but a Kansas twister descends, carrying Alec into the Rapture. Believing he has only been separated from Margrethe, he searches for her in heaven. But heaven is not as ideal as he imagined: "I had always pictured Heaven as a place of guaranteed beatitude—not filled with the same silly frustration so common on earth," or with angels arrogant because of their superior position and power. Heinlein bases his description of heaven on the imagery of Revelation. The throne of God is "magnificent, carved out of a single diamond with its myriad facets picking up Jesus' inner light and refracting it in a shower of fire and ice in all directions." The wall of the Holy City is "of iridescent jasper but it has a dozen footings in horizontal layers that are more dazzling than the wall itself: sapphire, chalcedony, emerald, sardonyx, chrysolite, beryl, topaz, amethyst . . . so dazzling everywhere that it is hard for a human to grasp it" (333).

Since Margrethe is not there, Alec asks to be thrown into hell. He learns, however, that hell is a planet and no one is really in the Pit. Satan has "tail and horns and fierce eyes, a pitchfork in lieu of a scepter, a gleam from braziers glinting off Its dark red skin." But he turns out to be Jerry Farnsworth, whom Alec had met in one of the worlds. Jerry calls Alec "another Job":

Yahwah came to Me and offered the same wager He had made over Job, asserting that He had a follower who was even more stubborn than Job. I turned Him down. . . . It was not until I saw you and Marga trudging along Interstate Forty

... that I realized that Yahweh had found someone else with whom to play His nasty games (403).

As Jerry argues about the injustice of the Judeo-Christian code, Alec begins to doubt it himself.

Yahweh is only Jerry's brother; there is a Final, higher Power, called the Chairman. Because the Chairman orders Yahweh to be more consistent, Alec and Margrethe find themselves in Eden Texas, a "bucolic place." Alec concludes, "I have what I want. I would not want to be a saint in Heaven if Margrethe was not with me; I wouldn't fear going to Hell if she was there.... Heaven is where Margrethe is."

Ironically, even though Heinlein is not known as a religious writer, the voyage is effective in *Job* because it allows for serious theological issues to be posed and extensively argued within constant adventure and humor. In general, the voyage as a form permits the characters to have a second chance and to explore heaven and hell without the realism necessary in science fiction. However, as Tolkien argued, the lack of realism destroys the credibility. In addition, the form necessitates long dialogues and minor characters to convey ideas, often at the expense of interest and action.

## ANIMAL STORIES

Another ancient form for fantasy is the beast fable, and a central element in fantasy is the presence of talking animals, sometimes as the only characters. They are used for several reasons. First, as C. S. Lewis points out, the animal character has the advantages of both the human child and adult. Since they have a child's carefree life with no domestic or other responsibilities, the writer does not need to explain such details as where the food comes from. On the other hand, they are like adults because they can do what and go where they wish (*On*, 36). They can also portray personality types succinctly. While in the medieval beast fables, animals served to satirize human foibles and teach morals, in fantasy they can convey psychology and character types more briefly and to a wider audience. Lewis gives the example of Mr. Badger in *The Wind in the Willows*, "that extraordinary amalgam of high rank, coarse manners, gruffness, shyness, and goodness. The child who has once met Mr. Badger has ever afterwards ... a knowledge of humanity and of English social history which it could not get in any other way" (*On*, 36).

In addition, when a writer uses animals in fantasy, he creates a world we wish were true: an Eden where lion and lamb can lie down together and where animals talk. Tolkien observes that although the beast fable satisfies our desire to communicate with animals, the animals are only masks for humans ("On Fairy," 15). On the other hand, Blount argues that "animals are an acceptable disguise . . . for plain speaking, leaving the reader the choice of appreciating what is said at its face value or letting it affect him more deeply" (58). For example, when Eustace turns into a dragon in *Voyage of the Dawn Treader*, the reader can ultimately see his peeling away layers of scales as an image of salvation.

Animals are frequently used as aids and comforters. Lewis considers it important to have such protectors side by side with terrible creatures (*On*, 40). Birds, for example, often lead children or warn them of danger. In *The Sword Bearer* the pigeon who "brought Anthropos out of chaos as it brooded over the abyss" serves as a guide. A silwar bird in Leeson's *Path of the Promise Keeper* keeps Harold from eating poisonous food and water, because "silwars have the job of warning Earthlings about the tricks and deceit of the Dark Ones."

### *The Book of the Dun Cow* and *The Book of Sorrows*

The advantages of animal characters are found in two of the most successful contemporary religious fantasies, Walter Wangerin's *The Book of the Dun Cow* and *The Book of Sorrows*. In the first book, Chaunticleer the Rooster, as leader of the coop, has the "priestly" role of crowing the canons several times a day. In his coop also live assorted animal characters such as the dog, Mundo Cani; John Wesley Weasel, Lord Russel Fox, and Ebenezer Rat. The animals are Keepers of the evil, serpent-like Wyrm, who lives underground in a bottomless pit but surfaces when Keepers in a small part of earth are killed. The animals, however, do not know who Wyrm is or why he exists. They "fight against a mystery," including his son Cockatrice and the Basilisks.

In *The Book of Sorrows*, Chaunticleer goes to the underworld to kill Wyrm and find the dog. But he discovers that Wyrm is physically dead already, with Mundo Cani's bones inside his eye. However, Wyrm, now in spirit form, overtakes Chaunticleer's body as hundreds of worms. John Wesley Weasel thus allows the Wolves to fight Chaunticleer. But Chaunticleer stabs himself, realizing Wyrm has been inside him.

The Dun Cow is sent as a messenger or "angel" from God so the Keepers will not be alone. The name Dun Cow comes from a Gaelic folklore manuscript from 1100 A.D., so named because it was bound in brown cowhide (Thoet, *The Book of the Dun Cow Teacher's Guide*, 29). The Cow comforts him, speaks without words, breathes on him, provides shelter and refuge, and gives the "milk of remarkable nourishment." Most important, she bears his sorrow:

Horns strangely dangerous on one so soft stood wide away and sharp from either side of her head. Her eyes were liquid with compassion—deep, deep, as the earth is deep. Her brow knew his suffering and knew, besides that, worlds more. But the goodness was that, though his wide brow knew so much, yet it bent over his pain alone and creased with it. . . . His grief had become her grief, his sorrow her own (140).

Eventually, she cuts off one of her "lethal looking" horns for Mundo Cani, who uses it to stab Wyrm's eye. As she gives up her horn, she says, "Modicae fidei—it is all for you."

Wangerin effectively uses the beast epic form popular in the ninth to fifteenth centuries. However, the animal characters, which were used in fables primarily for satire, are here more developed and not allegorical. While his animals have distinct, human-like personalities, they maintain their unique animal qualities and simple needs for existence. Wangerin also combines several traditional fantasy forms. First, the cosmology is an interesting mixture of Ptolemaic, Aristotelian, Hebraic, Norse, Arthurian, and Christian to contrast harmony and evil. Earth is fixed, flat, and at the center of the universe, while God exists in the empyrean halfway between earth and moon. Wyrm is the Midgardsorm of Norse myth, who encircles the earth and bites his tail. The wolves of chaos, also from Norse myth, seem about to win, but instead, Chaunticleer fights them, then takes his own life.

The books use other features of medieval literature such as a chivalric romance between Chaunticleer and Pertolote, feudalism, and symbolic weather. Rain, floods, and snow symbolize the coming of evil; night and heat illustrate a loss of faith. Wangerin also echoes the Arthurian legend when Chaunticleer asks that his battle spurs be thrown in the sea, and the Philomela myth when Wyrm plucks out Bird's tongue.

Perhaps the most successful aspect of the books is that the Christian ideas are not obvious, but rather the books echo concepts, such as sacrifice or sharing suffering, and presents them in a totally new form. Wangerin is also interested in showing what we can learn from animals and how God works in actual events around us. For example, the Dun Cow might remind one of the Holy Spirit. Wangerin thinks of the Dun Cow symbolically as a comforter, angel, and a sharer of suffering: "The symbolism I thought of with her was *sympathos* which is a Greek word meaning 'to suffer with'—or sympathy—and compassion which is the Latin 'suffer with' " ("Of," 8). His goal was to elicit feelings by making the reader identify with the characters and show how God can speak to us through animals ("Of," 6–7). He explains, "I didn't put forward ideas for the reader to find. The scenes and ideas arose naturally from the story itself. Of course, I would have to say the truth in order to make it unified. That implies telling the truth in order to bring out the truth" ("Of," 6).

Chaunticleer, the most strongly developed character, evokes our sympathy. As he did to the Apostle Paul, the Lord appears to Chaunticleer as a light at a time when he wants to avenge the animals who accuse him of his mother's death: " 'Get away from me,' the Rooster cried, 'or I'll die!' In the blinding light he saw himself, and he was a filthy piece of thing. . . . 'Why do you hurt me?' The light was a blaze. . . . 'Get up,' said the Lord." Then the Lord gives the rooster the land in the north to lead. Chaunticleer's priestly role is to encourage the animals and make them aware of the enemy. Yet he struggles in his role, especially when his own chicks die. He blames God for not only taking his sons but for making him ruler in the first place: "*O God, where are you?* Why have you hidden your face from us?"

Wangerin uses two other unlikely heroes, Mundo Cani and Ferric Coyote, both of whom are thin and cowardly but perform major roles in helping to combat evil. Mundo Cani (which means "dog's world") illustrates the importance of the meek and lowly, for he is described as the "ransom" for the other animals. Chaunticleer feels he is responsible for Mundo Cani's death:

That should have been *me*. . . . I should have gone down into the pit, not Mundo Cani. I should have died instead of him . . . . He was making ready to die for us, and I didn't understand that. I judged him a traitor. I made his last moments lonely, and I despised him (*Dun*, 252–253).

Pertelote advises him to ask forgiveness:

It is more than your life. It is that scrubbing of the past which you want so much, because it is confession. It is the new birth of the present, which you want so much, because it prepares for deliverance. The one is separated from the other by forgiveness. It is the honoring . . . of the worth in *his* life. Penance. You can tell him you are sorry. He will forgive you (252).

Wanting to be the animal's "saviour" himself, the rooster tries to redeem them from their troubles. But Chaunticleer finds that he can neither save Mundo Cani nor heroically kill Wyrm; Wyrm overtakes him instead. "Wyrm," explains Pertelote, "took his worth. Wyrm took his life. Wyrm left him the thing that he most hated—and when he looked for the one whom he loathed most of all, he saw himself." Through Chaunticleer, Wyrm is able to enter the animals' hearts so that, choosing evil, they decide to kill Chaunticleer.

Ferric Coyote, described as the "least of all God's Creatures on earth," also must play an important role by leading Chaunticleer to Wyrm. When the Coyote is on the verge of death and despair, the Dun Cow nourishes and cleanses him by licking him like a newborn. Because the Dun Cow forgave him, Ferric Coyote, in turn, forgives Chaunticleer for killing his wife and son: "When I was hurting the most, this beautiful Cow came to me. And somebody maybe should have punished me, on account of all the troubles that I caused. But she loved me. . . . She touched me, she fed me, she washed me." As he licks the worms from Chaunticleer, his tongue seems to scorch the rooster because of kindness: "Every stroke of the Coyote's tongue wakens a wickedness in the Cock, draws it through his memory in order to wipe it away. . . . It is as rough as gravel and scours the Rooster." Scenes such as this, within the reworking of the beast epic and ancient cosmologies, illustrate how Wangerin conveys many Christian principles through character and action.

### Other Contemporary Animal Stories

Robert Siegel's *Whalesong*, the life story—therefore "whalesong"—of a humpback whale, Hruna, similarly presents the idea of sacrifice and encourages the reader to see from a new point of view. Hruna must take the Lonely Cruise, a trip each whale takes at the beginning of adulthood. The Great Plunge is a special part of this journey that reveals the direction of his life and "the particular note of being the Spouter of Oceans sang at his conception." Siegel thus uses the whale to give a new form for his myth of creation. As described in Chapter 1, Siegel also illustrates the theme of sacrifice without lapsing into allegory.

Animals provide readers a new way of looking at other life forms. Siegel's use of the whale is effective not only because of its archetypal symbolism, but because the reader takes on the perspective of the whale. Siegel remarks, "In fantasy one hopes to give the reader an experience of what it's like to be something other than human. . . . By projecting our imagination into another form of existence we are able to gain a new or different perspective on human life" (Miller and Miller, 2). Because of this point of view, the reader's perspective on mankind is changed: humans are seen as the enemy because they harpoon or trap the whales and dolphins. For example, Hruna's first glimpse of men is disappointing to him: "Even though I knew they were small, I hadn't expected to find men so puny—all flippers and legs, like squids or octopuses."

The theme of man's separation from beasts as a result of the Fall is central to Siegel's novel *Alpha Centauri*. Rock Movers are called the Divided Kind "because they are divided from creatures as much as from their higher selves." They hate centaurs, satyrs, and fauns because in them "they see the human linked to the beast within." These mythical creatures are now hidden from us. Just as Rebecca the horse and Becky are "one," the centaurs symbolize the union of man and beast.

Jean Mosley's *The Deep Forest Award* uses animal fantasy for a younger audience to contrast the love and self-sacrifice of God's people with unbelievers. When Little Mocker, a baby Mockingbird, is lost and disabled, he accidently lands in Grassy Meadow. He is befriended by D. P. (Dump Pile) Rat, Squirrel, Head Frog, Skunky the storyteller, and Rabbit. Mrs. Racoon sets his wing, gives him hope, and tells him of the Keeper of All Creatures. Although you cannot see him, you can see where He has been, for the Keeper is "Everywhere at once" ready to help "and straighten us out when we make mistakes, if we want Him to. And he loves us all the time, whether we're lovable or not. A great friend." Mrs. Racoon describes his creatures as being linked together in a chain but free to move: "When you're a link in the chain, you can still go any place, any time, anywhere." Since bad things have slipped into the world and "haven't been stomped out yet," Little Mocker and Mrs. Racoon vow to stomp them out, each "in his own best way . . . and they stomped symbolically all around the little room."

In Grassy Meadow, Deep Forest, and the area near Rustling Brook, creatures love and help each other. But the Next Country, which lies adjacent to it, is polluted and disorganized; the animals are unfriendly, mean, and unhappy because they do not know about the Keeper. Unfortunately, it is difficult to "know where the boundaries of the Next Country are." Little Mocker yearns to return home to begin his singing lessons. Ironically, he learns how to sing in the Next Country, where the animals despise his joyful songs. But when he sings for his friends in Grassy Meadow, they "are strangely moved as if they had listened to music that came from somewhere beyond the bird's throat, beyond the treetops, up, up to the realms of the Keeper of All Creatures Himself." While he feels guilty for stealing tunes, he is assured that he combines them in a new way. His songs are his way of "stomping" out evil, and his gift of singing should be used for the Keeper.

The Deep Forest Award, given to the animal contributing most to others, goes this year to Rabbit, who diverts the attention of Dog from his friends so they can rescue Skunky: "There is no greater deed than that of one person risking his life for another." The other animals' abilities allow them to work for the good of all. For example, D. P. Rat finds things they can use in the Dump Pile, such as the Little Toy Computer that answers every question with the word "Love." Mrs. Racoon decides Keeper is using the Computer to send a message to them. Rabbit and Little Mocker thus decide they must return to Next County because the difference between the two lands is Love: "We've got to go back to the Next County," says Rabbit, "and teach them the ways of love, clean up that river and forest floor, stop that fighting, and tell them of the Keeper."

### Quest for the Faradawn

The theme of man's responsibility to animals is central to Richard Ford's *Quest for the Faradawn*. This book also successfully uses the method of "transposing" the Biblical story of creation, fall and Christ. Ashgaroth the Great One, Lord of Good, fought Dreagg the Mighty, Ruler of Evil in the Efflinch Wars. The victorious Ashgaroth banned the bitter Dreagg to the Halls of Dragorn. As a memorial to his triumph, Ashgaroth created a "jewel" which he blessed "with the gifts of life and he gave colour, shape and form to this life": green growing things, flowers and vegetables, mountains, sea, and creatures of life. "And there was harmony and peace amongst the life he had created. . . . Earth shone out as the creation of the Lord of Good." In the time "Before-Man," "the land was one vast forest and the earth was full of strange creatures with magical powers."

But the strong light goaded Dreagg into feeding from the fluids in the Halls, thus renewing his strength. His most important influence was to make the animals fight and suffer. Therefore, Ashgaroth renewed his struggle with the Lord of Evil, creating the Elves to fight Dreagg and "restore peace and innocence." Elves were formed from wind and stars and made of Magic. Their "essence is of the depth of the mighty sea and the spirit is amongst the green growing things of the woods and the trees and their souls are of the wild forgotten mountains." They appear as light from hundreds of stars because of the silver glow of their bodies, and they are "full of a restless vibrant energy." Three Elves were made Lords of the Mountains, Seas, and Forests.

But Magic was not enough to Combat Dreagg's influence. To aid the Elves, Aragorn gave them Magic and Logic; but because the latter is so powerful, he divided it into three seeds, one placed in a casket given to each Elflord. All three must be released together to be powerful. Dreagg nurtured the greed of Ammdar, the most powerful Elflord, until he rejected Ashgaroth and chose Dreagg as Lord. Desiring the seeds, Ammdar sought Elflings to aid in his quest; these became Goblins or Fallen Elves: "The hideous puffy features were twisted and contorted and the slavering viscous lips had pulled themselves into an attitude of hatred and contempt."

Ammdar, Lord of the Forest, obtained the Three Seeds of Logic. When he offered the gift of Logic to the animals in return for their acceptance of him as Ruler of Evil, they remained loyal to Ashgaroth. In revenge, Ammdar created Man or Urkku, who would have no regard for animals. Man had pure Logic but not the Magic given to the Elves. Believing himself ruler of Earth and its Creatures, Urkku was cruel to the animals, and earth became a "barren waste." The Evil One "used deceit and trickery to play on the minds of the Urkku." Eventually, the Elves were driven out to the secret places of the Earth.

However, Eldron or The Friends are Urkku who "turned towards Ashgaroth and he opened their eyes so that they had glimpses of the Earth even as the Elves and the animals do and they saw the magic in the mountains and the trees and the sea and they were as one with the animals" (129). Unfortunately, they are few, have been "ridiculed, and a great anger is in them as they see the suffering and horror inflicted by their fellow race on the animals." After a Goblin named Degg destroyed Ammdar, the animals begged Ashgaroth for help against Man. Therefore,

Ashgaroth promised them that when the time was right and the stars in the heavens were in their true place then would he send a Saviour who was truly of the Duain Elrondin, so that in him lay both Magic and Logic and to this Savior he would show the way and through him would they be saved (130).

As the story begins, two Urkku leave a baby in the Silver Woods under Great Oak. He is rescued by Brock the Badger who names him Nab ("friend"). In the Silver Woods live such legendary heroes as Rufus the Fox who outsmarted hounds; Perryfoot the Fleet, a brown hare famous for speed and humor; Bibbington the Brash, a Hedgehog who once lived with Urkku; and Wythen the Wise Owl. Although the animals help him and teach him their particular skills, Nab is allowed to develop independently, especially his opinions toward the Urkku. The animals feel an affection for Nab which they find hard to explain, and many give up their lives for him. Because of their legend about an Urkku Savior who comes to their woods, they believe Nab is this Savior. Born of Eldron, he has logic, but he also has Magic because his spirit came from Ashgaroth. Most important, raised by animals, he does not have the cruelty of Man.

Nab must obtain from each of the three Elflords a casket in which is Faradawn, the essence or the Grain of each Kingdom. Because the fragile world of the Urkku is breaking down, he must accomplish this task quickly. The Urkku cut down and clear Silver Woods, gassing and clubbing the animals to death. The rest of the world shows similar signs of collapse: countries are at war with each other and within themselves as supplies become scarce, and a strange disease begins to spread. He is given the Belt of Ammdar to help defeat the evil that Ammdar brought on the world and to contain the three caskets. Nab is told to have "faith in the powers of Ashgaroth," and in his eyes burns the "fury of Ashgaroth." The group begins their quest on Christmas day. Nab's companions are Perryfoot the Fleet, Sam the Dog, Brock, Warrigal and Owl, and Beth, an Eldron girl.

Beth first met Nab by a stream, and ever since she "had not felt truly at peace with herself.... Something about the boy had sparked off within her a restlessness that had troubled her." Like a disciple of Christ, she willingly leaves her home and her parents because something was calling her and she had to go; what it was she did not know but that it was there she could not doubt. There was no real choice, for if she did not go she would be unable to live with herself for the rest of her life. (149)

The world seems new to her, "as if she had just been born." Now she is on the side of the creatures and a participant in their world.

Nab must eventually travel to the sacred Peak Ivett and speak with Ashgaroth, who is like a "warm welcoming golden glow." Ashgaroth tells him to fill each casket with water from a pool, then sprinkle the water over the shawl he had been wrapped in as a baby. The shawl bursts into light: "All the colours and patterns had come together to form a picture of the world . . . all over the picture were lines which shone with a pure white light; a network of lines each leading to a point on the map" (301). Simultaneously, these lines or silver paths appear on the earth, but only the Eldron and animals can see them. They begin to journey along them, escaping into tunnels that open in the ground as earth is shaken by blasts. As Nab and his friends descend, they drift into sleep in Ashgaroth's arms. "They did not grow old for Ashgaroth had frozen the passage of time for them." When they awake they are in a new world, "free of the Urkku, a world of infinite colour and magic." Ashgaroth and the Elves bring the world back to its natural state. The Elves remain on earth, and the others are granted the immortality of Elves.

In the author's concluding note, we are told that the story was narrated to the writer by Nab, now old. Many of the Eldron "have denied their true nature and grown similar in their ways to the old Urkku." Nab tells him that we are children of the Eldron and still have a choice about how we will act. Thus the story "is not yet ended."

This book contains almost all the elements of religious fantasy discussed thus far. As with the other beast stories, the reader is so drawn into sympathy with another species that he sees man from a negative viewpoint. While the mythology might remind one of the Biblical creation and fall of Satan, it is complicated enough to avoid simple allegory. Nab is a savior and yet undergoes no redemption; but he and his friends are "reawakened" after the quest to an afterlife. The religious parallels, then, are not overt and are blended well with the fantasy elements, particularly the animal characters and the theme of man's responsibility to creation.

## HISTORICAL FANTASY

A unique form might be called historical fantasy. Two recent books, *Noah* (Traylor) and *Many Waters* (L'Engle), for example, fictionalize the Biblical story of the flood but add elements such as mythology, supernatural creatures, and science fiction. Traylor chose the pre-Flood world because of the potential for interesting scientific questions and speculation about the world system (14). Based on reputable experts, her book speculates about the identity of the "sons of God" mentioned in Gen. 6:1, 2 and the nephilim (giants) in Gen. 6:4.

Traylor sets her story in the imaginary world of Adamlanda (Adlandia or Atlantis) and the towns Sun City and Cronos. This is an Edenlike world with many beautiful "green pockets of wilderness" where huge varieties of creatures live in harmony. There are dragonflies with wings the span of a man's arm, twelve-foot turtles, a talking dolphin, and an eighteen-foot bear. All animals live without fear of man.

Adala, Lamech's daughter, is seduced by Poseidon, the god of Sun City, capital of the Nephilim. When Poseidon questions Noah to test his knowledge, Traylor is given an opportunity to compare the fall of man to the fall of the angels. Whereas some angels, knowing both good and evil, chose evil through choice, man fell through deception. Nephilim are the offspring of women and angels of Lucifer, whom they worship. They are Overlords, tall, wise, generous, and just, but they "sometimes used their might to cruel ends, and fell prey to the self-deception of their own pride." This unpredictability confused their subjects. Most citizens worship and admire the Overlord Lord and Prince (Lucifer), except for eccentrics like Lamech. These people claim "a truth 'higher' and 'older' than the wisdom of the gods" and believe the planet is evil and the gods corrupt. Traylor thus combines mythology with Biblical history.

Obad, Adala's betrothed, and her brother Noah go to Poseidon to get her back. Although Obad and Adala are sacrificed, Noah lives for a while with Obad's father, Shubag, where he learns from a Voice that he is to be a prophet. Traylor portrays Christ as "The Stranger" to convey the theme of the reality of the unseen world and living by faith. This Stranger comes to Noah and dresses Noah's wound caused during his eviction from Poseidon's temple:

It was a man's face, to be sure, but of such guileless character, the effect of it was startling. Above a neatly trimmed beard and slender nose were calm gray eyes and a smooth forehead. The cheeks, framed by a fall of dark, shoulder-length hair, were ruddy . . . and the man's hands were rugged but soothing (176).

The pain subsides in a moment, then the Stranger gives Noah the plans for the Ark of Safety. He also reveals that angels kept Poseidon from chasing Noah from Sun City: "Were your eyes not blind you would have seen my servants all about you, greater far and stronger than all the hosts of Lucifer. . . . But you are called to walk not as the world walks—by faith and not by sight" (178).

Traylor describes the building of the ark for 100 years, the mocking by Noah's neighbors and relatives, and their rejection of his preaching; the growing violence, immorality and corruption of civilization; the rumblings and changes in the earth itself; the changes to the earth due to the pull of the moon; and, at last, the flood and subsequent events. Traylor's inclusion of the birth and marriage of his three sons— Shem (and Sindra), Japheth (and Elbeth), and Ham (Carise)—allows her to develop the theme of Ham's rejection of his father's religion.

Traylor also includes aspects of science fiction. Because of their special knowledge, the Nephilim have a futuristic civilization. In their desire to be like gods, they perform genetic manipulation and animal experimentation. In a "lust for immortality," they transplant body parts, resulting in legendary creatures such as minotaurs, centaurs, satyrs, mermaids, and mermen. The Temple to the Sun uses Solar Energy, and nuclear energy propels their ships. Compared to wheels within wheels, their military sky-machines "each had a metallic rim which revolved about a stationary plate, and within the rims were rows of eye-like, circular windows, lit brilliantly by interior lumination." Their "religion," called the Way of the Sun, requires worship of created things rather than Yahweh, the Creator. In addition, the Overseers abuse and desecrate nature, destroying the "divinely established orders of created things."

Similarly, L'Engle's book *Many Waters* is based on the Flood story but uses a different perspective. Sandy and Dennys, characters from her space-time trilogy, interrupt their parents' experiment on virtual particles (particles which have a "tendency to life" or "almost particles"). "Tessering" or a time-space jump called a quantum leap transports them to the pre-Flood desert, where they are taken in by Noah's family. Because they are not supposed to change history, their only role seems to be to reconcile Noah and his grandfather Lamech. The twins fall in love with Noah's daughter Yalith, who is spared from the flood by being taken to God as Enoch was. The title thus alludes not only to the flood but also the verse "Many waters cannot quench love, neither can the floods drown it."

Because Traylor tells the story from Noah's point of view, she focuses more on the historical aspects of the flood story. Her book might be labeled predominantly historical fiction, with fantasy aspects added. L'Engle, on the other hand, employs the time travel device used in her other books and tells the story from the point of view of the twins. Because the twins leave before the flood occurs, there are few details about the building of the ark, compared to Traylor. The Biblical account mentions wives but gives no names, so both writers invent wives for Noah and the sons. Otherwise, they do not change the Biblical account.

Finally, both writers add fantasy elements to the Biblical account. For her setting, Traylor invents the allegorical land of Adamlanda and includes a map, whereas L'Engle's is a sandy pre-Flood desert. They depict the Nephilim as supernatural creatures, though differently. However, in both, in keeping with the Genesis account, the Nephilim seduce pretty human girls and displease Noah's family. Both include other legendary creatures. But while Traylor's are the result of animal experimentation, L'Engle simply includes unicorns, manticores, and griffins without giving their origin.

Parke Godwin's *The Last Rainbow*, the third book of his Arthurian novels, similarly combines elements of history with fantasy, legend, and myth. It takes place in the early days of Christianity when pagan gods were still worshipped. The central character, Patricius, is a priest sent to convert the tiny Faerie folk who live in Prydn (now the British isles) before the time of King Arthur. "Faerie" are "like the German trolls, little folk who lived under earthen mounds," according to the Saxons. "Some did not believe in them at all." Patricius goes to them to "find the Grace I preach . . . find where it is, dig for it. . . . Hold it up and say, 'Here! Here is ultimate truth'!"

The "Edenic" Faerie folk believe in Earth Mother, her husband Lugh Sun, and a Moses-like queen Mabh who led her folk to the promised land of Prydn: "Miracles and magic: that was religion to the Faerie, that and the quaintly unstable marriage of sun and earth." They "have a deep need for magic" and no sense of linear time. Thus Patricius discovers he must not preach at them but tell stories, using "the words and pictures that had meaning for them" and that they can relate to. So he tells the Bible stories of miracles in their own way "as stories of magic." Believing they need the "strongest possible magic" to supply their needs, the people turn to "Father-God's magic." They trust this magic to vanquish their fear of Blackbar, or iron.

But Patricius changes, too. He becomes one of the Faerie by changing his name to Padrec and marrying Dorelai, their leader. Once self-righteously believing that he will change their lives, he realizes he does not know the whole truth: "The world, real and spirit, was larger than his idea of it." While he breaks many of his vows, he feels happier and closer to God than he ever did: "How strange it is to err in love and through an error to find the right." Whereas his faith had been self-centered, Dorelai made no division: "Earth, sky, body, faith were all one. She existed in a wholeness from which . . . he had riven her."

Several events help him experience the concepts he had only preached. First, having a son, Crulegh, helps him understand for the first time the meaning of love which to him had only been a word: "I have read of God's only begotten Son until the phrase blurred in my soul's sight." Then, during the Holy War, when he watches the crucifixion of his friend Drust, he recognizes that a man who preaches about crucifixion "should see it once to know what he's prating of." He forces "himself to look up at the reality of what he'd learned as symbol. . . . A butterfly spread on black cloth by a zealous but clumsy collector, the exquisite, fragile beauty trembling a moment before the pinioned life left it" (275). Drust maintains his belief until the end, while Padrec does not: "All his faith, all his Christianity came down to that agonized but pure death and showed his own heart wanting." In anguish, he smears himself with Drust's blood, "the blood of the lamb." He also believes the Faerie people fought for God only to be rewarded with defeat, abandonment, and no land to live in. Dorelei, like Moses, desires to find the land where the Rainbow points, "The Road of the Gods." This is their promised land "where the magic lives, even beyond world-edge," " the land of the young" where no one grows old, and the grass is always green. It is called Tir-Nan-Og, a name used in Gwynn Jones' Celtic poem of that name to also refer to the true spirit's home, the ideal community. By following both the Rainbow and clues in an ancient nursery rhyme, they are led to the barrow of Mabh. Mabh lifts Dorelei up by the hand into the sunlight until she is high enough to see the true, round shape of Mother Earth, the mountains, rivers, and glens drawn together "into the whole": "She saw where and why they all joined, saw their common purpose, and cried out in her joy." Through daylight, night, storms, and over sea, they soar until Dorelei sees Tir-Nan-Og, "huge, young and green, with her own copper-brown folk on the shore . . . waiting." Dorelei leads them to this Promised Land, Virginia.

Padrec, on the other hand, goes his own way, eventually renewing his faith: "I thought to turn my back on my Father's house but found in truth that neither He nor it would leave me." He becomes bishop to the Christian Irish and eventually known as Saint Patrick. Godwin's book thus retells history by using legend, myth, and the elements of enchantment. Padrec's crisis of faith is both developed and integral to the story, and the naivete and freshness of the Faerie folk allow him to see Christianity from a new perspective.

## SCIENCE FICTION

Another form only a few contemporary authors have successfully used for theological themes is science fiction. Fantasy and science fiction differ basically in that rational, instead of supernatural, explanation is used in the latter. Science fiction traditionally is distinguished from other types of fantasy in that it is more limited by the laws of science or what might be scientifically feasible in the future. Thus "magical" occurrences must be given rational explanation. In contrast, Tolkien says fairy tales are concerned not with possibility but desirability.

After World War II when attitudes toward science changed, there was a shift in emphasis in science fiction, and it began to deal with religious themes. Contemporary science fiction is often negative towards religion or creates new religions. However, it is an ideal form to deal with religious themes because it is, by nature, more interested in ideas such as the future of mankind or the ethical implications of science than many other genres. It is thus a natural type of literature to speculate about religion on other planets or in the future. Madeleine L'Engle writes, "I often seek theological insights in reading science fiction because this is a genre eminently suited to explorations of the nature of the Creator and creation ... because to think about worlds in other galaxies, other modes of being is a theological enterprise" (*Walking*, 134–135).

Lewis said it was David Lindsay "who first gave me the idea that the " 'scientification' appeal could be combined with the 'supernatural' appeal" (*Letter*, 205). *Voyage to Arcturus* is a "remarkable thing, because scientifically it's nonsense, the style is appalling, and yet this ghastly vision comes through" (*On*, 145). In this novel, Lindsay expresses the idea that the Creator is the Devil and thus all creation is evil and an illusion. Only the soul is good in some way. Tolkien describes *Voyage to Arcturus* as more "powerful" and "mythical" than *Out of the Silent Planet*, with more religion and morals in it than story (*Letters*, 34). Lewis also got his narrative form from other ancient works such as Bernardus Silvestris' *Cosmographia* and Plato's *Myth of Er*. Space fiction allowed Lewis to go beyond normal limits of perception without the work becoming dream vision or allegory. Through space travel, humans can leave earth and experience something new such as uncorrupted creatures. In addition, events take on cosmic significance.

In "On Science Fiction," Lewis identifies several types of science fiction story. The first uses a futuristic setting as a backdrop for a love, spy, wreck, or crime story that could just as well have taken place anywhere. Thus Lewis warned that there should be a good reason for using this setting: "to develop a story of real value which could not have been told ... in any other way" (*On*, 57). The second type is interested in space travel or other undiscovered scientific techniques as real possibilities. The third is more speculative and less scientific, imagining what something, such as another planet, might be like. The fourth type is eschatalogical, exploring the destiny of man. Finally, "mythopoeic" literature is about "gods, ghosts, ghouls, demons, fairies, monsters" because the author's goal is to create the effect of wonder and beauty. This last type needs to be only superficially plausible because "suggestiveness" is what matters.

Cordwainer Smith, who wrote in the 50's and 60's, is often cited as an example of a "Christian" science fiction writer. However, he does not overtly make science fiction an apology for Christianity, and the religious parallels in his stories are not obvious. Instead, his works have been described as "outrageous" allegory or "codes" that emphasize love.

Central to his universe is an elite group called the Instrumentality, a term derived from Roman Catholic and Episcopal theology for the priest's performance of the sacraments.

One example of religious echoes in his stories can be seen in "Under Old Earth." Some readers might be reminded of the story of Noah, but Smith makes the details so bizarre that most readers may not see the parallels. On one of the Douglas-Ouyang planets is a preserve called the Gebiet where there are no rulers or punishment. People fled here seeking the freedom of drugs, women, parties, and games as a cure for the "weary happiness of mankind." In Beziek, "all things are allowed," including a wild dance and music produced by congohelium, "matter and antimatter laminated apart by a dual magnetic grid." One of the "ancient ones," Lord Sto Odin, visits Gebiet to judge it before he dies. But mud-laden water begins to rush onto the continent until it sinks. Centuries later, Lady Alice More begins the Rediscovery of Man by bringing disease, risk, and misery back to increase man's happiness.

More recently, several books are set in the future when there is space travel and colonization of other planets. While there has not been much adult science fiction, it seems to be a popular form for youth books because it attracts younger readers. The theme of many of the science fiction novels that have been written for both young and adult readers is faith versus concrete proof of the supernatural.

David Lawrence's *The Wheels of Heaven*, for example, not only focuses on the theme of belief based on evidence but exemplifies the techniques of science fiction used to establish credibility. A scientist named Singer accidentally synthesizes Poly CFP—polymerized cyanide ferroporphyrin—catalyzed by blood, sweat, and tears. When it is bombarded by appropriately modified sound waves of exactly 163 decibels and 431 cps, objects disappear. To see why, Singer and the narrator Albert Blake, a poet and scientist, attach themselves to the compound by making armbands out of the substance. Shrinking to the size of an atom, Blake sees matter at the molecular, atomic, and subatomic levels. He discovers there are "intelligent, willful, purposeful forces operating on each electron" and governing their motions. They are, in turn, controlled by God.

In a dream vision, Christ appears to Blake and explains the meaning of his atomic journey. When God calls each of these beings by name, they do his bidding. Since there are also "mind-boggling" numbers of them, and everything has such beings, all things are under the control of God's will. In addition, Blake raises the possibility that large amounts of unobserved matter do not behave according to laws because they cannot be detected. Thus miracles, answers to prayer, and influences on one person or even a nation can occur to suit God's purposes. Finally, Blake is told that some people believe all of this without being given proof like he has. He is therefore called to tell others.

This book, like most science fiction, aims at believability. The narrator gives the exact dates of events, emphasizing that he recorded everything that happened on his journey as soon as he returned to the laboratory. The experiment itself is outlined and explained in detail. In fact, the narrator even apologizes for the "barrage of scientific terminology." Over half the book is spent giving the details of how the discovery was made, and about twenty pages are spent giving a detailed description of what he sees. Blake interprets what he saw by explaining how the exact numbers of electrons, neutrons, protons, and so on theoretically would have appeared. He also develops his explanations by referring to the atomic theories of Bohr, Rutherford, Heisenberg, and Einstein, to journal articles and formulae, and finally to a noted professor's interpretation of the events as "relativistic time-dilation."

Mark Durstewitz's *Code Red on Starship Englisia* similarly presents the problem of faith without "scientific" proof but for a younger audience. The main character, Howard Prynne, questions the existence of "Elohim" and does not understand "why a god who was powerful enough to create the universe would want to bother with an insignificant organism like man" or have a "real and intimate relationship" with him. While servicing his spaceship, Howard is dragged into space by the thruster system. Begging Elohim, "whoever he is," to save him, Howard is surrounded by a dazzling light. An angel Elohim sends tells him he will be saved. Unknown to Howard, his superiors have taped the encounter. But his captain at first tries to convince him the experience was an illusion and accidently erases the tapes. However, Howard, who knows inside it is true, eventually decides faith is what is important: "You can't prove that [Elohim] does or doesn't [exist] by scientific data. You have to look into the unseen. . . . Faith is based on evidence inside you."

As with many of the books written for young readers, this book is brief, and thus there is little character development, descriptive details, and scientific explanation. In fact, this is a good example of a story that wouldn't necessarily have to use science fiction at all except to attract certain readers; the spaceship is simply a "backdrop" for Howard's inner conflict.

Stephen Lawhead's two Empyrion books take place in the year 2285. Orion Treet, a historian, is sent to Empyrion, a planet in Epsilon Eridani, a star system 11 light years away. Colonized by people from earth, it has been cut off from civilization, and he is to investigate why. Lawhead says he wanted to write a book long enough to "create a sense of a different world" ("Stephen," 24). Treet finds the humans there are 3,000 years ahead of earth and have a rigid class system.

Lawhead describes the two cultures that exist on Empyrion as a metaphor for what good versus evil are like and examination of the theme "the development of spiritual maturity against the decision not to mature" ("Stephen," 23–24). One culture lives under a great climate-controlled dome, worships Trabant Animus, Lord of the Astral Planes, and follows the Credo of Cynetics. The priests issue Sacred Directives, a body of ancient writings, and record transgressions. Anyone who deviates from the Clear Way (Path of Obedience) is punished. In contrast, the Fieri, who live in a utopia, believe in a Supreme Being who is concerned about men: "The Fieri's beliefs had created a vital, thriving society of nearly eight million Souls in love with truth and beauty and kindness to one another." The Fieri were cast out of the Dome during a great war, and only some survived a nuclear attack. Treet prevents a second attack by helping them destroy Dome.

In Lawhead's science fiction novel *Dream Thief*, Spence Reston has an inner conflict which is integrated with the story's focus, that of mind control. The setting shifts from space station Gotham to Mars and eventually India. Long ago, we discover, when Mars became uninhabitable, Ortu and others from Mars once came to India as gods. Ortu uses a tanti (consciousness altering device) to manipulate dreams, control other's minds, and hopes to ultimately rule the world by making the tanti into a machine capable of broadcasting to the world. He has nurtured men's belief that their salvation will come from benevolent beings from the stars, "a savior from beyond their world."

As Ortu's primary victim, Spence must examine his past motives and beliefs, using his will to avoid succumbing. Not only does the danger here seem truly threatening, but the question of what belief is and how it is shaped is examined. Spence's struggle as he wavers in his belief is also developed throughout the book, as described in Chapter 2.

Two books deal with the consequences of biotechnology. In Wallace Henley's *City Under the Sands*, a group of scientists, with the aid of the KGB, set up an underground city. Their goal is to eventually create a "posthuman" society which, through biological engineering and evolution of a new species, is "above evil." This underground center would monitor and control humans by means of stimoreceivers (electronic devices) planted in the amygadala of the brain. In addition, they would use brain surgery and genetic engineering to create three classes of society: Peacemakers, Producers, and Primary Beings. A god called Sovereign, which is also being created, is a biocomputer. A combination of living tissue and computer technology, it would create life and determine its destiny.

Amidst this background of biotechnology, the Christianity is overtly stated. The main character, Tilman, a newspaper reporter who is eventually led to this underground city while investigating a death, is a Christian. He tries to convert Singlelaub, the head of this Trinity II society. The story ends with Singlelaub's answered prayers for his daughter, whose brain has been damaged by experimentation.

*Weeping in Ramah* by J. R. Lucas is similarly set in the future when abortion is widely accepted, fetuses are used for scientific experiment, and hospital bio-ethical committees decide which patients should die. These patients are kept alive so their organs can be used for others. In addition, fetal bioproducts such as skin cream are produced. However, a small underground group of Christians secretly try to rescue the aborted babies.

Another theme of contemporary religious science fiction is persecution of the future church. The church is depicted as in exile or an army behind enemy lines which must sabotoge its opponent. In Dilwyn Horvat's *Operation Titan*, for example, there was a war between the League of the Church and the Empire lasting 12 years. Twenty Knights of the church, who safeguard the Faith and keep the truth from being lost, were tortured, imprisoned, and killed. The Church thus went underground to Ekklesia, the planet city whose location must be kept secret on a computer disk. If the disk is taken, the secrets of the Church will be laid bare and Christians will be slaughtered. There are only seven remaining knights, one of whom has become a traitor and has gained access to information from the computer about Church officials on the planet Titan. Now in danger, these officials must be rescued and taken to Ekklesia. As with many such novels, however, the religious parallels are obvious because this book specifically mentions God and quotes from the Bible.

*The Captive Planet* is similarly about the resistance of a small group who refuse evil. A rebel sect called The Way of Tsu refuses allegiance to the Dominion by establishing a secret colony. They serve the Source and Power who "*is* God." Doomen, evil-empowered, walking corpses, have taken over various planets, and King Padeus of the rebel group returns to the planet Tsu to expel the Doomen.

Finally, in the short story "The Director" by James Howard, Christians live on reservations separated from the outside world because they are considered insane and refuse to conform to the "world order." While the cities in the outside world are dead, "empty stretches of rock and glass with no life in them," the Christians still have forests and joy. For example, their leader-priest, Kyle, "was in love with life. He felt a deep joy inside him that seemed to be renewed each morning so that it spilled over and he felt a need to share it with trees and animals." The inhabitants of the outside world have made themselves immortal through drugs, rejuvenation cycles, and "psyche control," in contrast to the Christians who "believe death is just a door. It's a beginning in a place where there is no death and no fear." But a conspiracy of Christians is spreading outside the reservation to end psyche control and "make the human race human again."

In conclusion, science fiction is an ideal genre to deal with religion because of the thematic possibilities and the popularity of the form itself. It may pose religious issues such as the conflict between science and religion, reflect on the nature of the cosmos as revealed by science, speculate on the creation of the universe, and show other planets and their religions. Or it can deal, as Lewis did in *Perelandra*, with the problem of peculiarity—how can one setting furnish truth about the love shown by God? How is one person, nation, or race the center of God's plan for the universe? Finally, the science aspect appeals to readers because they trust it, while the fiction aspect is appealing and entertaining.

However, as the contemporary novels discussed here seem to illustrate, the number of themes explored through religious science fiction have been limited. Because God as Magic is such a central ingredient in religious fantasy and plausibility is so vital to science fiction, perhaps some writers find it easier to choose fantasy as the ideal form for conveying their ideas. A key pitfall to avoid is the class of science fiction Lewis mentioned, which uses the futuristic setting merely as a backdrop for a character's conversion.

## MYTH

Finally, the ideal form of fantasy for Lewis is what he called "myth." Whereas myth is usually associated with falsehood, Lewis uses the term differently. In *An Experiment in Criticism*, Lewis distinguishes six characteristics of myth:
(*a*) It exists despite who tells it because it is independent of its literary form and particular details. (*b*) The narrator's skill in creating suspense or surprise is also not important. It is enthralling for its own sake and has a contemplative purpose. (*c*) We only observe the characters rather than identify with them, as in most stories, because "they are like shapes moving in another world." (*d*) It contains fantasy elements—creatures, the supernatural, impossible, and out of the ordinary. These sentient animals or characters are larger than life. (*e*) It is solemn and grave, never comic. (*f*) The experience is grave, awe-inspiring, and numinous because some terribly important thing has been communicated (43–44). Thomas Howard in "The Uses of Myth" adds several other characteristics: the story takes place in a remote setting; is detached from the ordinary; has roots in experience; invokes high things such as majesty, courtesy, purity and sacrifice; and pays attention to plain things ("Uses," 20–23).

In *An Experiment in Criticism*, Lewis explains how myth does not exist in words. First, he tells the basic plot of the Orpheus and Euridice story, plus the mere plot summaries of two other stories. The first story makes a powerful impression on most readers by making them feel the story's inherent quality, but the other two are dull and boring. The appeal of the Orpheus story is obviously something beyond its literary form because just the plot can strike us and move us deeply: "Myth does not essentially exist in *words* at all but as 'a particular pattern of events' " ("Preface," *George MacDonald: An Anthology*, xxvi-xxvii). This pattern is important, not how the events are told to you. Thus we need only hear a brief summary to feel the quality inherent in it. The plot "is only really a net whereby to catch something else. The real theme may be, and perhaps usually is, something that has no sequence in it, something other than a process and much more like a state or quality" (*On*, 18).

So once you have grasped the "soul" of the story, which is the myth itself, you can do away with the vehicle that conveyed it. Because myth allows us to go beyond the limitations of language, it must be experienced, not read for any abstract or intellectual meaning. The underlying form is spiritual rather than theoretical:

In the enjoyment of a great myth we come nearest to experiencing as a concrete what can otherwise be understood only as an abstraction . . . if I remind you . . . of Orpheus and Eurydice, how he was suffered to lead her by the hand but, when he turned around to look at her, she disappeared, what was merely a principle becomes imaginable. You may reply that you never till this moment attached that "meaning" to that myth. Of course not. You are not looking for an abstract "meaning" at all. If that was what you were doing the myth would be for you not true myth but a mere allegory. You were not knowing, but tasting. . . . The moment we *state* this principle, we are admittedly back in the world of abstraction. It is only while receiving the myth as a story that you experience the principle concretely (Lewis, *God in the Dock*, 66).

Roland Hein believes a similar example of the effects a religious man feels in the presence of myths can be found in a passage in MacDonald's "The Golden Key" (134). In the presence of the Old Man of the Fire, Tangle

had a marvellous sense that she was in the secret of the earth and all its ways. Everything she had seen, or learned from books; all that her grandmother had said or sung to her; all the talk of the beasts, birds, and fishes . . . all was plain: she understood it all, and saw that everything meant the same thing, though she could not have put it into words again (172).

One of the chief reasons for Lewis' conversion to Christianity was his realization that it is impossible to perceive reality apart from experiencing it: "As thinkers we are cut off from what we think about: as tasting, touching, willing, loving, hating, we do not clearly understand. The more lucidly we think, the more we are cut off: the more deeply we enter into reality, the less we can think" (*God*, 65). Once we begin to examine our experience of reality, we are cut off from the object and left with only an abstraction, a mental construct.

Since man will always be limited in his knowledge, having a gap between experience and perception, in order to truly experience, perceive, and know, man needs "both reason, the natural organ of truth, plus imagination, the organ of meaning and the condition of truth" (*Rehabilitations and Other Essays*, 157). Imagination was seen by Lewis as a means to truth, a path to God: "For this end I made your senses and for this end your imagination, that you might see my face and live" (*Pilgrim's*, 171).

We must thus combine reason with imagination to come close to understanding what is real. Truth is larger than our imperfect minds can comprehend, and there is a larger universe than we can see. This is why, says Madeleine L'Engle, she tries to write about things beyond or on the other side of intellect. Since our intellect is limited, we must go beyond it to find truth. And imagination can take us beyond this finite, restricted world of provable fact (*Circle*, 228, 112). She feels that today children are taught about the tangible world—called the "real" and "practical"—but that there has been no emphasis on imagination (fantasy, myth, fairy tale) which will give truth (236–237).

"Myth" is consequently being reworked in current fantasy writers as a result of the failure of "scientism" to know everything. Lewis believed that the only way to unite the two modes of experience is to see every object in its relevant context, and the only way to suggest that context and restore the relationships is through metaphor. For Lewis, the most perfect form of metaphor, and thus the closest approach to truth, is myth. Highest truths need to be expressed in symbols, not rationally but imaginatively understood.

Myth is a form of literature, the purpose of which is thus to express and help us understand what we cannot rationally or intellectually know or express in any other way, serving as a bridge between thought and the real world: "In the enjoyment of a myth we come closest to experiencing what can otherwise only be understood as an abstraction" (*God*, 66). It incarnates reality for the reader. L'Engle says fantasy allows us to communicate ideas "too big, too violent, too brilliant to be rendered directly" (*Circle*, 211). Since we cannot look at the sun (flame of reality) directly, she writes, myth allows us to approach it. It conveys truth and helps us get at reality and experience the abstract concretely by showing and not being dependent on fine details, explanation, or eloquent abstraction. Hein agrees:

Successful myths rise to probe the ultimate mysteries of existence, simultaneously arousing the reader's wonder and awakening in him a desire that these insights might be true. The reader becomes convinced that they bring him into closer proximity to the Ulitmate Mystery, which stands considerably beyond the reach of any system of abstract principles (155).

Throughout Lewis' writing, myth is always shown to point to what is objectively real, things more solid. Ransom discovers that what had been mythology on earth is real and living in another world: "Our mythology is based on a solider reality than we dream." On Perelandra he feels as if he is "enacting" a myth. The small coiled dragon with scales of red gold suggests to him that things like dragons which have for centuries appeared on earth only as "myth" might be scattered through other worlds as realities. In Narnia, mythological creatures such as Naiads, Dryads, Fauns, Satyrs, Dwarves, Giants, Centaurs, and Talking Beasts are shown as living realities in that world.

Because the moral should not be able to be abstracted, expressed conceptually, and restated but rather inheres in the myth, Lewis considers myth "higher" than allegory. While allegory has one meaning, myth has varying meanings that "will grow for different readers and in different ages" (*Letters*, 271). In addition, "what shows that we are reading myth, not allegory, is that there are no pointers to a specifically theological, or political, or psychological application. A myth points, for each reader, to the realm he lives in most. It is a master key; use it on what door you like" (*On*, 85). Moreover, the story has several different and true meanings that cannot be separated from the framework: "What flows into you from myth is not truth but reality (truth is always *about* something, but reality is that *about which* truth is) and therefore every myth becomes the father of innumerable truths on the abstract level" (*God*, 66).

According to Tolkien, "the significance of a myth is not easily to be pinned on paper by analytical reasoning. It is at its best when it is presented by a poet who feels rather than makes explicit what his theme portends." If one is not careful, he "will kill what he is studying by vivisection, and he will be left with a formal or mechanical allegory. . . . myth is alive at once and in all its parts, and dies before it can be dissected" ("Beowulf: The Monsters and the Critics," 12). He also believes myth has inherent truth:

Myth is invention about truth. We have come from God, and inevitably the myths woven by us, though they contain error, will also reflect a splintered fragment of the true light, the eternal truth that is with God. Indeed only by myth-making, only by becoming a "sub-creator" and inventing stories, can Man ascribe to the state of perfection that he knew before the Fall (Carpenter, *Tolkien: A Biography*, 147).

Myth not only allows us to get at truths we could not otherwise obtain, but, as Lewis points out, also expresses principles deep within us and which we have always known:

Myth goes beyond the expression of things we have already felt. It arouses in us sensations we have never had before, never anticipated having, as though we had broken out of our normal mode of consciousness and "possessed joy, not promised to our birth." It gets under our skin, hits us at a level deeper than our thoughts or even our passions, troubles oldest certainties till all questions are re-opened, and in general shocks us more fully awake than we are for most of our lives ("Preface," *George*, 10–11).

Lewis gives examples of stories that add to life and give us new experiences and sensations because of the marvelous quality of the other world: parts of the *Odyssey, Hymn to Aphrodite*, the *Kalevala, The Faerie Queen*, Malory, Novalis' *Heinrich von Oferdingen, The Ancient Mariner*, "Christabel," Beckford's *Vathek*, Morris' Prologue to *The Earthly Paradise*, MacDonald's "The Golden Key" and *Phantastes*, Eddison's *Worm Ouroborous, Lord of the Rings*, Lindsay's *Voyage to Arcturus*, Mervyn Peake's *Titus Groan*, some of Ray Bradbury's stories, and W. H. Hodgson's *The Night Land (On Stories*, 66). Such stories, which are rare, "are actual additions to life; they give, like certain rare dreams, sensations we never had before, and enlarge our conception of the range of possible experience" (Lewis, *On*, 66). He calls these "mythopoeic," "a mode of imagination which does something to us at a deep level." Fantasy, then, has the potential to affect the reader in several ways, as will be described in the final chapter.

*Chapter* **6**

# "A Far-off Gleam": The Effects of Fantasy

The "eucatastrophe"... may be a far-off gleam or echo of *evangelium* in the real world (J. R. R. Tolkien, "On Fairy Stories").

Besides giving the reader new moral perspectives, putting him on the road to God, and giving him new sensations and experiences, there are other effects of fantasy: recovery, restoration, satisfaction of desires, and consolation.

## RECOVERY

As previous chapters have emphasized, religious fantasy shows as real the realm of the supernatural and uses many techniques for describing it so that we can view it and Christian concepts in a new way. Ryken identifies one purpose of fantasy as "shock treatment": "Visionary literature, with its arresting strangeness, breaks through our normal way of thinking and shocks us into seeing that things are not as they appear." It convinces us "that reality cannot be confined to the physical world that we perceive with our senses" (*How*, 169). Thus one of the effects of fantasy is to change the reader's view of religion, himself, and the world around him.

In *The Forbidden Door*, when the Green Dragons are nice to the children, Laura thinks to herself how many things "were being turned upside down in her mind." Tolkien calls this effect "recovery," a cleansing of our eyes so that we return to the "real world" with renewed awe and pleasure, an enlarged perspective, and see things in a new way. Tolkien says, "Recovery (which includes return and renewal of health) is a regaining—regaining of a clear view.... We need ... to clean our windows, so that the things seen clearly may be freed from the drab blur of triteness or familiarity" ("On Fairy," 57). Recovery involves seeing things apart from ourselves and thus free from familiarity and possessiveness; Tolkien considered this the main theme of *Lord of the Rings*.

Tolkien describes one type of fantasy as MOOREFFOC, a term he borrowed from Chesterton's description of Dickens. The word is simply "coffee room" backwards, the way it would appear on the inside of a cafe. This effect illustrates the way common and inanimate objects can come alive when simply seen from a different perspective or when really looked at for the first time ("On Fairy," 58). An example would be using a "time telescope" to see London in the past or future. But Tolkien believes this type of fantasy is limited because it only gives the reader a fresh vision. In contrast, "creative fantasy" creates things anew.

For example, in reading *Phantastes*, Lewis found a work that did not make the real world seem dull. Instead, the "bright shadow" came into the real world and transformed common things without changing itself: "I saw the common things drawn into the bright shadow" (*Surprised* 180–181). After reading fantasy, we similarly return to the real world with a relish for life. Lewis says fairy land gives the actual world "a new dimension of depth" and sends us back to the real world with renewed pleasure. The reader "does not despise real woods because he has read of enchanted woods: the reading makes all real woods a little enchanted" (*On Stories*, 38). In discussing Tolkien's works, Lewis says the

value of the myth is that it takes all the things we know and restores to them the rich significance which has been hidden by "the veil of familiarity." The child enjoys his cold meat (otherwise dull to him) by pretending it is buffalo, just killed with his own bow and arrow. And the child is wise. The real meat comes back to him more savoury for having been dipped in a story; you might say that only then it is the real meat. If you are tired of the real landscape, look at it in a mirror. By putting bread, gold, horse, apple, or the very roads into a myth, we do not retreat from reality: we rediscover it (*On Stories*, 90).

Chesterton agrees that fairy tales give "a certain way of looking at life" and Nature which he calls "spell," "enchantment," and "magic" (*Orthodoxy*, 53). They restore a childlike wonder at the world. Actually, it is adults who need fairy tales, not children (*Orthodoxy*, 54). Children still have a sense of awe and wonder at the universe and find life interesting or even nonsensical, whereas adults find earth humdrum (Lewis, *Lunacy and Letters*, 26–70). For example, in *The Magic Bicycle*, John is given a Magic Bicycle, a gift of magic from the Kings that symbolizes the power of God. He is dangerous to Daimones because he is a child with the ability to wish and believe in magic, an ability his uncle clearly lacks. John is told, "You can't fight the battles of the Deeper World with the weapons of our lesser world. You need Magic to stop Tragic."

There is also a need for the ability to wonder at the universe simply because it *is*. By expanding on creation, an author can glorify it. Chesterton wrote often about common objects like cheese or chalk because he was resolved to write against Pessimists and Decadents: "The object of the artistic and spiritual life was to dig for this submerged sunrise of wonder; so that a man sitting in a chair might suddenly understand that he was actually alive and be happy" (Lewis, *The Autobiography of G. K. Chesterton*, 91). Stories of magic showed him that "life is not only a pleasure but a kind of eccentric privilege" (*Orthodoxy*, 64). They give us the kind of astonishment and wonder at the world that the ancients had, convincing him that "this world is a wild and startling place, which might have been quite different, but which is quite delightful" (58).

Even repetition to him seemed to show the vitality in life rather than monotony. If man ever gets to the point that he cannot experience wonder and view things except as dull, then he must see them as things "entirely unfamiliar and almost unearthly" (*Everlasting Man*, 17). He writes,

Religion has for centuries been trying to make men exult in the "wonders" of creation, but it has forgotten that a thing cannot be completely wonderful so long as it remains sensible. So long as we regard a tree as an obvious thing, naturally and reasonably created for a giraffe to eat, we cannot properly wonder at it. . . . Everything has in fact another side to it, like the moon, the patroness of nonsense. . . . This is the side of things which tends most truly to spiritual wonder. . . . This simple sense of wonder at the shapes of things, and their exuberant independence of our intellectual standards and our trivial definitions, is the basis of spirituality as it is the basis of nonsense (*Defendant*, 422).

Recovery leads to Spence Reston's conversion in Stephen Lawhead's *Dream Thief*, as he and his friends have a special farewell meal called Essila. Spence

looked through new eyes at the world, and what a world he saw. . . . He saw narrow, tapering shapes of the leaves with the delicate saw-toothed edge individually and precisely drawn and duplicated. Each was a thing of exquisite, inexplicable beauty . . . . Everywhere he looked he saw some new wonder, some commonplace revealed in a way he had never seen it before. The ordinary had been transformed into the extraordinary, the normal into the supernormal (353–354).

Similarly, in Harold Myra's *Escape From the Twisted Planet*, David returns to earth from interplanetary voyages with a resolve to save it from the Twisted One:

What joy to be relaxed, to be attuned to the One who had made it all. He exulted in the colors, the ice, the black branches etched against the blue sky, even the new, metallic-gold Pontiac parked in his neighbor's drive. He exulted because Aelor wanted him to like colors, to like things, to rejoice with Him in His creation (187).

## RESTORATION

By giving meaning to the world and human existence, fantasy restores certain values we have lost. Since the Fall, Lewis believed, man has separated subject from object, the phenomenal from the invisible, numinous world, and how he experiences from what he experiences. The first result of this split was the de-mythologization of the physical world, which has taken us further away from the meaning of objects. In his Preface to D. E. Harding's *Hierarchy of Heaven and Earth* Lewis writes,

At the outset [the ancient world view] the universe appears packed with will, intelligence, life, and positive qualities; every tree is a nymph and every planet a God. Man himself is akin to the gods. The advance of knowledge gradually empties this rich and genial universe: first of its gods, then of its colours, smells, sounds, and tastes, finally of solidity itself as solidity was originally imagined (9).

In the ancient world, however, reality was still seen in terms of myth, and man was united with nature. Since then, a "reductionism" has occurred, as well as a tendency to classify things as either subjective or objective. Many people believe that only science can put us in touch with reality, considering any other type of thought simply subjective and therefore invalid. We begin to even further strip the universe of its significance, says Lewis, when we claim that nothing really exists behind Nature either. As a result, our present world has become drained of qualities of the supernatural and wonderful.

But another, perhaps even worse result of the de-mythologization is that man himself has been emptied of all meaning: "The masters of the method soon announced that we were just as mistaken . . . when we attributed 'souls,' or 'selves' or 'minds' to human organisms, as when we attributed Dryads to the trees. . . . We, who have personified all other things, turn out to be ourselves mere personifications" (Lewis, "Preface," 9–10).

The modern view of space is an example of the contrast between our perceptions and that of the medieval period: "Nothing is more deeply impressed on the cosmic imaginings of a modern than the idea that the heavenly bodies move in a pitch-black and dead-cold vacuity. It was not so in the Medieval Model" (Lewis, *Discarded*, 119). Whereas we feel, when we look at the night sky, that we are peering *out* to cold, vast, dark space, the Medieval observer felt like one looking *in* to a "vast, lighted concavity filled with music and life." In Lewis' space trilogy,

although Ransom had always thought of space as black, vacuous dead-
ness, he instead finds it a bright, empyrean ocean of life and radiance
pouring into him every moment. His concept of "space" is thus transformed to that of "heaven."

A scene similar to Lewis' can be found in Chant's *Red Moon and Black
Mountain*. In the Starlit Land of Kedrinh, Nicholas is shaken by the size,
number, and brilliance of the stars: "They were like great motionless
snowflakes, like frosty flowers . . . The biggest and brightest star in our
sky is nothing to those; and hundred thousand such pepper the background, dim and unconsidered. . . . the great ones swelled and sank,
bloomed, dimmed, and bloomed again" (15). The mountains appear to
him as "an absence, a void of darkness by comparison with the life and
movement above them."

Many fantasy writers are consequently trying to regain a consciousness like that of ancient times. Thomas Howard believes writers have
turned to fantasy for images because they are lacking in our modern
world:

The chances of a writer finding inside the modern world an imagery that will
suggest the big, real, whole world are slim. The writer will have eventually to
lift his sights away from the shards and catch once more the vision that was
born in olden days when an imagery of heroes and elves and gods was alive
("Myth," 208).

L'Engle calls fantasy the sign of order and meaning in the universe
(*Circle*, 223). It shows the relevance of old beliefs in such values as
hierarchy, order, and majesty. Many newer writers thus continue to use
symbols, images, and archetypes from the medieval views of the universe, the most common being the Music of the Spheres and the Great
Dance. According to Lewis, while modern man seeks to discover meaning in reality, the Medieval model had a "built-in significance" (*Discarded*, 204).

The Music of the Spheres is a Medieval description of the universe
used frequently today to convey harmony and worship. According to
the Pythagorean model, the sun, moon, and planets revolve in concentric circles around the earth, each fastened to a sphere or wheel. They
are aligned in exact mathematical relationships and revolve at such constant speeds that each creates sound waves, proportionate to its speed
of orbit, as it moves through space. Each planet sings one note, creating
one, never-ending chord. Thus the orbits were pictured as a huge lyre
or violin with strings curved in circles, tuned by the hand of God and
creating a symphony of sound. The Platonists believed that the music
was created by the singing of the Intelligences who sat on each sphere.
Lewis says in this model "you must conceive of yourself looking up at

a world lighted, warmed, and resonant with music." Even in the book of Job, we are told "the morning stars sang together and all the angels shouted for joy" (38:6–7).

When Johannes Kepler, a seventeenth century astronomer, learned that the planets move in elliptical, not circular, paths with different speeds, he calculated the changing speeds, size, and shape of each planet to determine what tone each gave off. According to this theory, the Music of the Spheres was a continuous but ever-changing song. Recently, professors at Yale have used computers and synthesizers to record the sounds Kepler predicted. In their simulation, Mercury whistles like a shrill piccolo, Venus hums, Earth moans, Mars sings a fast-moving tune with a wide range of tones, Uranus ticks, Neptune clicks, and Jupiter thumps (Blanksteen, "Two Professors Record Synthesized Music from the Planets").

It is not surprising, then, that Narnia is created when Aslan makes "the most beautiful noise Digory had ever heard." Other voices blend in harmony with it, but in "higher, cold, tingling, silvery voices" which become stars, constellations, and planets. There is a relationship between the notes Aslan sings and what is created. Deep, prolonged notes produce fir trees, while light, rapid notes produce primroses. The idea of God creating the universe through singing it into being is also found in Tolkien's *The Silmarillion*. Eru creates the Ainor, or Holy Ones, as offspring of his thought and "propounds" to them musical themes. Harmoniously, they sing before him a Great Music, calling forth a new World. In contrast, evil and proud beings sing their own music, resulting in discord.

Contemporary writers similarly use music to illustrate harmony. Christ is called Singer in Calvin Miller's trilogy *The Song, The Singer*, and *The Finale*. In Livingston's *Journey to Aldairoon*, God is called the Singer of the Song of the Morning: "Everything that lives is of the utmost importance, because each has its unique part prepared for it in the Song; each is important to the whole." The "ancient Powers still sing the Song of the Morning, the great Song which is the universe in being." Rafe's search for his place in the world is also compared to music. Just as each star has "its place in the pattern" and knows its place, and "filling that place gave harmony to the Great Song," so too he has a place. When you learn your name "you shall know your own Melody, your part of the Song of the Morning;" at the end of life you will go "into the Realm of Light, into a deeper cycle of the Song of the Morning."

In *Shardik* the Singing is a ceremony offered to show that those who worship Shardik also offer their lives of their own accord and desire to draw near to him. The priestess says, "By worshiping him thus we put a narrow, swaying bridge across the ravine that separates his savage nature from our own; and so in time we become able to walk without stumbling through the fire of his presence." When Kelderek hears the song he seems "to himself to have been lifted to some plane on which there was no more need of prayer, since the harmony that is continually present to the mind of God had been made audible to his own prostrate, worshiping soul."

The entire novel *Whalesong*, by Robert Siegel, is one humpback's song, his unique life story that is added to and repeated. The older he gets, the longer and more complex the song becomes until it takes several hours to sing. When Hruna the Whale takes the "Deep Plunge" to find out the direction his life will take, he is surrounded by a sea of light and a low hum: "I could now focus upon the light and see it moving even while it remained still. Then it became one long, low indescribable sound. I started to weep. . . . The Light sang to me, a voice musical and soft" (65).

In Siegel's other novel, *Alpha Centauri*, music illustrates the ideal. Scopas, the seer of the centaurs, begins to hum:

and soon a swelling of sound rose from all throats . . . and joined as streams join together in a river. The sounds were all different but harmonized. Becky understood no words, only a melody or theme that moved from within the circle toward the outside and back again. All the centaurs stood very still, their heads alone swaying, their faces lifted to the sky. The music was at once the most beautiful and sorrowful she'd ever heard (162–163).

After they finish Becky experiences an unexplainable joy, and everything, "every leaf and blade of grass" seems "much stiller, much more *there* than it had been. Lights and colors and fragrances from the wood were more intense. Time moved slowly, more distinctly" (63).

At another celebration, the music of the centaurs make the "hair on Becky's neck" rise up:

The walls shook and the ground trembled beneath her. A low vibration climbed within range of hearing. In a few moments her head was filled to bursting with it. It brought tears to her eyes and flooded her with a mellow golden light such as she'd seen on a winter's afternoon. It breathed through her like spring air heavy with lilac, and reminded her of things old, far away, and sad. And then of things tremendously glad as she imagined infinite numbers of stars and planets reeling in a brilliant dance (155).

Just as creation and the created universe was an act of music and in a state of music, it also was believed to be in a perpetual Dance. Like the music metaphor, the dance was used by mystics and poets like Dante, Sir John Davies, and Milton to show the harmony, order, freedom, and measured movement of the universe. While each being produces a precise note that fits into the harmony of the universe, each path makes up a perfect whole. Many cults also believed that any pomp on earth reflects this dance in order to participate in it and brings about the union of God and man. The Dance thus became a metaphor in literature for the joy and unity of all creation, where every person, animal, plant, and stone plays a vital part. It also shows joy and celebration.

Both metaphors are used in John White's *The Iron Sceptre*, when Mary sees lights take the shape of swirling, transparent skirts of hundreds of giant dancers, swirling and swishing like a thousand scintillating lights. They dance to a high, pure music with "icicle tinklings so chillingly delicate they made you shiver, and the clean singing of stellar winds. The thin sounds swept the refuse from her mind." She draws a "breath of joy" because they are dancing for Gaal, who is the center. Then the "stars sang wondermusic, music that made you want to laugh and cry, or to leap and shout, both at the same time." Suddenly, out of Mary's own throat "came music she had never heard before, music that came from the stars yet also from the center of her heart as she sang of the glory of Gaal."

In Lawhead's *Dream Thief*, while eating the Essila dinner which symbolizes loving others and mingling souls, Spence senses the presence of the Source and witnesses the Great Dance of Heaven:

He saw his own world as one minute fleck against the darkness and knew that his life, and the lives of every man who had ever lived, was but a single faltering step in the Great Dance of Heaven. The Dance flowed and ebbed according to the will of the Maker, and all moved with him as he moved. There was not a solitary figure in the Dance that was not in his plan—from the seemingly random shuttling of atoms colliding with one another through the limitless reaches of empty night, to the aimless scrabblings of an insect in the dust, to the directionless meandering of a river of molten iron on a world no human eye would ever see—all was embraced, upheld, encompassed by the Great Dance (355).

In *Tales of the Kingdom*, when the Sacred Flames reveal a person's true nature, a dance takes place during the celebration. Musicians begin to play, while a circle of dancers within the Sacred Flames join hands. The "dance would begin slowly, then build . . . turn in perfect order, then move faster and faster and faster." The subjects sing, "I'm clean! I'm clean! / The King has made me clean!" Then the circle moves faster and faster as they sing, dance, and rejoice.

Madeleine L'Engle uses Medieval metaphors frequently in her fantasy novels. In *A Swiftly Tilting Planet*, the unicorn Gaudior remarks that the "Echthroi would distort the melody and destroy the ancient harmonies. When you are loving, that lovingness joins the music of the spheres." When Charles Wallace rides Gaudior "through the time-spinning reaches of a far galaxy," he realizes "that the galaxy itself was part of a night orchestra, and each star and planet within the galaxy added its own instrument to the music of the spheres. As long as the ancient harmonies were sung, the universe would not entirely lose its joy" (72).

In *A Wind in the Door* one of the children's tasks is to get Sporos to become part of the pattern. Sporos is a "farandola," part of a mitochondrion, but the word actually means a type of dance. The Echthroi tempt him to do the tarantella, a wild, disordered dance associated with madness. In contrast, the birth of a star appears to Meg as an "ordered and graceful" dance with the "impression of complete and utter freedom, of ineffable joy . . . wind, flame, dance, song, cohered in a great swirling, leaping, dancing, single sphere."

Charles Wallace is sick because his farandola are dying. Thus Meg, Calvin, and Mr. Jenkins must journey inside his mitochondrion to get Sporos to mature and deepen. This journey literally illustrates that we are part of and affect one another. Mr. Jenkins, for example, realizes that he is both himself and yet a "miniscule part" of Charles Wallace. L'Engle also uses the ancient concept of the microcosm paralleling the macrocosm. The mitochondrion is a "planet" to the farandola. Farandolae are dying and making the mitochondria sick, just as we know the earth is dying because of pollution, war, and death.

Finally, in *Many Waters*, the stars, moon, seraphim, and humans join "in great organ tones of harmony." They join hands and "dance in rhythm with the song," weaving "patterns under the stars, touching hands, moving apart, twirling, touching, leaping" until "the harmony of the spheres and the dance of the galaxies inter[weave] in radiance" (225).

## SATISFACTION OF DESIRES

Not only does fantasy restore the ancient way of viewing the universe, but it also fulfills many of our deepest wishes. Tolkien believes fantasy satisfies our desires to "survey the depths of space and time," "to hold communion with other living things," and to escape death (*"On Fairy*, 13, 67). Thus it deals with not possibility but desirability. For Lewis, marvelous literature evoked and satisfied his intense longing. In *The Weight of Glory*, Lewis says we all have a desire for a "far off country" like an inconsolable secret—"a desire for something that has never actually appeared in our experience" (4). We cannot hide it because we mistakenly identify what we long for as beauty or a memory; but these are only the "scent of a flower we have not found, the echo of a tune we have not heard, news from a country we have never yet visited" (5).

As described in *Surprised By Joy*, Lewis all his life experienced this longing for a beauty that lies "on the other side" of existence, as do many of his characters. Such feelings also appear in many contemporary works. In White's *The Tower of Geburah*, when Wesley comes face to face with Gaal, "a flood of longing swept through him to know" him." In *Escape From the Twisted Planet*, as David surveys an unfallen planet, he feels the "same emotion as when, on earth, he stood in a field staring at a fully blossomed dogwood—so beautiful it made him ache inside. Mere touching or staring at those blossoms could not satisfy the burning to share the tree's beauty" (133). Similarly, In *The Secret Garden* Burnett says one has the feeling of immortality while standing "in a wood at sunset and the mysterious deep gold stillness slanting through and under the branches seems to be saying slowly again and again something one cannot quite hear" (187). This same feeling comes to Dickon when he sees Springtime for the first time and stares "with a sort of growing wonder in his eyes."

Fairy land thus arouses in the reader's mind

a longing for he knows not what. It stirs and troubles him (to his life-long enrichment) with the dim sense of something beyond his reach and, far from dulling or emptying the actual world, gives it a new dimension of depth. He does not despise real woods because he has read of enchanted woods: the reading makes all real woods a little enchanted. This is a special kind of longing (Lewis, *On Stories*, 38).

Lewis mentions that some associate fantasy with escapism, retreat into fantasy, and wish fulfillment rather than facing the real world. But, he argues, it is realistic stories that create discontentment with life, whereas fantasy creates a different kind of longing, "askesis," or a spiritual exercise (*On Stories*, 37). Tolkien points out that the charge of escapism is rooted in the confusion about what is real or the misconception that progress is better than the archaic. Instead, fantasy deals not only with what is real and fundamental, but it is desirable to escape the modern world. He distinguishes between the Escape of the Prisoner and Flight of the Deserter. The former longs to go home, just as through fantasy one realizes his slavery to fact and liberates his spirit. Our world is not more real than the secondary world. Why are smoke stacks and cars more real than centaurs or dragons? In a way, then, fantasy can be a flight to rather than from reality.

Fantasy also fulfills a longing for the supernatural. When asked the reason for the popularity of Tolkien, Clyde Kilby responded that he thought "our present world had been so drained of elemental qualities such as the numinous, the supernatural and the wonderful that it had been consequently drained of much—perhaps most—of its natural and religious meaning" (*Tolkien*, 79). Similarly, Protestant minister William Boyle believes contemporary fantasy satisfies the public's desire for the spiritual: "There's a natural longing in our hearts for God and our creator, so when you touch on areas of spirituality, I think you see a longing for a meaning outside of ourselves" (Short, *The Gospel from Outer Space*, 17). When asked why people are not lining up outside churches instead of movie theaters, Boyle replied that maybe "organized religion hasn't been able to communicate that message to the public. Not as well as an ET, anyway." Similarly, Carl Sagan writes,

The interest in UFO's and ancient astronauts seems at least partly the result of unfulfilled religious needs. The extraterrestrials are often described as wise, powerful, benign, human in appearance, and sometimes they are attired in long white robes. They are very much like gods and angels, coming from other planets rather than from heaven, using spaceships rather than wings. There is a little pseudoscientific overlay, but the theological antecedents are clear. . . . Indeed, a recent British survey suggests that more people believe in extraterrestrial visitations than in God (*Broca's Brain*, 67).

In his book *The Gospel from Outer Space*, Frank Short examines modern religious films in this same context. One can see in these films, he believes, "watered down" versions of Christianity, plus a longing for an answer to spiritual questions and a search for meaning and direction from outside earth. One example is *Close Encounters of the Third Kind*, in which aliens attempt to communicate with earth. Short argues that the religion of outer space points upward. "Close Encounters" not only begins with characters longing for something to happen, reflecting a spiritual need, but zeroes in on a certain place and time—Devil's Tower— where they feel compelled to go to communicate with the spaceship. He likens this place to Bethlehem.

Tolkien identifies our "oldest and deepest desire" as the Great Escape: the Escape from Death. This longing is fulfilled in many books by depicting the reality of heaven and an afterlife. According to G. K. Chesterton, humans have an "instinct for a heaven that shall be as literal and almost as local as a home," an idea pursued by mythmakers. This place is the "shrine of the god or the abode of the blest" (*Everlasting*, 211–212). Lewis says that because Heaven is "outside our experience . . . all intelligible descriptions must be of things within our experience" (*Weight*, 6). Thus the scriptural picture of heaven is just as symbolical as the terms we use, except the "scriptural imagery has authority."

In Smith's *Captive Planet* the contrast between the real world and the afterlife is called This Side and the Other Side. Those who walk in the "Power with the Source . . . live to be very old" and give up their lives when they "are called and enter life" in the Other Side. Thus they do not fear death. Similarly, Queen Alinea in Stephen Lawhead's *The Sword and the Flame* tells about a great, faraway kingdom of the Most High where they will be with him when they die: "It is a wondrous place and more beautiful than anything you have ever seen. You will leave your body—you will not need it anymore, because you will have a new body—and go live in happiness forever." Quentin is thus assured he will see Durwin again "in a place without separation or the painful intrusion of death."

In *Alpha Centauri*, the First Ones, who led the centaurs to earth, take the Great Journey or Change. They face west, "singing music from before the beginning of time," then the "shining spirit passes on. The frail body, like a dry leaf" or cocoon is carried on the waves to the west, where the sun beats it to copper. The First Ones consider death to be the "end of life, for which all life prepares one . . . a door to another life."

In Harold Myra's *The Choice*, Risha (Eve) dies an old woman, finally free of the guilt of her disobedience in the Garden of Eden. The novel ends with her new life in another world, just as it begins with her creation in Eden. As her skull is about to be split by an enemy soldier, she feels herself rising from her chair

with new power, with new young flesh expanding from her bones, shoving aside the flaccid skin and the thin crackling hair like an old, loose garment being dropped at her feet. She felt herself running in joy to a ledge above a vast sea where Kael was laughing with Erlin, and then they were all being led by the living stones and by Shia up and up and through, hearing Aaael's whispers, moving with the grace and spirit of young colts among the celestial glories (167).

Several books associate blue with heavenly things, just as in the Romantic poets, blue was often used as a symbol of the union of the earthly and divine. In *The Sword Bearer*, when John runs to the bookstore basement, he opens a door and is surrounded by and "inconceivably lovely" blue light: "Everything changed. His pain was gone. It was as though he had been dreaming and that now he had suddenly woken up. Or as though he had been awake but had walked into a dream" (40). This light takes John's fears away, but makes him feel guilty and ashamed. In contrast, the Mystery of Abomination is associated with red light.

In *The Forbidden Door*, the Blue Road is a symbol of the road to heaven and eternal life. In the middle of the green seas is a road of blue water: "The closer it drew to the horizon the brighter it grew. And as they looked, Laura and David felt they had never before known what blue was. The edges of the pathway were well defined and stopped abruptly where they met the sea's waves" (72). It leads "home to the Great One. All who have obeyed His laws come here in the end, whether torn and slain in battle, twisted with age, or felled by plague—all come." For example, a family of Dark Dragons requests that if they are killed by their people, they be allowed to go to the Blue Road. Their desire is granted because all who wish it are free to go there. When Laura steps on the Road, she knows "that all her life long she would feel those gentle ripples in her heart until she, too, could go Home." She watches an elderly dragon spread his wings and fly straight up the Blue Road, and the light from the water shines brilliantly. Picturing death in her own world—hearses, mourning, grief, and darkness—Laura wonders "which world was wrong." All worlds, in fact, have a Blue Road, "whether it can be seen or not, and they all lead Home." In contrast, the Dark Dragons' road is grey.

Life after death is conveyed in several books by using blood as a means of resurrection. In *In the Hall of the Dragon King*, Quentin awakens the sleeping King Eskevar from a trance. After wounding himself in a battle with a dragon, Quentin reaches up to touch Eskevar's lifeless face. When a drop of blood falls from his cut hand, the King comes to life. In *The Iron Sceptre*, Gaal stabs his ankle and wipes some of the blood on Mary McNab's big toe, thumb, and ear lobe: "You are different inside," he tells her. "You're mine now—mine all the way through!" He then gives her a vial of this blood to break the power of the witch and deliver King Kardia by smearing some on his toe. When the children splatter this blood before the witch's throne, the statue-like figures before her begin to move, and the witch melts.

When the witch rises again in the form of a dragon, Gaal explains to Kardia that she will kill him. The children feel this is not fair; Gaal is not like that. What did Kardia do wrong? Is Gaal mad? Doesn't he care? Why does he have to die? When Kardia is killed by the dragon as predicted, like Arthur he is laid on a barge and his sword thrown back in the lake. The children drift slowly to the misty end of the lake, where they become diffused in the golden radiance of Gaal's Palace in the Bayith of Yayin (Hebrew for "house of wine"). Gaal tells them he has conquered death and commands Kardia to arise. He springs up through his satin pall without disturbing it:

For a moment Mary thought he must be a ghost, but she touched him and found him solid and full of strength. . . . He was young again, young and vigorous, his hair and his beard jet black, and his cheeks glowing with health. . . . He was, as Kurt put it, "more real and more solid than he had ever been" (388).

## CONSOLATION

Finally, more important than the satisfaction of our desires is what Tolkien calls the Consolation of the Happy Ending or Eucatastrophe. Tolkien believes fantasy has a happy ending because the religious view perceives real consolation occurring after death or the end of the world. Fantasy, however, does not deny "dystastrophe" (sorrow and failure);

instead, the highest function of fairy stories is Eucatastrophe, "a sudden glimpse of the underlying reality or truth" ("On Fairy," 70–71). It is "the sudden happy turn in a story" that "pierces you with a joy that brings tears," "a catch of the breath, and a beat and lifting of the heart," and this joy "is a sudden and miraculous grace never to be counted on to recure" ("On Fairy," 68; *Letters*, 100). According to Tolkien, this emotion comes through in *The Hobbit* when Bilbo cries, "The Eagles! The Eagles are coming." Because we are chained by death we feel relief, perceiving that "this is indeed how things really do work in the Great World for which our nature is made" (*Letters*, 100). The eucatastrophic vision "denies . . . universal final defeat and in so far is *evangelium*, giving a fleeting glimpse of Joy" and an "echo of evangelium in the real world" ("On Stories," 68, 71).

Here again we return to myth, for myth gives a gleam of the Gospel in which the Eucatastrophe is true. Myth is a medium of divine revelation, helping us understand what cannot be known through facts or history. Thus every great myth has at its center the revelation of God. In *The Pilgrim's Regress*, a voice tells John,

Child, if you will, it *is* mythology. It is but truth, not fact: an image, not the very real. But then it is My mythology. The words of Wisdom are also myth and metaphor; but since they do not know themselves for what they are, in them the hidden myth is master, where it should be servant: and it is but of man's inventing. But this is My inventing, this is the veil under which I have chosen to appear even from the first until now (*Pilgrim's*, 171).

Lewis calls Myth "at its best, a real though unfocussed gleam of divine truth falling on human imagination" (*Miracles*, 139). In *Everlasting Man*, Chesterton observes that pagan mythology is an attempt to reach divine reality solely through imagination. Before his conversion, Lewis realized that pagan stories hinted at truth which later became history in the Incarnation. Yet he could not understand the purpose of Christ, the crucifixion, and resurrection. Tolkien and Dyson replied that since he was affected by the sacrifice in pagan mythology, why not accept it in Christianity? When Lewis called myth lies, Tolkien objected. We invent terms for objects based on our perception of them. Prodded by friends like Tolkien and Hugo Dyson, Lewis decided that the Christian story is a myth like other great myths except the Bible is myth become fact. God's truth first appeared in mythical form, then became incarnate as History:

The story of Christ is simply a true myth: a myth working on us in the same way as the others, but with this tremendous difference that *it really happened*: and one must be content to accept it in the same way, remembering that it is God's myth where the others are men's myths: i.e. the Pagan stories are God expressing Himself through the minds of poets, using such images as He found there, while Christianity is God expressing Himself through what we call "real things." Therefore it is *true*, not in the sense of being a "description" of God (that no finite mind could take in) but in the sense of being the way in which God chooses to (or can) appear to our faculties. The doctrines we get *out* of the true myth are of course *less* true: they are translations into our *concepts and ideas* of what God has already expressed in a language more adequate, namely the actual incarnation, crucifixion, and resurrection. (Hooper, *They Stand Together,* 427)

The Gospels themselves, then, tell the greatest story of all, the Eucatastrophe of the Resurrection, producing a tearful Christian joy by mingling Joy and Sorrow. This joy at the end of the story is a fundamental principle. Randall Helms writes that a " successful fantasy . . . by dealing in its own terms with the themes of the Gospels and the rest of the Bible, could bring to the reader 'exactly the same quality, if not the same degree' of the Christian 'joy' Tolkien says is the gift of fairy-story" (*Tolkien*, 35). In the Bible, writes Tolkien, is a story with all the characteristics of good fantasy—the marvelous, eucatastrophe, and consistency—and it is true:

The Gospels contain a fairy-story, or a story of a larger kind which embraces all the essence of fairy stories. They contain many marvels—peculiarly artistic, beautiful, and moving: "mythical" in their perfect, self-contained significance; and among the marvels is the greatest and most complete conceivable eucatastrophe. But this story has entered History and the primary world; the desire and aspiration of sub-creation has been raised to the fulfillment of Creation. The Birth of Christ is the eucatastrophe of Man's history. The Resurrection is the eucatastrophe of the story of the Incarnation. This story begins and ends in joy. It has pre-eminently the "inner consistency of reality." There is no tale ever told that man would rather find was true ("On Fairy Stories," 71–72).

This similarity between fantasy and the Gospels, perhaps more than any other, gives this genre its legitimacy and true purpose.

# Bibliography

Abrams, M. H. *The Mirror and the Lamp*. New York: W.W. Norton & Co. Inc., 1953.

Adams, Richard. *Shardik*. New York: Avon Books, 1974.

Addison, Joseph. "The Spectator," Tuesday, July 1, 1712. In *Addison and Steele Selections From the Tatler and the Spectator*, edited by Robert J. Allen, 2d ed. New York: Holt, Rinehart & Winston General Book, 1970.

"Allegorical Fantasy: Mortal Dealings with Cosmic Questions." *Christianity Today* 8 (June 1979): 14–18.

Allnutt, Frank. *The Force of Star Wars*. Van Nuys, CA: Bible Voice, 1977.

Aurelio, John. "The Greatest Feat." In *Visions of Wonder: An Anthology of Christian Fantasy*, edited by Robert H. Boyer and Kenneth J. Zahorski, 215–227. New York: Avon Books, 1981.

_____. *Story Sunday*. New York: Paulist Press, 1978.

Basney, Lionel. "What About Fantasy?" *Christianity Today* 26 (May 1976): 18.

Bettelheim, Bruno. *The Uses of Enchantment*. New York: Vintage, 1976.

Bibee, John. *The Magic Bicycle*. Downers Grove, IL: Inter Varsity Press, 1983.

Blamires, Harry. *Cold War in Hell*. rev. ed. Nashville: Thomas Nelson Inc., 1984.

_____. *The Devil's Hunting Grounds*. rev. ed. Nashville: Thomas Nelson Inc., 1984.

_____. *Highway to Heaven*. rev. ed. Nashville: Thomas Nelson Inc., 1984.

Blankstein, Jane. "Two Professors Record Synthesized Music from the Planets." *Cincinnati Enquirer* 6 (May 1979): K–8.

Blish, James. *A Case of Conscience*. New York: Ballantine/Del Rey/Fawcett Books, 1958.

Blount, Margaret. *Animal Land: The Creatures of Children's Fiction*. New York: Avon Books, 1974.

Bunyan, John. The Pilgrim's Progress. rev. ed. New York: Washington Square, 1961.

Burnett, Frances Hodgson. *The Secret Garden*. New York: Dell Publishing Co. Inc., 1938.

Carpenter, Humphrey. *The Inklings*. Boston: Houghton Mifflin Co., 1979.

_____. *Tolkien: A Biography*. Boston: Houghton Mifflin Co., 1977.

Carroll, Lewis. *Alice's Adventures in Wonderland and Through the Looking Glass*. rev. ed. New York: NAL/Signet, 1960.

Carter, Lin. *Imaginary Worlds*. New York: Ballantine/Del Rey/Fawcett Books, 1973.

Chant, Joy. *Red Moon and Black Mountain*. New York: Bantam Books Inc., 1970.

Chesterton, G. K. "A Defense of Nonsense." *The Man Who Was Chesterton*. New York: Doubleday Publishing Co., 1960.

_____. *The Autobiography of G. K. Chesterton*. New York: Sheed and Ward, 1936.

_____. *The Common Man*. New York: Sheed and Ward, 1950.

_____. *The Defendant*. London: R. Brimley Johnson, 1901.

_____. *Everlasting Man*. rev. ed. New York: Doubleday Publishing Co., 1955.

_____. *Lunacy and Letters*, edited by Dorothy Collins. New York: Sheed and Ward, 1958.

_____. *Orthodoxy*. New York: Doubleday Publishing Co., 1959.

_____. *Sidelights*. rev. ed. Freeport, NY: Books for Libraries, 1968.

_____. *Tremendous Trifles*. New York: Sheed and Ward, 1955.

Coleridge, Samuel Taylor. *Biographia Literaria*. Edited by George Watson. rev. ed. London: Everyman's Library, 1965.

Cox, Harvey G. *The Feast of Fools*. Cambridge: Harvard University Press, 1969.

Dante. *The Divine Comedy*. Translated by John D. Sinclair. New York: Oxford University Press, 1969.

Donaldson, Stephen R. *Daughter of Regals and Other Tales*. New York: Ballantine/Del Rey/Fawcett Books 1984.

_____. *The Illearth War*. New York: Ballantine/Del Rey/Fawcett Books, 1977.

_____. *Lord Foul's Bane*. New York: Ballantine/Del Rey/Fawcett Books, 1977.

_____. *The One Tree*. New York: Ballantine/Del Rey/Fawcett Books, 1982.

_____. *The Power That Preserves*. New York: Ballantine/Del Rey/Fawcett Books, 1977.

_____. *White Gold Wielder*. New York: Ballantine/Del Rey/Fawcett Books, 1983.

_____. *The Wounded Land*. New York: Ballantine/Del Rey/Fawcett Books, 1980.

*Dragonraid*. Colorado Springs: Adventure Learning Systems, 1984.

Durstewitz, Mark. *Code Red on Starship Englisia*. Elgin, IL: David C. Cook Publishing Co., 1983.

_____. *Starforce: Red Alert*.

Edwards, James. R. "Letter." In *Bulletin of the New York C. S. Lewis Society* (January 1986): 5.

"Fantasy: A Habit of Mind. An Interview with John White." *Axis* (Spring 1986): 7–10.

Fickett, Harold. "A Conversation with Poet/Novelist Robert Siegel." *Christianity Today* 21 (November 1980): 36–37.

Flatter, Charles. "Folktales: The Enchanted Lesson." *American Educator* (Summer 1984): 30–33.

Foque, Friedrich H. La Motte. *Undine*. Translated by Edmund Gosse. Library of World Literature Series, 1985.

Ford, Richard. *Quest for the Faradawn*. New York: Dell Publishing Co. Inc., 1982.

Frye, Northrop. *Anatomy of Criticism*. Princeton: Princeton University Press, 1957.

Gallico, Paul. *The Man Who Was Magic: A Fable of Innocence*. Garden City: Doubleday Publishing Co., 1966.

Galloway, John T. *The Gospel According to Superman*. Nashville: Holman Bible Publishers, 1973.

Glut, Donald. *The Empire Strikes Back*. New York: Ballantine/Del Rey/Fawcett Books, 1980.

Godwin, Parke. *The Last Rainbow*. New York: Bantam Books Inc., 1985.

Grahame, Kenneth. *The Wind in the Willows*. rev. ed. New York: NAL/Signet, 1969.

Grant, George. "Sacramentalism in the Speculative Fiction of Tim Powers." Humble, TX: Believers' Fellowship, 1985.

Brothers Grimm. "Bearskin," The Complete Grimm's Fairy Tales. New York: Pantheon, 1944.

Hales, E. E. Y. *Chariot of Fire*. New York: Doubleday Publishing Co., 1977.

Harding, D. E. *Hierarchy of Heaven and Earth*. London: Faber and Faber, 1952.

Harris, Gordon. *Apostle from Space*. Plainfield, NY: Logos International, 1978.

Hein, Rolland. *The Harmony Within*. Grand Rapids: Christian University Press, 1982.

Heinlein, Robert A. *Job: A Comedy of Justice*. New York: Ballantine/Del Rey/Fawcett Books, 1984.

Helms, Randall. "All Tales Need Not Come True." In *Studies in the Literary Imagination* 14 (Fall 1981): 31–45.

_____. *Tolkien and the Silmarils*. New York: Houghton Mifflin Co., 1981.

Henley, Wallace C. *City Under the Sands*. Locust Valley, NY: Living Flame Press, 1986.

Holbrook, David. "The Problem of C. S. Lewis." In *Writers, Critics, and Children*, edited by Geoff Fox et. al. New York: Agathon, 1976.

Homer. *The Odyssey*. Translated by W.H.D. Rouse. rev. ed. New York: Nal-Mentor, 1937.

Hooper, Walter. *Past Watchful Dragons*. New York: Macmillan/Collier, 1971.

_____. "Preface." In *Narrative Poems*, by C. S. Lewis. New York: Harcourt Brace Jovanovich, Inc., 1969.

_____, ed. *They Stand Together*. New York: Macmillan Publishing Co., 1979.

Horvat, Dilwyn. *Operation Titan*. Westchester, IL: Crossway, 1984.

Howard, James. "The Director." In *Strange Gods*, edited by Roger Elwood, 131–157. New York: Pocket, 1974.

"How to Beat the Beaten Path: An Interview with Clyde Kilby." *Christianity Today* 9 (Sept. 1977): 30–32.

Howard, Thomas. "Myth: Flight to Reality." In *The Christian Imagination: Essays on Literature and the Arts*, edited by Leland Ryken, 201–210. Grand Rapids: Baker Book House, 1981.

_____. "The Uses of Myth." *Mythlore* 7 (March 1980): 20–23.

Hughes, Robert Don. "Crossing Over: A Tale of Two Markets." *Axis* (Spring 1986): 17+.

_____. *The Power and the Prophet*. New York: Ballantine/Del Rey/Fawcett Books, 1985.

_____. *The Prophet of Lamath*. New York: Ballantine/Del Rey/Fawcett Books, 1979.

————. *The Wizard in Waiting*. New York: Ballantine/Del Rey/Fawcett Books, 1982.

Huttar, Charles A. "C. S. Lewis' Narnia and the 'Grand Design.' " In *The Longing for a Form*, edited by Peter J. Schakel, 119–135. Grand Rapids: Baker Book House, 1977.

Jewett, Robert, and John Shelton Lawrence. *The American Monomyth*. Garden City: Doubleday/Anchor, 1977.

Kilby, Clyde S. *Images of Salvation in the Fiction of C. S. Lewis*. Wheaton, IL: Harold Shaw Publishers, 1978.

————. "Mythic and Christian Elements in Tolkien." Unpublished Paper, Wheaton College, 1971.

————. *Tolkien and The Silmarillion*. Wheaton, IL: Harold Shaw Publishers, 1976.

Kingsley, Charles. *The Water Babies*. New York: Macmillan, nd.

Kotzwinkle, William. *E. T. The Extra-Terrestrial*. New York: Berkley Publishing Group, 1982.

Landini, Cristoforo. *Commentary on Dante*. (Venegia, 1484)

Lawhead, Stephen. *Dream Thief*. Westchester, IL.: Crossway, 1983.

————. *Empyrion: The Search for Fierra*. Westchester, IL: Crossway, 1985.

————. *Empyrion II: The Siege of Dome*. Westchester, IL: Crossway, 1986.

————. *In the Hall of the Dragon King*. Westchester, IL: Crossway, 1982.

————. *The Sword and the Flame*. Westchester, IL: Crossway, 1984.

————. *The Warlords of Nin*. Westchester, IL: Crossway, 1983.

Lawrence, David. *The Wheels of Heaven*. Westchester, IL: Crossway, 1981.

Leeson, Muriel. *The Path of the Promise Keeper*. Chicago: Moody, 1984.

————. *The Promise Keeper*. Chicago: Moody Press, 1975.

LeGuin, Ursula. *The Language of the Night: Essays on Fantasy and Science Fiction*. New York: Berkley Publishing Group 1979.

L'Engle, Madeleine. *A Circle of Quiet*. Greenwich: Fawcett Crest, 1972.

————. *A Swiftly Tilting Planet*. New York: Farrar, Straus & Giroux Inc., 1978.

————. *A Wind in the Door*. New York: Dell Publishing Co. Inc., 1973.

————. *A Wrinkle in Time*. New York: Dell Publishing Co. Inc., 1962.

————. *Many Waters*. New York: Farrar, Straus & Giroux Inc., 1986.

————. *Walking on Water: Reflections on Faith and Art*. Wheaton, IL: Harold Shaw Publishers, 1980.

Lewis, C. S. *The Allegory of Love*. London: Oxford, 1936.

————. *A Preface to Paradise Lost*. London: Oxford University Press, 1942.

————. *Christian Reflections*, edited by Walter Hooper. Grand Rapids, MI: Wm. B. Eerdmans Publishing Co., 1967.

————. *The Discarded Image*. Cambridge: Cambridge University Press, 1964.

————. *Dymer*. London: Dent, 1926.

————. *English Literature in the Sixteenth Century Excluding Drama*. London: Oxford University Press, 1954.

————. *An Experiment in Criticism*. Cambridge: Cambridge University Press, 1961.

————. *God in the Dock*, edited by Walter Hooper. Grand Rapids, MI: Wm. B. Eerdmans Publishing Co., 1970.

————. *The Great Divorce*. New York: Macmillan Publishing Co., 1946.

_____. *That Hideous Strength*. New York: Macmillan, 1946.

_____. "Introduction." In *Phantastes*, by George MacDonald. Grand Rapids, MI: Wm. B. Eerdmans Publishing Co., 1964.

_____. *The Last Battle*. New York: Macmillan/Collier, 1956.

_____. *Letters of C. S. Lewis*, edited by W. H. Lewis. New York: Harcourt Brace Jovanovich Inc., 1966.

_____. *Letters to Malcolm: Chiefly on Prayer*. New York: Harcourt Brace Jovanovich Inc., 1964.

_____. "Letter to Cynthia Donnelly." *Bulletin of the New York C. S. Lewis Society* (March 1985): 7.

_____. Letter to Jenkins. 22 January 1939. Marion Wade Collection, Wheaton College, IL.

_____. Letter to Miss Jacob. 3 July, 1941. Marion Wade Collection, Wheaton College, IL.

_____. *The Lion, the Witch, and the Wardrobe*. New York: Macmillan/Collier, 1950.

_____. *Miracles*. New York: Macmillan Publishing Co., 1947.

_____. *On Stories and Other Essays on Literature*, edited by Walter Hooper. New York: Harcourt Brace Jovanovich Inc., 1982.

_____. *Out of the Silent Planet*. New York: Macmillan, 1945.

_____. *Perelandra*. New York: Macmillan Publishing Co., 1944.

_____. *The Pilgrim's Regress*. Grand Rapids, MI: Wm. B. Eerdmans Publishing Co., 1943.

_____. "Preface." In *George MacDonald: An Anthology*. New York: Macmillan Publishing Co., 1947.

_____. "Preface." In *Hierarchy of Heaven and Earth*, by D. E. Harding. London: Faber and Faber, 1952.

_____. *Rehabilitations and Other Essays*. London: Oxford, 1939.

_____. *The Screwtape Letters*. New York: Macmillan Publishing Co., 1961.

_____. *Spenser's Images of Life*. Cambridge: Cambridge University Press, 1967.

_____. *Surprised By Joy*. New York: Harcourt Brace Jovanovish Inc., 1955.

_____. *They Asked for a Paper*. London: Geoffrey Bles, 1962.

_____. *The Voyage of the "Dawn Treader."* New York: Macmillan/Collier, 1952.

_____. *The Weight of Glory and Other Addresses*. Grand Rapids, MI: Wm. B. Eerdmans Publishing Co., 1949.

Lewis, W. H., ed. *Letters of C. S. Lewis*. New York: Harcourt Brace Jovanovich Inc., 1966.

Lindsay, David. *Voyage to Arcturus*. New York: Ballantine, 1963.

Livingston, Douglas. *Journey to Aldairoon*. Westchester, IL: Crossway, 1984.

Lockhead, Marion. *The Renaissance of Wonder*. San Francisco: Harper & Row, Publishers Inc., 1977.

Lucas, George. *Star Wars*. New York: Ballantine/Del Rey/Fawcett Books, 1976.

Lucas, J. R. *Weeping in Ramah*. Westchester, IL: Crossway, 1985.

MacDonald, George. *A Dish of Orts*. London: Edwin Dalton, 1908.

_____. "The Fantastic Imagination." In *The Gifts of the Child Christ*, vol. I, edited by Glenn Sadler, 23–28. Grand Rapids, MI: Wm. B. Eerdmans Publishing Co., 1973.

_____. "The Golden Key." In *The Gifts of the Child Christ*, vol. I, edited by

Glenn Sadler, 151–177. Grand Rapids, MI: Wm. B. Eerdmans Publishing Co., 1973.

————. *Phantastes and Lilith*. rev. ed. Grand Rapids: Eerdmans, 1964.

Mains, Karen. "Fantasy and Christian Truth." Mythcon XVI, Wheaton College, 27 July 1985.

Mains, Karen and David. *Tales of the Kingdom*. Elgin, IL: David C. Cook Publishing Co., 1983.

Manlove, C. N. *Modern Fantasy: Five Studies*. Cambridge: Cambridge University Press, 1975.

Mason, David. *The Deep Gods*. New York: Lancer, 1973.

Melrose, Andrea, ed. *Nine Visions: A Book of Fantasies*. New York: Seabury, 1983.

Miller, Calvin. *Guardians of the Singreale*. San Francisco: Harper & Row, Publishers Inc., 1982.

————. *The Finale*. Downers Grove, IL: Inter Varsity Press, 1979.

————. *The Singer*. Downers Grove, IL: Inter Varsity Press, 1975.

————. *The Song*. Downers Grove, IL: Inter Varsity Press, 1977.

————. *Star Riders of Ren*. San Francisco: Harper & Row, Publishers Inc., 1983.

————. *War of the Moonrhymes*. San Francisco: Harper & Row, Publishers Inc., 1984.

Miller, Carol, and Susan Miller. "Exploring Myth." *Wheaton Alumni* 15 (June 1984): 1–3.

Milton, John. *Paradise Lost and Selected Poetry and Prose*. rev. ed. San Francisco: Rinehart, 1951.

Molson, Francis. "Ethical Fantasy for Children." In *The Aesthetics of Fantasy Literature and Art*, edited by Roger Schlobin, 82–104. Notre Dame: University of Notre Dame, 1982.

Mosley, Jean Bell. *The Deep Forest Award*. Westchester, IL: Crossway, 1985.

Murphy, Patrick D. "C. S. Lewis' *Dymer*: Once More with Hesitation." *Bulletin of the N. Y. C. S. Lewis Society* (June 1986): 1–7.

Myra, Harold. *The Choice*. Wheaton, IL: Tyndale House Publishers, 1980.

————. *Escape From the Twisted Planet*. Waco, TX: Word Inc.

Nichols, Ruth. *The Marrow of the World*. New York: Athenum Publishers, 1972.

Norweb, Jeanne. *The Forbidden Door*. Elgin, IL: David C. Cook Publishing Co., 1985.

"Of Books and Birds." *Mythellany* 1 (1983): 4–8.

Pinzon, Scott. "Drunk on the Wild Sweetness." *Axis* (Autumn 1955): 7.

Powers, Tim. *Dinner at Deviant's Palace*. New York: Ace, 1985.

Puttenham, George. "The Art of English Poesy." In *The Renaissance in England*, edited by Hyder E. Rollins and Herschel Baker, 640–646. Lexington, MA: D. C. Heath & Co., 1954.

Quinn, Dennis. "The Narnia Books of C. S. Lewis: Fantastic or Wonderful." *Childrens' Literature* 12:105–121.

Richardson, Don. *Peace Child*. Atlanta: Regal, 1975.

————. *The Revelation of Jesus Christ: An Interpretation*. Atlanta: John Knox Press, 1939.

Ryken, Leland. *How to Read the Bible as Literature*. Grand Rapids, MI: Zondervan/ Academie, 1984.

_____. *The Literature of the Bible*. Grand Rapids, MI: Zondervan/Academie, 1974.

_____. *Triumphs of the Imagination*. Downers Grove, IL: Inter Varsity Press 1975.

Sagan, Carl. *Broca's Brain*. New York: Ballantine/Del Réy/Fawcett Books, 1980.

"Satan's Fantasy." *Dove*. Faith Ministries, Pittsburgh.

Sayers, Dorothy. *Further Papers on Dante*. London: Methuen, 1957.

_____. *The Mind of the Maker*. rev. ed. New York: Harper & Row, Publishers Inc., 1979.

_____. *The Whimsical Christian*. New York: Macmillan Publishing Co., 1978.

Schaeffer, Francis A. *Art and the Bible*. Inter Varsity Press: Downers Grove, IL, 1973.

Scheer, Andrew. "Malice in Wonderland?" *Moody Monthly* (July-Aug. 1985): 31–35.

Shea, John. *Stories of God: An Unauthorized Biography*. Chicago: Thomas More Press, 1978.

Shelley, Percy Bysshe. "A Defence of Poetry." In *Shelley's Poetry and Prose*, edited by Donald H. Reiman and Sharon B. Powers, 480–508. New York: W. W. Norton & Co. Inc., 1977.

Short, Robert. *The Gospel From Outer Space*. San Francisco: Harper & Row, Publishers Inc., 1983.

Shumaker, Wayne. "The Cosmic Trilogy of C. S. Lewis." In *The Longing for a Form*, edited by Peter J. Schakel, 51–63. Grand Rapids, MI: Baker Book House, 1977.

Sidney, Sir Philip. "The Defense of Poesy." In *The Renaissance in England*, edited by Hyder E. Rollins and Herschel Baker, 605–624. Lexington, MA: D. C. Heath & Co., 1954.

Siegel, Robert. *Alpha Centauri*. Westchester, IL: Cornerstone, 1980.

_____. *The Kingdom of Wundle*. Westchester, IL: Crossway, 1982.

_____. *Whalesong*. Westchester, IL: Crossway, 1981.

Silvestris, Bernardus. *Cosmographia*. Translated by Winthrop Wetherbee. rev. ed. New York and London: 1973.

Smith, Cordwainer. *The Best of Cordwainer Smith*. New York: Ballantine, 1975.

_____. *The Instrumentality of Mankind*. New York: Ballantine, 1979.

Smith, Gregory. *Captive Planet*. Minneapolis: Bethany House Publishers, 1986.

Spencer, Chris. *Starforce—Red Alert*. Westchester, IL: Crossway, 1984.

Spenser, Edmund. *Poetical Works*. Edited by E. de Selincourt. London: Oxford University Press, 1970.

Spielberg, Steven. *Close Encounters of the Third Kind*. New York: Dell, 1977.

"Stephen Lawhead and Fantasy." *Axis* (Summer 1985): 21 + .

*Superman—the Movie—the Magazine*. New York: D.C. Comics, 1978.

Tennyson, Alfred. Poems of Tennyson. Edited by Jerome H. Buckley. Boston: Houghton Mifflin.

Thoet, Felicity. *The Book of the Dun Cow Teacher's Guide*. New York: Pocket Books.

Timmerman, John. "Fantasy Literature's Evocative Power." *Christian Century* (May 17, 1987): 533–537.

_____. *Other Worlds: The Fantasy Genre*. Bowling Green, OH: Bowling Green University Press, 1983.

Tolkien, Christopher, ed. *The Silmarillion*. Boston: Houghton Mifflin Co., 1977.
Tolkien, J. R. R. "Beowulf: The Monsters and the Critics." In *Modern Writings on Major English Authors*, edited by James R. Kreuzer and Lee Cogan. 1–32. Indianapolis: Bobbs-Merrill, 1963.
————. *The Hobbit*. New York: Ballantine, 1937.
————.*The Letters of J. R. R. Tolkien*. Ed. Humphrey Carpenter. Boston: Houghton, 1981.
————. "On Fairy Stories," *The Tolkien Reader*. New York: Ballantine/Del Rey/Fawcett Books, 1966.
————. *The Silmarillion*. Boston: Houghton Mifflin, 1977.
Traylor, Ellen Gunderson. *Noah*. Wheaton, IL: Tyndale House Publishers, 1985.
Urang, Gunnar. *Shadows of Heaven*. Philadelphia: Pilgrim Press, 1971.
Waggoner, Diana. *The Hills of Faraway*. New York: Atheneum Publishers, 1978.
Walsh, Chad. "Impact on America." *Light on C. S. Lewis*, edited by Jocelyn Gibb, 106–116. London: Bles, 1965.
Wangerin, Walter. *The Book of the Dun Cow*. New York: Harper & Row, Publishers Inc., 1978.
————. *The Book of Sorrows*. New York: Harper & Row, Publishers Inc., 1985.
White, John. *The Tower of Geburah*. Downers Grove, IL: Inter Varsity Press, 1978.
————. *The Iron Sceptre*. Downers Grove, IL: Inter Varsity Press, 1981.
————. *The Sword Bearer*. Downers Grove, IL: Inter Varsity Press, 1986.
White, John Wesley. *The Man from Krypton: The Gospel According to Superman*. Minneapolis: Bethany Fellowship, 1978.
Willard, Nancy. *Things Invisible to See*. New York: Bantam Books Inc., 1984.
Williams, Charles, and C. S. Lewis. *Taliessin Through Logres, The Region of the Summer, Stars, Arthurian Torso*. Grand Rapids, MI: Wm. B. Eerdmans Publishing Co., 1974.
Wolfe, Gary. "Symbolic Fantasy." *Genre* 8 (1975): 194–209.

# Index

**About the Author**

MARTHA C. SAMMONS is Associate Professor of English at Wright
State University in Dayton, Ohio. Her published books include *A
Guide through C. S. Lewis' Space Trilogy* and *A Guide through Narnia*.
Her articles have appeared in *Mythlore, The Bulletin of the N.Y. C. S.
Lewis Society,* and *Christian Scholar's Review.*

## DATE DUE

| | | | |
|---|---|---|---|
| JAN 2 7 '91 | | | |
| MAY | 9 '90 | | |
| MAY 2 1 2003 | | | |
| | | | |
| | | | |
| | | | |
| | | | |
| | | | |
| | | | |
| | | | |
| | | | |
| | | | |
| | | | |
| | | | |
| | | | |
| | | | |